NAZARENE   JEWISH   C

NAZARENE JEWISH CHRISTIANITY

From the End of the New Testament Period
Until Its Disappearance in the Fourth Century

by

Ray A. Pritz

THE HEBREW UNIVERSITY MAGNES PRESS, JERUSALEM

First Edition 1988
Reprinted 1992, 2010

Published by The Hebrew University Magnes Press
P.O. Box 39099, Jerusalem 91390
Fax 972-2-5660341
www.magnespress.co.il

ISBN 965-223-798-1
Printed in Israel

CONTENTS

PREFACE

This book arose out of a fascination with that elusive enigma called Jewish Christianity. I first encountered it under other names as a modern phenomenon. Many of its adherents would claim a continuity of community over the centuries in various places and forms. While this may prove to be a less-than-tenable position, it is clear that scattered across the pages of relations between Judaism and Christianity are numerous Jews who, for a wide spectrum of reasons, have attached themselves to the Christian faith. These too range widely, from the self-hating Donins and Pfefferkorns of the later middle ages to the Edersheims and Chwolsons of more recent times, men proud of their Jewish heritage and whose scholarly contributions left no small mark on the search for Christian origins. A comprehensive study of both phenomena is still desirable.

The subject of this book was suggested to me over Christmas dinner by Randall Buth. While I was surprised to find that no comprehensive monograph had been done on the Nazarenes, the present study is only a small step in that direction.

I would like to thank Prof. David Rokeah of the Hebrew University for his faithful advice and assistance both during and after the completion of this work. I am also grateful to Dr. Wesley Brown for putting at my disposal both the equipment and a quiet place to use it while I was preparing the final manuscripts. And finally, none of the work would have been accomplished without the generous financial assistance of the Memorial Foundation for Jewish Studies and the Warburg Foundation.

Jerusalem, 1987

Introduction

In the course of the last century there has grown an ever-increasing interest among Church historians in the phenomenon known as Jewish Christianity.[1] The relative newness of interest and complexity of the problem is shown by the large number of articles and chapters which have been written just attempting to establish a definition of Jewish Christianity.[2] In the end it may prove fruitless to define it because it is so varied, but all should agree that needless argument over the differing concepts of "Jewish Christianity" can be avoided. To the student of Early Christianity one thing becomes quickly apparent: in the early centuries there were many offshoot sects having some connection both to New Testament and to Jewish thought.

Even in the writings of some of the Church Fathers from the third and fourth centuries and later, this proliferation of "Jewish Christian" sects led to confusion and to the confounding of different sects under the name "Ebionite." So convenient (and subtle) was this that it has caused not a few modern scholars to make the mistake of thinking that if we can box in the phenomenon known as Ebionism we will have defined Jewish Christianity. But Ebionism was not the direct heir of the Jewish apostolic church; it was at best only third generation, and to reconcile its doctrines with those of the New Testament requires no small amount of mental gymnastics.

---

1 Major works (full references in bibliography) include those by Daniélou (*Théologie*), Schoeps (*Theologie u. Geschichte, Jewish Christianity, Urgemeinde*), Longenecker, Simon (*Verus Israel*), Strecker (*Judenchristentum*), Testa (*Simbolismo*), Pines (which must be read in conjuction with the articles by Stern), Schonfield (*Jewish Christianity*), Bagatti (*Church from the Circumcision*), *Judéo-Christianisme* (=*RSR* 60), *Aspects*, Elliot-Binns, Hoennicke, Hort, Pieper, Manns, Schlatter (*Synagoge u. Kirche*).

2 See G. Quispel, *VC* 22 (1968), 81–93; J. Munck, *NTS* 6 (1960), 103–116; A.F.J. Klijn, *NTS* 20 (1974), 419–431; R.A. Kraft, *RSR* 60 (1972), 81–92; *JBL* 79 (1960), 91–94; B.J. Malina, *JJS* 7 (1976), 46–57; R. Murray, *Heythrop Journal* 15 (1974), 303–310; S.K. Riegel, *NTS* 24 (1978), 410–415; G. Strecker, Appendix I in W. Bauer, *Orthodoxy and Heresy in Earliest Christianity* (1971), pp. 241–285; J.G. Gager *HTR* 65 (1972), 91–97; R.E. Brown, *Catholic Biblical Quarterly* 45 (1983), 74–79; R. Murray, *Nov Test* 24 (1982), 194–208.

All of the first Christians were Jews, either by birth or by conversion, and yet within a hundred years of the report that tens of thousands "from the circumcision" had believed in Jesus as Messiah, there remained only small, despised pockets of Jewish Christians, and of these a large percentage seem to have been adherents to various late-blooming hybrids of Christian teaching with that of some free-thinking individual. It has been the interest of the present writer for the past few years to trace whatever remains can be found of the heirs of that first Jewish church in Jerusalem, those who "continued in the apostles' doctrine." One event which would seem to provide the first link between that Jerusalem congregation and the Jewish Christianity of patristic writings is the reported flight to Pella of the Decapolis.[3] This move to Pella was undertaken, according to Epiphanius, by the sect known as the *Nazoraioi* (Nazarenes). Or, as Epiphanius would rather express it, the Nazarenes were the descendants of those Jerusalem believers who fled to Pella. If this notice of the Bishop of Salamis is correct,[4] then we have the desired link and identity of the Jewish Christian sect which we should investigate.

Curiously enough, investigative scholarship has dealt almost entirely with Ebionism,[5] and to date no comprehensive monographic work has been dedicated to the Nazarenes,[6] nor even to such later "Jewish Christian" sects as the Symmachians or Elkesaites. It is the aim of the present work to start filling these lacunae.

3   Eus. *HE* III 5,3; Epiph. *pan.* 29 7,7; 30 2,7; *de mens. et pond.* 15. See Appendix III.
4   The information of both Eusebius and Epiphanius was derived from the mid-second century writer Hegesippus (perhaps himself a Jewish Christian, although this has lately been called into doubt).
5   This imbalance is largely due to the availability of the material generally thought to be Ebionite in the Ps. Clementine literature.
6   Only J.B. Wirthmüller's *Die Nazoräer* (Regensburg, 1864), made an attempt, but it was far from comprehensive. See also A. Schmidtke, *TU* 37/1 (1911).

Chapter One

The Name of the Sect

The earliest documentary reference to "Nazarene" as applied to a person is in the New Testament, and refers to Jesus.[1] We do not find it in Paul's writings, which are commonly acknowledged to be the earliest of the New Testament canon, just as we do not find there the name "Christian," (which is found only in Acts 11:26, 26:28, and 1 Pet. 4:16). Likewise, the earliest reference to a *sect* of Nazarenes occurs in Acts 24:5, when it is used by Tertullus, Paul's "prosecutor." While it can be argued that the lawyer Tertullus invented the name for the occasion,[2] there is a tradition as early as Tertullian[3] that an early name for Christians was Nazarenes, and his claim is borne out by the earliest name in the various semitic languages. Obviously the name of the sect came from the title NAZORAIOS/-NAZARENOS, evidently applied to Jesus from the beginning of his public ministry.

Matthew 2:23
While it is not central to the theme of this study, it will prove worthwhile to take a look at the origins of this name. The key verse is Matthew 2:23, in which it is stated that Joseph brought Jesus to live in Nazareth that it might be fulfilled which was spoken by the prophets "He shall be called a Nazarene." The difficulty

---

1 Ναζωραῖος: Matt. 2:23, 26:71; Luke 18:37; John 18:5,7, 19:19; Acts 2:22, 3:6, 4:10, 6:14 (9:5 in 1 [or 2] MSS), 22:8, 26:9.

2 Weiss, *TU* 9 (1893), *ad loc.* See below.

3 *Adv. Marc.* iv 8. Cf. Eus. *onomas.*, s.v. Nazareth; Epiph. *pan.* 29 1,3; 6,2ff (where he specifically cites Acts 24:5); Jerome, *de situ* 143. While the name seems most frequently applied to Christians from without, one may note the use of the name in the so-called "Canons of Hippolytus," also called the "Canons of the Church of Alexandria," where, in the 10th and 14th canons the name Nazarene is used (*PG* 10, 959–962; H. Achelis, *TU* 6 (1891), Heft 4; R.–G. Coquin, Patrologia Orientalis XXXI 2 (1966); Eng. trans. in ANCL 9, 137–141). The canons were composed in Greek in perhaps the later 3rd century. However, they survive only in an Arabic version of a Coptic translation, and it is most likely that the present form of our word came about in the translating, the original Greek having read χριστιανός/οί.

is, of course, that no particular prophet says any such thing. It is a commonplace of scriptural criticism that Matthew quotes "the prophets,"[4] which may mean the general sense of prophecy rather than one particular reference. While this may be true, the general sense itself is based on specific prophetic statements. What passage or passages of the Old Testament are both messianic in content and somehow connected to the name of Nazareth?

The solutions which have been proffered are legion, and it is happily not necessary to go through them all here,[5] since this has been done recently by R.H. Gundry[6] who deals with the various solutions in their natural groupings. After treating several minor suggestions and noting their failings, he considers two major theories. First, the references in Judges 13:5,7, and 16:17 to the naziriteship of Samson; and secondly, the recent idea that the name came from an earlier Mandaean name perhaps through John the Baptist. The first possibility was already noted and rejected by Epiphanius (*pan.* 29 5,7),[7] who sought a connection to the name Nazareth. As Gundry rightly notes, the most serious objection to this theory is that Jesus was not in fact a nazirite: "The Son of Man has come eating and drinking; and you say 'Behold, a gluttonous man, and a drunkard'" (Luke 7:34).

Gundry raises several serious objections to the second suggestion, of which we need mention only a few. Neither the disciples of Jesus nor those of John the Baptist are called Nazarenes in the gospels. John himself occupies a relatively small place in Mandaean literature, and all that it does tell us could easily have been taken from New Testament tradition. And finally, at the very root of the question, a close look at Mandaean practices shows that they were probably not even a Jewish sect at all,[8] and therefore not valid candidates for the forebears of Christianity.

As a solution to the origin of the name and the quote in Matt. 2:23, Gundry, like the present author, returns to the old but still valid reference to Isaiah 11:1, although he — like not a few ancient writers before him — prefers to see the verse as referring more to the *sense* of the prophets than exclusively to one prophecy.[9]

---

4 As compared to the other four places in the first two chapters, where the prophet is singular: 1:22–23, 2:5–6, 2:15, 2:17–18.

5 See the bibliographies provided in the studies of P. Winter, *NTS* 3 (1956/57), 138 n. 2; H. Schaeder, *ThDNT* 4 (1942), 874–879; E. Schweizer in *Judentum Urchristentum Kirche* (1964), 90–93; E. Zuckschwerdt, *ThZ* 31 (1975), 65–77. See now also H.P. Rueger in *ZNTW* 72 (1981), 257–263.

6 *The Use of the Old Testament in St. Matthew's Gospel* (Leiden, 1967), 97–104.

7 For all *panarion* 29 references, see the text and translation given below, in Appendix I and chap. 3 respectively.

8 Gundry, citing Brandt in *ERE VIII*, 380, mentions that they did not circumcise, observe the Sabbath, offer animal sacrifice, or turn to Jerusalem in prayer.

9 It is implied in *pan.* 29. Jerome, *comm. in Is.* (on 11:1 = *PL* 24, 144): *Illud quod in Evangelio Matthaei omnes quaerunt Ecclesiastici, et non inveniunt ubi scriptum sit, "Quoniam Nazaraeus*

Epiphanius provides an interesting area for speculation, in writing about the Nazarenes, saying that before the Christians were called Christians they were, for a short time, also called Iessaioi.[10] He suggests at first — without any explanation — that the name came from Jesse, the father of David. Then he wavers, and concedes that it might have come from the name of Jesus, giving the impression that he has only the fact of the early name before him without anything but his own conjectures to explain it.[11] Now if it is true that Nazarenes is an earlier name than Christians, as we are told by several Church fathers,[12] we must assume that the two pre-"Christian" names were in use simultaneously, if Epiphanius is correct. The Greek name, Christian, was first applied in Antioch, probably the earliest mission to non-Jews, and it is well known that "Christian" was originally used by non-Christians to designate believers among the Gentiles, while "Nazarenes" was already used in Palestine to describe Jewish adherents to the new messianic sect.

Few passages in the Old Testament are more messianic — even in their early interpretation by Jewish exegetes[13] — than Isa. 11:1–10. The phrase in ques-

vocabitur" (*Matth. II,23*), *eruditi Hebraeorum de hoc loco assumptum putant*, which may indicate that he had found it in an earlier work. One would like to know who the *eruditi Hebraeorum* are. Are these his Jewish contacts and Hebrew teachers (who presumably would be loath to aid Jerome in his search for the source of this messianic prophecy)? Or perhaps it is the Nazarenes themselves, either in direct contacts with them or in their commentary on Isaiah? Cyril of Alexandria = J. Reuss, *Matthäus-kommentare aus der Griechischen Kirche* (*TU* 61, [1957]), 158 (Cyril, fr. 16); B. Rabanus Maurus (*PL* 107, 765); Paschasius Radbertus, *Exp. in Matth.* II, 3 (*PL* 120, 148), discussed below, chap. 5; Rupertus (c. 1075–1130) (*PL* 168, 1346). It is noteworthy— as a statement of the general poverty of Christian knowledge of the Hebrew scriptures —that no Christian commentator on Isaiah before the Renaissance (other than Jerome) shows any knowledge of the נצר of Isa. 11:1 and its possible significance.

10 *Pan* 29 1, 3–9; 4, 9. This name appears elsewhere only in a later contemporary of Epiphanius, Nilus, Bishop of Ancyra (d. ca. 430), in *de monastica exercitatione*, 3 (*PG* 79, 721), but he is not referring to a Christian sect. See Hilgenfeld, *Ketzergeschichte*, 99; *Judentum u. Judenchristentum* (1886), 27–28, and chap. 3 below.

11 1,4: οἶμαι; 4,10: ὅμως after giving both etymologies.

12 Above, n. 3. We should note that the *NT* record alone is insufficient to explain the agreement on this fact among the early fathers, since the title "Christians" appears far earlier in the Acts narrative than "Nazarenes."

13 The Targum reads ויפוק מלכא מבנוהי דישי ומשיחא מבני בנוהי יתרבי. "There shall come forth a king from the sons of Jesse, and a Messiah will grow from the sons of his sons." Verses 6 and 10 are also interpreted messianically by the Targum. In Sanh. 43a we read of five disciples (תלמידים) of Jesus, one of whom is called Netzer. It has been suggested to me by Mr. J. Shulam that we should read תלמודים instead of תלמידים. The passage which follows then preserves sayings (or polemic) of Jesus (or of his disciples about him) and their supporting scriptures. Isa. 11:1 plays a central part here (even if one does not accept Shulam's hypothesis). This is a baraita dating no later than about 200. Elsewhere in talmudic literature Isa. 11:1 is referred to, with only one or two exceptions, only in a messianic context or reference. See on 11:1: Midrash Lamentations I, 51; Tanḥuma (Buber) Vayeḥi 110; on 11:2: GenR III 4; XCIX 8; Midrash Ruth VII 2; on 11:4: Midrash Ruth V 6; Midrash Song of Songs VI 10, 1; Shoḥer Tov 72; and on 11:10: GenR XCVIII 9; Tanḥuma, Vayeḥi 10; Shoḥer Tov 21.

tion reads ויצא חטר מגזע ישי ונצר משרשיו יפרה. One immediately notices the juxta-position of the words *yišaf* (Jesse) and *nezer* (branch). This, I believe, can support Epiphanius' statement that the two names were both used before Christian. New Testament references are not lacking to indicate that this verse occupied a posi-tion of some importance in the early Church. Acts 13:22-23 reads: "He raised up David to be their king, concerning whom He also testified and said, 'I have found David the son of Jesse, a man after My own heart, who will do all My will.' From the offspring of this man, according to promise, God has brought to Israel a Savior, Jesus."[14] It is not difficult to imagine that Isa. 11:1 formed a central part of the earliest Jewish Christian polemic,[15] and that its centrally important words gave the followers their first name or names. Neither one of these words in itself would have any meaning for the Gentile world, but since Paul decided early to "preach Christ crucified" (1 Cor. 1:23, 2:2), the name Christ provided ready material from which the Greeks could give a name. And of course the name Christos—messiah—for those who knew anything of Jewish thought (and the LXX) embodied the essence of Isa. 11:1.

Acts 24:5

About the year 57 Paul was brought to Caesarea and tried before Felix, then governor of Judaea. The lawyer for the prosecution was one Tertullus, who spoke on behalf of Ananias the high priest and certain "elders." According to the record in Acts 24, as Tertullus began to state his accusations against Paul, he said, "We have found this man a pestilent fellow, and a mover of sedition among all the Jews throughout the world, and a ringleader of the sect of the Nazarenes." This is the first time that we read the name *Nazoraioi* in reference to Christians as a group. As mentioned above, it is not impossible that Tertullus is in fact the author of the title. But this seems unlikely. For one thing, in his reply Paul seems to ac-cept the title without hesitation and even to equate it with the honored term, "the Way"[16] (v. 14, ὁμολογῶ δε τοῦτό σοι ὅτι κατὰ τὴν ὁδὸν ἣν λέγουσιν αἵρεσιν οὕτως λατρεύω τῷ πατρῴῳ θεῷ). Also, Tertullus probably would not use a term before Felix which was unknown or meaningless. It is more likely that the at-

14 See also Rom. 15:12, where Paul quotes Isa. 11:10 about the root of Jesse. From Rev. 5:5 and 22:16 it appears that one of the earliest titles of Jesus was the "root of David." And here we may also draw attention to Rom. 11:16–18, where the root referred to is, in context, quite con-ceivably the Messiah.

15 Cf. Justin, *Dialogue* 86; 87 (*PG* 6, 681B, 681D–683A); *First Apology* 32 (*PG* 6, 379); *Orac. Sib.* I 383; VI 16 (H–S II, 712; 719).

16 The term appears again in 24:22. Compare also Acts 9:2; 18:25, 26; 19:9, 23; 22:4; and pos-sibly 16:17; 2 Pet. 2:2, 15, 21. The name gives every impression of being one applied by the first Christians to themselves, based perhaps on sayings such as those later recorded in Matt. 7:14 and John. 14:4–6. See E. Repo, *"Der Weg" als Selbstverzeichnung des Urchristentums* (Helsinki, 1964).

torney for the prosecution would choose a somewhat derogatory term, which, like most sect names, has been given from the outside. It would seem, then, that the earliest Jewish Christians called themselves something like "disciples (or followers) of the Way," while their opponents called them Nazarenes, most likely on the basis of some generally known (and despised) characteristic, such as their insistence on the fulfillment of a particular verse of prophecy.[17]

It is important to note that the name Nazarenes was at first applied to *all* Jewish followers of Jesus. Until the name Christian became attached to Antiochian non-Jews,[18] this meant that the name signified the entire Church, not just a sect. So also in Acts 24:5 the reference is not to a sect of Christianity but rather to the entire primitive Church as a sect of Judaism. Only when the Gentile Church overtook and overshadowed the Jewish one could there be any possibility of sectarian stigma adhering to the name Nazarene within the Church itself. This should be borne in mind when considering the total absence of the name from extant Christian literature between the composition of Acts and 376, when the *panarion* was written. Even after the name *Christianoi* had been commonly accepted by Christians as the name they called themselves,[19] it would require some passage of time until the earlier name would be forgotten and those who carried it condemned as heretics.

It might be objected at this point that if it is true that Nazarenes was the

---

17 It must be kept in mind in all of this that Jesus was the first to be called by the name Nazarene. If it is true that it is based on Isa. 11:1, then *a priori* it must have been first applied to him by those who believed in him. If it was polemic which gave a name to the first Christians, it was a polemic with the person of Jesus at its very center.

18 This is usually thought to be 40–44, but see H.B. Mattingly, *JTS* 9 (1958), 26–37, who argues convincingly that the date may be set c. 60.

19 This was at a relatively late date. Before the middle of the 2nd century, the name is used in such a way once in the *Didache* (XII 4) and frequently by Ignatius (Phila. 6,1; Magn. 4; 10; Trall. 6; Rom. 3; Polyc. 7). This latter may be explained by Ignatius' situation in Antioch, where, we are told (Acts 11:26) the disciples were first called Christians. After the middle of that century the name is accepted more frequently by Christian authors. Cf. *Martyrdom of Polycarp* 10; *Ep. to Diognetus, passim* (but this work is likely later); Justin Martyr, *First Apology* 3; 4, and *passim* (but note that even this is a defense against the accusations of the persecutors of the "Christians"; his terminology is usually something like "those who are accused of being Christians"). J.B. Lightfoot defended the earlier usage of the name by Christians (*The Apostolic Fathers* II, 1 (New York, 1973 [1889]), pp. 415–19), but he opposed a scholar of no less weight, R.A. Lipsius, *Über den Ursprung u. den ältesten Gebrauch des Christennamens* (1873). The words of Lightfoot on the scholarship of his time should be immortalized (pp. 418): "Some apology is due for occupying so much space in controverting an opinion which future generations will probably be surprised that anyone should have maintained . . . One is tempted sometimes to despair of the intellectual temper of an age in which such a phenomenon is possible. But extravagances like this are the price paid for the lessons which the critical activity of our time has taught us."

earliest name for Christians, then we should expect to find the name more frequently in patristic literature before Epiphanius, more often certainly than the
isolated notices of Tertullian and Eusebius. To be sure, it is strange (not to say
frustrating) that the name is so universally ignored. The easy answer to this, of
course, is to say that there is no recollection of the name (and sect) of the
Nazarenes because there was no such sect until a later one was described by
Epiphanius and visited by Jerome (if indeed these two fathers were not simply ex-
ercising their fantasies). But such an answer is too easy and is precluded by the
accumulated weight of evidence.

In searching for a more profound explanation, one is tempted to fall back on
the lost notices of antiquity. If only we had the lost works of Papias or Hegesippus or Ariston of Pella or even Origen, two or three of whom lived in the right
area and had some knowledge of Hebrew. . . This line of wishful thinking is not
wholly without validity, but it is weakened by its vulnerability to the counter-reply
that those writers whose works *are* extant (and voluminously) and who *did* still
have access to now-lost treatises, should be expected to know of the name of the
Nazarene sect. Of course, Tertullian and Eusebius did know the name, and as I
have stated above, the single notice in Acts 24 is too flimsy to serve as the sole
source for their assertions.

But perhaps the solution is simpler than this. Perhaps it is linguistic. If any early Church father wrote in Hebrew, the work is unknown to us. It is true that
Eusebius tells us of Hegesippus that he knew Hebrew and even used it,[20] but as
far as we know his *Hypomnemata* were written only in Greek. The difficulty is
that Hebrew, Aramaic, or any other Semitic language would have had the potential of preserving naturally the early name (as, in fact, the Talmud does),[21] but for
someone writing in Greek it was more natural, upon finding the name Nazarenes
referring to the (early) catholic Church, to change its form to the known and accepted *Christianoi*. Of course the lamentable fact that precious few of those
Greek fathers would have been able to read a document in a semitic language
only decreases the likelihood that the name Nazarene could have been preserved
in their writings.

So on the one hand it seems likely that the name was preserved somewhere
between Acts and Tertullian, but on the other it is equally likely that it was infrequently mentioned in non-Semitic script, which may be accounted for by the
predominance of Greek in early Church writing. It is no less important to keep in
mind that any sect that did persist after the year 70 would almost certainly have
been small, and given its basic orthodoxy of theology (including its acceptance of
Paul), it posed little threat. Since it also preserved one of the several names at-

---

20 *HE* IV 22, 8.
21 The discussion of the name נוצרים/ם in the Talmud is taken up in chap. 7.

tested to in the New Testament at a time when the greater Church itself had not settled on its own name, there would have been small reason to attack it; no more reason, at least, than an essentially orthodox small group known as "brethren" or "disciples of the Way."

Pliny's Nazerini

While treating the name of the sect, we may deal here with a short notice by Pliny the Elder which has caused some confusion among scholars. In his *Historia Naturalis*, Book V,[22] he says: *Nunc interiora dicantur. Coele habet Apameam Marysa amne divisam a Nazerinorum*[23] *tetrarchia, Bambycen quae alio nomino Hierapolis vocatur, Syris vero Mabog.*[24] This was written before 77 A.D., when the work was dedicated to Titus. The similarity of the name with the Nazareni has led many to conclude, erroneously, that this is an early (perhaps the earliest) witness to Christians (or Nazarenes) by a pagan writer. Other than this, be it noted, there is no pagan notice of Nazarenes.

The area described is quite specifically located by Pliny. It is south of Antioch and east of Laodicea (Latakiya) on the River Marysas (Orontes) below the mountains known today as Jebel el Ansariye (a name which may preserve a memory of this sect). The town of Apamea[25] was a bishopric in the time of Sozomen and an archbishopric in the medieval period. A fortress was erected there during the first Crusade.[26] Today the region is inhabited by the Nuṣairi Moslem sect (which believes that women will not be resurrected, since they do not have souls).

If to the Nazerini and Nuṣairi and Nazoraioi/Nazareni we add the Nasaraioi

---

22 The exact reference can be confusing. Mayhoff gives V 23; Brotier has V xix (xxiii); and Rackham in the Loeb series has V 81 (xix).

23 As alternate readings Mayhoff lists Nazerivorum Ra, Nazeruiorum r.

24 Rackham (Loeb): "Now let us speak of the places inland. Hollow Syria contains the town of Kulat el Mudik (Apamea), separated by the river Marsyas from the tetrarchia of the Noṣairis (Nazerini); Bambyx, which is also called the Holy City (Hierapolis), but which the Syrians call Mabog . . . "

25 Located also by Strabo, 16, 2.10/11 (=p. 753).

26 Sozomen, *HE* VII 15; J. Martin, *Atlas zur Kirchengeschichte* (1970), Maps 61 and 60A. See also A.H.M. Jones, *The Cities of the Eastern Roman Provinces* (1971), map facing p. 226. Apamea in Syria should be distinguished from at least three other towns of the same name, one in Bithynia, one in Pisidia, and the third also in Syria, on the Euphrates west of Edessa (Martin, index, s.v.). At first glance it might appear that Pliny himself has mixed up the two Syrian Apameas, since he immediately follows it with Bambyce (Hierapolis), which is not far south of the Euphrates Apamea. However, we need see no confusion here, since his list is alphabetical (as pointed out by Jones/Seyrig, *op. cit.*, 261). (Also, Pliny covers this other Apamea in V xxi [89]). Here we may record without comment the notice by Hippolytus (*ref. omn. haer.* IX 13, 1, followed by Theodoret, *haer. fab.* II 7) of an Elkesaite named Alcibiades who lived in "Apameia of Syria."

of Epiphanius and the Nazorei of Filaster, we have all the ingredients for a scholastic free-for-all.

The confusions may have started quite early. At the turn of this century, R. Dussaud[27] noted a passage in the *Ecclesiastical History* of Sozomen (VII 15) in which he tells of some "Galileans" who helped the pagans of Apamea against the local bishop and the Christians.[28] Dussaud rightly called into question the likelihood that the Galileans—that is, Jewish Christians—would side with the pagans in a dispute over the keeping of idols, and he suggested that the people referred to were "certainly either Nuṣairi or Nazerini, whom Sozomen has confused with the Nazarenes."[29] Sozomen's source here is unknown. Dussaud further suggested[30] that the writer Greg. Aboulfaradj (*Chron. Syr.* I 173) in the year 891 confused the Nuṣairi with the Mandaeans (נאצוראייא *Natzoraia*) and was followed by others.

Can Pliny's Nazerini be early Christians? The answer depends very much on the identification of his sources, and on this basis the answer must be an unequivocal No. It is generally acknowledged that Pliny drew heavily on official records and most likely on those drawn up for Augustus by Marcus Agrippa (d. 12 B.C.).[31] Jones has shown that this survey was accomplished between 30 and 20 B.C.[32] Any connection between the Nazerini and the Nazareni must, therefore, be ruled out, and we must not attempt to line this up with Epiphanius' Nazoraioi.[33] One may, however, be allowed to see the Nazerini as the ancestors of today's Nuṣairi, the inhabitants of the ethnic region captured some seven centuries later by the Moslems.

27 *Histoire et religion des Noṣaires* (1900), p. 17, n. 3. His arguments are summarized in English by R. Basset in *ERE* IX (1917), s.v. Nusairis.

28 *PG* 67, 1457: Σύρων δὲ μάλιστα οἱ τοῦ ναοῦ ᾽Απαμείας τῆς πρὸς τῷ ᾽Αξίῳ ποταμῷ. Οὓς ἐπυθόμην ἐπὶ φυλακῇ τῶν παρ᾽ αὐτοῖς ναῶν, συμμαχίαις χρήσασθαι πολλάκις Γαλιλαίων ἀνδρῶν, καὶ τῶν περὶ τὸν Λίβανον κωμῶν. Τὸ δὲ τελευταῖον ἐπὶ τοσοῦτον προελθεῖν τόλμης, ὡς Μάρκελλον τὸν τῇδε ἐπίσκοπον ἀνελεῖν. Λογισάμενος γὰρ ὡς οὐκ ἄλλως αὐτοῖς ῥάδιον μετατεθῆναι τῆς προτέρας θρησκείας, τοὺς ἀνὰ τὴν πόλιν καὶ τὰς κώμας ναοὺς κατεστρέψατο. (The event can be dated c. 390.)

29 Dussaud's suggestion was rejected by his colleague, H. Lammen, "Les Noṣairis," in *Études religieuses* (1899), 6, n. 1, but he himself wanted to line Pliny's Nazerini up with the Nazoraioi of Epiphanius, an untenable hypothesis, as will be presently clear.

30 *Op. cit.*, p. 12.

31 B.W. Bacon, *Studies in Matthew* (1930), pp. 163; Jones, *op. cit.* (as revised by H. Seyrig), pp. 260ff, and esp. 503–508.

32 *Op. cit.*, p. 261.

33 The Nasaraioi of Epiph. *pan.* 19 are discussed below in chap. 3.

Chapter Two

Christian Sources before Epiphanius

In setting the literary background for the notices of Epiphanius and Jerome by determining earlier patristic knowledge of the Nazarene sect, we must first note that no source mentions the Nazarenes by name as a distinct group. Necessarily, then, any evidence will be derived or inferred and not obtained from direct testimony. In light of this, it is best to state at the outset that the aim of this chapter is to establish the fact of the Nazarenes' continued existence into or near the fourth century. We shall be able to work from two directions: Firstly, from references where a Jewish Christian sect is described but not named, we can compare the description with what is known to us of Nazarene doctrine, and then try to identify a Nazarene presence. Secondly, we can find use or knowledge of the Gospel according to the Hebrews. This latter path, of course, depends on a positive identification of the Gospel according to the Hebrews with the Nazarene sect and is taken up separately in Chapter Six.

Justin Martyr

In his *Dialogue with Trypho the Jew* Justin gives us the following information:
"'But if some, even now, wish to live in the observance of the institutions given by Moses, and yet believe in this Jesus who was crucified, recognising him to be the Christ of God, and that it is given to him to be absolute judge of all, and that his is the everlasting kingdom, can they also be saved?' he [Trypho] inquired of me."[1]
"And Trypho inquired again, 'But if someone, knowing that this is so, after he recognises that this man is Christ, and has believed in and obeys him, wishes, however, to observe these institutions, will he be saved?' I said, 'In my opinion, Trypho, such a one will be saved, if he does not strive in every way to persuade

---

1 46,1 (*PG* 6, 573): Ἐὰν δέ τινες καὶ νῦν ζῆν βούλωνται φυλάσσοντες τὰ διὰ Μωϋσέως διαταχθέντα καὶ πιστεύσωσιν ἐπὶ τοῦτον τὸν σταυρωθέντα Ἰησοῦν, ἐπιγνόντες ὅτι αὐτός ἐστιν ὁ Χριστὸς τοῦ θεοῦ, καὶ αὐτῷ δέδοται τὸ κρῖναι πάντας ἁπλῶς, καὶ αὐτοῦ ἐστιν ἡ αἰώνος βασιλεία, δύνανται καὶ αὐτοὶ σωθῆναι; ἐπυνθανετό μου. Translations from Justin are by G. Reith in ANCL 2.

other men — I mean those Gentiles who have been circumcised from error by Christ, to observe the same things as himself, telling them that they will not be saved unless they do'."[2] After explaining that some Christians condemn these, he says that as far as he is concerned if they "wish to observe such institutions as were given by Moses... along with their hope in this Christ... yet choose to live with the Christians and the faithful... then I hold that we ought to join ourselves to such, and associate with them in all things as kinsmen and brethren."[3] Justin goes on to indicate that for him the test is whether they believe in the Christ or not, and not whether or not they keep the Law.

This is all fairly general, and primarily it tells us that in Justin's day there were still Jews who believed in Jesus as the Messiah. Among these, evidently, there were some who tried to persuade Gentile Christians to keep the Law and some, by inference, who did not. But for Justin there is one further criterion: Christ must be more than mere man; he must have been pre-existent with God. "'For there are some, my friends,' I said, 'of our[4] race, who admit that he is Christ, while holding him to be man of men; with whom I do not agree, nor would I, even though most of those who have [now] the same opinions as myself should say so'."[5] This strongly worded statement should be contrasted with the tolerance of the previous ones. The fact that these people "admit that he is Christ" is an indication that Justin is still speaking of Jews, and of these there are "such as have confessed and known this man to be the Christ, yet who have gone back from some cause to the legal dispensation, and have denied that this man is Christ," who, he says, "shall by no means be saved."[6]

2   47, 1f (*PG* 6, 576): Καὶ ὁ Τρύφων πάλιν. Ἐὰν δέ τις, εἰδὼς ὅτι ταῦτα οὕτως ἔχει, μετὰ τοῦ καὶ τοῦτον εἶναι τὸν Χριστὸν ἐπίστασθαι δηλονότι, καὶ πεπιστευκέναι καὶ πείθεσθαι αὐτῷ, βούλεται καὶ ταῦτα φυλάσσειν, σωθήσεται; ἐπυνθάνετο. Κἀγώ ΄ Ὡς μὲν ἐμοὶ δοκεῖ, ὦ Τρύφων, λέγω ὅτι σωθήσεται ὁ τοιοῦτος, ἐὰν μὴ τοὺς ἄλλους ἀνθρώπους, λέγω δὴ τοὺς ἀπὸ τῶν ἐθνῶν διὰ τοῦ Χριστοῦ ἀπὸ πλάνης περιτμηθέντας, ἐκ παντὸς πείθειν ἀγωνίζηται, ταῦτα αὐτῷ φυλάσσειν, λέγων οὐ σωθήσεται αὐτούς, ἐὰν μὴ ταῦτα φυλάξωσιν.

3   47 (*PG* 6, 577): Ἀλλ᾽ ἐὰν αὐτοὶ διὰ τὸ ἀσθενὲς τῆς γνώμης καὶ τὰ ὅσα δύνανται νῦν ἐκ τῶν Μωϋσέως ... μετὰ τοῦ ἐπὶ τοῦτον τὸν Χριστὸν ἐλπίζειν ... καὶ αἱρῶνται συζῆν τοῖς Χριστιανοῖς καὶ πιστοῖς ... καὶ προσλαμβάνεσθαι, καὶ κοινωνεῖν ἁπάντων, ὡς ὁμοσπλάγχνοις καὶ ἀδελφοῖς, δεῖν ἀποφαίνεσθαι.

4   ἡμετέρου; some choose to read ὑμετέρου, making the reference clearly to Ebionite doctrine (see note *ad loc.* by Reith, who cites Maranus, presumably in his note in *PG* 6, 581f, q.v.). It seems to me that even the reading ἡμετέρου, taken in context, must give the same sense. Note that Trypho immediately (49,1) finds this doctrine more reasonable than that of Justin and those who agree with Justin.

5   48 (*PG* 6, 580–581): Καὶ γὰρ εἰσί τινες, ὦ φίλοι, ἔλεγον, ἀπὸ τοῦ ἡμετέπου γένους ὁμολογοῦντες αὐτὸν Χριστὸν εἶναι, ἄνθρωπον δὲ ἐξ ἀνθρώπων γενόμενον ἀποφαινόμενοι. οἷς οὐ συντίθεμαι, οὐδ᾽ ἂν πλεῖστοι ταυτά μοι δοξάσαντες ἔποιεν.

6   47: τοὺς δὲ ὁμολογήσαντες καὶ ἐπιγνόντας τοῦτον εἶναι τὸν Χριστόν, καὶ ἡτινιοῦν αἰτίᾳ μεταβάντας ἐπὶ τὸν ἔννομον πολιτείαν, ἀρνησαμένους ὅτι οὗτός ἐστιν ὁ Χριστός, καὶ πρὶν τελευτῆς μὴ μεταγνόντας, οὐ δόλως σωθήσεσθαι ἀποφαίνομαι.

Suffice it to say at this point that Justin, around the beginning of the second half of the second century, recognizes two kinds of Christians of the Jewish race whom he differentiates on christological grounds. One group, whom Justin condemns, holds doctrines which line up well with what is known to us of Ebionite teaching. The other group differs from Justin's orthodoxy only in its continued adherence to Mosaic Law.

Origen

Some twenty years after Justin issued his *Dialogue,* the pagan author Celsus wrote his "True Discourse" against the Christians. This work was answered by Origen, about seventy years later, in the *Contra Celsum,* which supplies us with all extant fragments from the work of Celsus. Both Celsus and Origen show a firsthand acquaintance with viable Jewish Christian communities.[7] What is of interest to us here is a statement in the fifth book (chap. 61):[8]

> Let it be admitted, moreover, that there are some who accept Jesus, and who boast on that account of being Christians, and yet would regulate their lives, like the Jewish multitude, in accordance with the Jewish Law, — and these are the twofold sect of the Ebionites, who either acknowledge with us that Jesus was born of a virgin, or deny this, and maintain that he was begotten like other human beings....

This reference to the *two* kinds of Ebionites must remind us of the testimony of Justin, and it is not without significance that here again they are to be separated on the basis of Christology, and that one of the two sects holds the orthodox line in the disputed matter while the other denies anything divine in Jesus' origins.[9] If the more orthodox Jewish Christians (who can only be faulted for keeping the Law) are Nazarenes,[10] then we have an early misuse of the name Ebionite to include all Jewish Christian Law-keepers.

---

7   Cf. *C. Cels.* II 1; 3; 4.

8   Translation by F. Crombie in ANCL 23. *PG* 11, 1277; Ἔστωσαν δέ τινες καὶ τὸν Ἰησοῦν ἀποδεχόμενοι, ὡς παρὰ τοῦτο Χριστιανοὶ εἶναι αὐχοῦντες. ἔτι δὲ καὶ κατὰ τὸν Ἰουδαίων νόμον ὡς τὰ Ἰουδαίων πλήθη βίουν ἐθέλοντες. (οὗτοι δ' εἰσὶν οἱ διττοὶ Ἐβιωναῖοι, ἤτοι ἐκ Παρθένου ὁμολογοῦντες ὁμοίως ἡμῖν τὸν Ἰησοῦν, ἢ οὐχ οὕτω γεγεννῆσθαι, ἀλλ' ὡς τοὺς λοιποὺς ἀνθρώπους).

9   See also V 65, where Origen again mentions a plurality of Ebionites (Ἐβιωναῖοι ἀμφότεροι). He says that these do not accept the letters of Paul, a statement which contradicts what Jerome tells us of the Nazarenes (*in Isa.* 9:1). However, this does not have to negate the possibility that the more "orthodox" sect of Ebionites in V 61 are Nazarenes. For one thing, Origen has brought in the confusion of two sects under one name; for another, the word ἀμφότερος does not necessarily have to be understood as "both" — it can also be a less specific "all" (see Liddell-Scott, s.v., II). On the virgin birth, compare *hom. in Luc.* 17 (GCS 35, 115), where Οριγεν σεεμσ το ινδιψατε τηατ *all* "Ebionites" reject it (noted by Lawlor, *Eusebius* II, p. 98).

10 This was suggested by H. Grotius, *Annotationes in Mattheum* (London, 1679) (cited by Spenger in *PG* 11, 1277f): "Et Origenes, cum duplices facit Ebionaeos, in disputatione contra

While looking at Origen, we may consider the statements he makes concerning the man from whom, perhaps, he learned some of his Hebrew. "My Hebrew master also used to say that those two seraphim in Isaiah, which are described as having each six wings, and calling to one another and saying 'holy, holy, holy is the Lord God of Hosts,' were to be understood of the only-begotten Son of God and of the Holy Spirit."[11] "For my Hebrew teacher also used to teach thus, that as the beginning or end of all things could be comprehended by no one save only our Lord Jesus Christ and the Holy Spirit, so under the form of a vision Isaiah spoke of two seraphim alone...".[12] The passage referred to is Isa. 6:2-3 in both notices, and one is left to wonder if this expression of the trinity came from an individual or from some commentary. The original Greek of Origen would seem to have read ὁ ἑβραῖος (the Hebrew) which Rufinus took to mean a person and thus translated Hebraeus magister (Hebrew teacher). But could ὁ ἑβραῖος possibly indicate some sort of Jewish Christian commentary? Jerome quotes from such a work on Isaiah at least five times, a work which he specifically attributes to the Nazarenes.[13] In a later work against Origen by Antipater, Bishop of Bostra (fl.454), we have an indication that this citation by Origen is indeed from a written work.[14] Evidently, however, neither Rufinus nor Antipater had any further information on which to base their interpretations; each simply interpreted as seemed best to him.

If we return to Jerome for a moment, we may be able to decide which of the two has understood Origen correctly. In each instance where Jerome cites the Nazarene commentary on Isaiah he relates to it in a neutral — if not in fact respectful — manner. However, in his own commentary on the prophet (in which all of the Nazarene citations appear), when he arrives at Isa. 6:2-3 he openly at-

---

Celsum ... Ebionaeorum nomine laxius abutens sub priore illa nota Nazaraeos, ut credibile est, describit."

11 De Principiis I 3, 4: translation by F. Crombie in ANCL 10, from the Latin text of Rufinus (GCS 22, 52f; PG 11, 143; which also give the extant Greek text from Justinian Ep. ad Mennam): Dicebat autem et Hebraeus magister quod duo illa Seraphin, quae in Esaia senis aliis describuntur clamantia adinvicem et dicentia: "Sanctus, sanctus, sanctus dominus Sabaoth", de unigenito filio dei et de spiritu sanctu essent intellegenda. Ἔλεγε δὲ ὁ Ἑβραῖος τὰ ἐν τῷ Ἠσαΐᾳ....

12 De Princ. IV 1, 26 (=IV 3.14), GCS 22, 346; PG 11, 400 (no Greek text extant): Nam et Hebraeus doctor ita tradabat: pro eo quod initium omnium vel finis non posset ab ullo conpraehendi nisi tantummodo a domino Iesu Christo et ab spiritu sancto, idcirco aiebat per figuram visionis Esaiam dixisse duos Seraphin solos esse....

13 See A.F.J. Klijn, "Jerome's Quotations from a Nazoraean Interpretation of Isaiah," RSR 60 (1972), 241-255, and below in chap. 4.

14 Quoted by John Damascene in his Parallela Rupefucaldina, Tit. 75 (PG 96, 505), cited by P. Koetsche in GCS 22, 52f: περὶ μὲν γάρ τοι τῶν χερουβὶμ ἢ τῶν Σεραφὶμ οὐδὲν δυνάμεθα λέγειν διὰ τὸ μαθεῖν τὸν συγγραφέα παρὰ τοῦ Ἑβραίου, ὅστις καί ἐστιν ὁ παρ' αὐτοῦ σημαινόμενος Ἑβραῖος, ὅτι ὁ υἱὸς καὶ τὸ πνεῦμα τὸ ἅγιον τούτοις σημειοῦνται.

tacks Origen's interpretation, while making no mention of any Hebraeus.[15] Indeed, Jerome attacks this interpretation on two other occasions,[16] and both times he attributes the error directly to Origen without a hint that the Alexandrian had taken it from elsewhere.[17] As far as Jerome was concerned, the heresy was Origen's. One may be allowed to surmise that had Jerome found this exegesis in the Nazarene commentary he would have been less absolute in his attribution of it to Origen.

One other simple consideration should settle the matter. In both passages the verb is in the imperfect tense. In the Greek preserved by Justinian we read ἔλεγε, translated by Rufinus as *dicebat* (I 3,4), while in the other passage we have *tradebat*, where the Greek presumably read παρεδίδου. This use of the imperfect tense would have been inappropriate if Origen were citing a written source (even one he had lost), but it is clearly in keeping with information heard from someone. We must conclude that Origen did have some contact with an individual of Jewish birth who believed in Jesus and whose Christology may not have been so damnable as Jerome would make out. He was clearly not an Ebionite, but whether he was a Nazarene or simply an isolated Jewish member of the greater Church we cannot say.

Eusebius

Finally we turn to Eusebius, who also makes mention of a dichotomy of "Ebionites." After describing the ones whom we know from Justin and Origen who "held him [Christ] to be a plain and ordinary man who had achieved righteousness merely by the progress of his character and had been born naturally from Mary and her husband, [who] insisted on the complete observation of the

---

15 *In Is.* III (on 6:2) (*PL* 24, 94f): *Impie ergo quidam duo Seraphim Filium et Spiritum Sanctum intellegit, cum iuxta evangelistam Ioannem et Paulum apostolum Filium Dei visum in maiestate regnantis, et Spiritum sanctum locutum esse doceamus. Quidam Latinorum duo Seraphim vetus et novum Instrumentum intellegunt, quae tantum de praesenti saeculo loquuntur.*

16 Ep. 61 (*ad Vigilantium*), 2 (*PL* 22, 603): *Origenes haereticus ... erravit ... quod his majus est, Filium Dei, et Spiritum Sanctum in commentariis Isaiae, Seraphim esse testatus est.*
    Ep. 84 (*ad Pammachium et Oceanum*), 3 (*PL* 22, 745): *Arguite potius ubi haeresim defenderim, ubi pravum Origenis dogma laudaverim. In lectione Isaiae (Cap. 6), in qua duo Seraphim clamantia describuntur, illo interpretante Filium et Spiritum Sanctum, nonne ego detestandam expositionem in duo Testamento mutavi?*

17 One must mention here the possibility that Jerome was referring only to another reference by Origen to the same matter (*Homiliae in visiones Isaiae* I, 2: *Quae sunt ista duo seraphim? Dominus meus Jesus et Spiritus Sanctus* [*PG* 13, 221]). It is inconceivable, however, that Jerome was unfamiliar with the two passages in *de Principiis*, a work over which he fought with Rufinus and which he himself translated literally. It is more likely that he blamed Origen for adopting an unacceptable interpretation, no less a sin than initiating one.

Law, and did not think that they would be saved by faith in Christ alone and by a life in accordance with it,"[18] he goes on to describe another kind of Ebionite.[19]

> But there were others besides these who have the same name. These have escaped the absurd folly of the first mentioned, and did not deny that the Lord was born of a Virgin and the Holy Spirit, but nevertheless agreed with them in not confessing his pre-existence as God, being Logos and Wisdom. Thus they shared in the impiety of the former class, especially in that they were equally zealous to insist on the literal observance of the Law. They thought that the letters of the Apostle ought to be wholly rejected and called him an apostate from the Law. They used only the Gospel according to the Hebrews and made little account of the rest. Like the former they used to observe the Sabbath and the rest of the Jewish ceremonial, but on Sundays celebrated rites like ours in commemoration of the Savior's resurrection. Wherefore from these practices they have obtained their name, for the name Ebionites indicates poverty of their intelligence, for this name means "poor" in Hebrew.

What are Eusebius' sources? In the section immediately preceding this one [26,2] he cites Irenaeus and Justin. In the passage which follows he names Gaius, the Roman presbyter of a century earlier. This latter would seem to be eliminated, however, by the wording of the transition between the passages.[20] Two other possible candidates are Tertullian and Hippolytus' *Refutation of all Heresies*.[21] Let us consider the last-mentioned first.

The information of Hippolytus about the Ebionites gives us precisely what Eusebius tells us about the first kind of Ebionites:[22] they believed that Jesus was a

---

18 *HE* III 27, 2 (Translations of Eus. *HE* are by K. Lake in the Loeb series): λιτὸν μὲν γὰρ αὐτὸν καὶ κοινὸν ἡγοῦνται, κατὰ προκοπὴν ἤθους αὐτὸ μόνον ἄνθρωπον δεδικαιωμένον ἐξ ἀνδρός τε κοινωνίας καὶ τῆς Μαρίας γεγεννημένον. δεῖν δὲ πάντως αὐτοῖς τῆς νομικῆς θρησκείας ὡς μὴ ἂν διὰ μόνης τῆς εἰς τὸν Χριστὸν πίστεως καὶ τοῦ κατ' αὐτὴν βίου σωθησομένοις.

19 *HE* III 27, 3–6: ἄλλοι δὲ παρὰ τούτους τῆς αὐτῆς ὄντες προσηγορίας. τὴν μὲν τῶν εἰρημένων ἔκτοπον διεδίδρασκον ἀτοπίαν, ἐκ παρθένου καὶ ἁγίου πνεύματος μὴ ἀρνούμενοι γεγονέναι τὸν κύριον, οὐ μὴν ἐφ' ὁμοίως καὶ οὗτοι προϋπάρχειν αὐτὸν θεὸν λόγον ὄντα καὶ σοφίαν ὁμολογοῦντες, τῇ τῶν προτέρων περιετρέποντο δυσσεβείᾳ, μάλιστα ὅτε καὶ τὴν σωματικὴν περὶ τὸν νόμον λατρείαν ὁμοίως ἐκείνοις περιέπειν ἐσπούδαζον. οὗτοι δὲ τοῦ μὲν ἀποστόλου πάμπαν τὰς ἐπιστολὰς ἀρνητέας ἡγοῦντο εἶναι δεῖν, ἀποστάτην ἀποκαλοῦντες αὐτὸν τοῦ νόμου, εὐαγγελίῳ δὲ μόνῳ τῷ καθ' Ἑβραίους λεγομένῳ χρώμενοι, τῶν λοιπῶν σμικρὸν ἐποιοῦντο λόγον. καὶ τὸ μὲν σάββατον καὶ τὴν ἄλλην Ἰουδαϊκὴν ἀγωγὴν ὁμοίως ἐκείνοις παρεφύλαττον, ταῖς δ' αὖ κυριακαῖς ἡμέραις ἡμῖν τὰ παραπλήσια εἰς μνήμην τῆς σωτηρίου ἀναστάσεως ἐπετέλουν. ὅθεν παρὰ τὴν τοιαύτην ἐγχείρησιν τῆς τοιᾶσδε λελόγχασι προσηγορίας, τοῦ Ἐβιωναίων ὀνόματος τὴν τῆς διανοίας πτωχείαν αὐτῶν ὑποφαίνοντος. ταύτῃ γὰρ ἐπίκλην ὁ πτωχὸς παρ' Ἑβραίοις ὀνομάζεται.

20 Cf. however, the suggestion of Lightfoot (*Apost. Fathers* I, 2, pp. 377–388) that the "Gaius" of Eus. here is just the *praenomen* of Hippolytus.

21 Eusebius specifically designates this as a work known to him, *HE* VI 22.

22 *Ref. omn. haer.* VII 34, 1–2 (*PG* 16, 3342). See also X 22, 1.

righteous man who kept the Law, and we will also obtain righteousness only by keeping it. For their beliefs about Christ we must unite the statement, "just like Cerinthus and Carpocrates they relate only myths" with the christological beliefs of Cerinthus given immediately before: "and he held that Jesus was not born of a virgin but rather of Joseph and Mary, a son born like all other men, and more righteous and wiser."[23] However, it is not necessary to stop with Hippolytus, who was a student of Irenaeus and is known to have borrowed freely from his master. So it is for the sections under consideration here. The order, the relative lengths, and the actual language used, show clearly that Hippolytus is here using Irenaeus, and in fact we probably have a good facsimile of the lost Irenaean Greek preserved in the *Refutation* for these chapters.[24]

But the source of Eusebius' information — Irenaeus or Hippolytus — can be resolved by looking carefully into Eusebius himself. A little earlier, in III 26, Eusebius deals with Menander. In fact, he is picking up a thread he dropped in II 13 and 14, when he wrote about Simon Magus. One could justly call II 15,1–III 23,7 an extended excursus, and this seems to be borne out by the way Eusebius returns to his subject: "Let us now resume the account. Menandros succeeded Simon the magician." So after dealing with Simon and Menander, the Bishop of Caesarea then treats the Ebionites, Cerinthians, and Nicolaitans. Irenaeus' order of treatment is as follows (*adv. haer.* I 23–26): Simon, Menander, Saturninus and Basilides, Carpocrates, Cerinthus, Ebionites, and Nicolaitans. The missing Saturninus, Basilides, and Carpocrates are taken up by Eusebius in IV 7,4 and 9, where he expressly cites Irenaeus as his source. For the rest of the heresies also, Eusebius specifically cites Irenaeus for all but Ebionites.[25] On this analysis alone we must give Irenaeus first consideration as Eusebius' primary source for the Ebionites.

There is a further reason. It is a notable fact that Eusebius never mentions a

---

23 *Ibid.* VII 33, 1. The Christology given for Carpocrates in chap. 32 is almost identical: τὸν δὲ Ἰησοῦν ἐξ Ἰωσὴφ γεγεννῆσθαι καὶ ὅμοιον τοῖς ἀνθρώποις γεγονότα δικαιότερον τῶν λοιπῶν γενέσθαι (*PG* 16, 3338).

24 This has long been recognized. Cf. *GCS* 26, 218–222, and W.W. Harvey, *Sancti Irenaei* (Cambridge, 1857), *ad loc.*, who uses Hippolytus extensively to restore Irenaeus. In the passage in question (*adv. haer.* I 26, 2=I 22, p. 212, in Harvey) the MSS of Irenaeus read *Qui autem dicuntur Ebionaei, consentiunt quidem mundum a Deo factum: ea autem quae sunt erga Dominum, non similiter ut Cerinthus et Carpocrates opinantur.* The *non* makes this exactly contrary to the notices of Hippolytus. However, there is good reason to emend the text. Harvey suggests it may have been an assimilation from the preceding Dominum; Grabius (*ad loc.*) refers to a suggestion by Cotelerius (*Const. Apos.* VI 6) to read *consimiliter*; Wenland in *GCS* 26, 221, suggests dropping the *non*. Without endorsing a specific solution, we shall proceed on the assumption that the original of Irenaeus lacked the negative. Against this, see Massueti in *PG* 7, 686.

25 Simon (and τῶν μετ' αὐτὸν κατὰ μέρος αἱρεσιαρχῶν, which surely includes Menander and probably the Ebionites), II 13, 5; Cerinthus, III 28, 6; Nicolaitans, III 29.

person named Ebion as one from whom the Ebionites received their name. Even Origen, who seems to have been the first to supply the fact that *ebyôn* means poor in Hebrew,[26] nevertheless seems, curiously, to have made one mention of Ebion.[27] Irenaeus alone, of all of Eusebius' possible sources for the Ebionite sect, never mentions an Ebion. The first to do so was either Tertullian or Hippolytus,[28] and after them this is the common story, *except* in Eusebius, until Epiphanius took over and gave Ebion an evil, tentacled personality.

Eusebius is primarily dependent on Irenaeus, but not exclusively. That is not his way. As he often does, Eusebius has included information and impressions from several sources, in this case Origen and perhaps Justin.[29] For example, returning to our present subject, Irenaeus gives no hint of two classes of Ebionites. Origen is the first to do so, and Eusebius is surely following him in this.

Another point at which Eusebius may be dependent on someone other than Irenaeus is in his statement that "these [other Ebionites] escaped the folly of the first mentioned, and did not deny that the Lord was born of a virgin and the Holy Spirit, but nevertheless agree with them in not confessing his pre-existence as God, being the Logos and Wisdom" (οὐ . . . προϋπάρχειν αὐτὸν θεὸν λόγον ὄντα καὶ σοφίαν ὁμολογοῦντες). The source for this may be either Justin or Origen. In the *Dialogue* passage (48,2) already cited, we read: "'now assuredly, Trypho,' I continued, '(the proof) that this man is the Christ of God does not fail, though I be unable to prove that he existed formerly (προϋπῆρχεν) as son of the Maker of all things, being God, and was born a man by the Virgin. But since I have certainly proved that this man is the Christ of God, whoever he be, even if I do not prove that he pre-existed (προϋπῆρχε)...'."[30] It will readily be seen that this

---

26 *De Princ.* IV 3, 8; *C. Cels.* II, 1. See also *hom. in Gen.* III 5; *in Matth.* XVI 12.

27 *In ep. ad Rom.* III 11 (*PG* 14, 957); as this is unique and inconsistent in Origen, could it be an interpolative change of Rufinus?

28 Tertullian: *de praes. haer.* X 8; XXXIII 5; 11; *de virg. vel.* 6, 1; *de carne Chr.* 14; 18; 24.

    Hippolytus: *ref. omn. haer.* VII 35, 1; *adv. omn. haer.* (= Ps. Tert.) 3 (depending on the determination of its date, this could be the earliest mention of Ebion and the source on which Tertullian expanded). Lightfoot, *op. cit.*, (n. 20 above), p. 418, n. 1, cites an article by Noedechen in *Jahrb. für Protest. Theol.* 14 (1888), 576ff, "in which the relations of Tertullian to Hippolytus are traced, showing that the African father is indebted to the Roman, and not conversely." While this suggestion has not found common acceptance, it does seem to me to be supported by the early date of Ps. Tert. and the known natural tendency for isolated bits of information to be proliferated by secondary sources, i.e., the single appearance of Ebion in Ps. Tert. has been taken over by Tertullian and used frequently.

29 This is somewhat against Lawlor (*op. cit.*, p. 98), who hesitatingly suggests Origen as the main source here, while conceding the use of Irenaeus (at III 27, 4).

30 *PG* 6, 580 (Reith translation): Ἤδη μέντοι, ὦ Τρύφων, εἶπον, οὐκ ἀπόλλυται τὸ τοιοῦτον εἶναι Χριστὸν τοῦ θεοῦ, ἐὰν ἀποδεῖξαι μὴ δύνωμαι ὅτι καί προϋπῆρχεν Ὑιὸς τοῦ Ποιητοῦ τῶν ὅλων, θεὸς ὤν, καὶ γεγέννηται ἄνθρωπος διὰ τῆς παρθένου. Ἀλλὰ ἐκ παντὸς ἀποδεικνυμένον, ὅτι οὗτός ἐστιν ὁ Χριστὸς ὁ τοῦ θεοῦ, ὅστις οὗτος ἔσται, ἐὰν δὲ μὴ ἀποδεικνύω ὅτι προϋπῆρχε, κτλ.

has several points of contact with Eusebius, not least of which is the use of the word προϋπάρχειν.[31]

The other possible source is Origen's in Ep. ad Titum:[32]

> But now one and the same must be believed also with regard to him who thinks something wrong about our Lord Jesus Christ, or according to those who say that he was born of Joseph and Mary, like the Ebionites and the Valentinians, or according to those who deny that he is the first born, God of all creation, Word, Wisdom, which is the beginning of the ways of God, before anything came into being, founded before the worlds and generated before the hills, but say that he was only a man....

The reader may decide for himself. The present writer would have to be swayed by the obvious parallel of "Deum et Verbum et Sapientam" to θεὸν λόγον ὄντα καὶ σοφίαν, where antequam aliquid fieret ("before anything came into being") could possibly have provided the basis for Eusebius' προϋπάρχειν.[33] The important point is that he has mixed together more than one source, and perhaps even several sources from several authors. The result is confused and confusing. While Eusebius is aware of more than one kind of 'Ebionite' in his sources, he has not succeeded very well in distinguishing their traits. So in III 27,1–2, we find the known, unorthodox kind of Ebionites, but in the following section (3–6) some of the traits which rightly belonged to the first group are erroneously assigned to the second, as indeed is the very name of the sect.

How did this confusion come about? Justin knew of two kinds of Jewish Christians but gives them no name in his extant works.[34] Irenaeus wrote against Ebionites but knew of no distinctions, christological or otherwise, within Ebionism itself. The same can be said of Tertullian and Hippolytus. When we

---

31 It should be noted that Eusebius was quite liable to use this word without any outside suggestion; see dem. ev. 5, 1: 6, 13; 7, 1; and de eccl. theol. 3, 3 and esp. 1, 13, where it is denied by "Hebrews" (PG 24, 852), whom Lampe, s.v. προϋπάρχω, takes to be Ebionites.

32 Trans. in K–R, 133. GCS 35, 285f: Sed nunc unum atque idem credendum est etiam de eo, qui de Domino nostro Jesu Christo falsi aliquid senserit, sive secundum eos, qui dicunt eum ex Joseph et Maria natum, sicut sunt Ebionitae et Valentiani, sive secundum eos, qui primogenitum eum negant, et totius creaturae Deum, et Verbum, et Sapientiam, quae est initium viarum Dei, antequam aliquid fieret, ante saecula fundata, atque ante omnes colles generatam, sed hominum solum eum dicentes....

33 This phrase is clearly from Prov. 8:23: antequam terra fieret (Vulg.), as are also the following Origen/Rufinus phrases from the same passages about sapientia. This very fact should cause us to hesitate as to the extent of Eusebius' dependence on Origen. The former's Greek bears little resemblance to the corresponding LXX. (But cf. Prov. 8:21 ἵνα μερίσω τοῖς ἐμὲ ἀγαπῶσιν ὕπαρξιν.)

34 See below, chap. 5, where it is shown that while Justin might have spoken of Ebionites, it is almost certain that he never made a negative mention of Nazarenes.

come to Origen, however (and return to the East),[35] we again find two classes of Jewish Christians which he calls Ebionites.[36] From this point on, the name Ebionite becomes a catch-all for Law-keeping Christians of Jewish background. It would seem that this tendency began somewhere in the first half of the third century. Other confusions in this second part of Eusebius' notice are reserved for the chapter on Epiphanius, which follows.

In summary we may say that Justin knows of two divisions of Jewish Christians, one of whom held an orthodox Christology with regard to the virgin birth and pre-existence of Jesus. Origen, who also knows of two groups, identifies the unorthodox group of Justin as Ebionites. While he calls his more orthodox Jewish Christians Ebionites also, he is inconsistent in this, and we may be justified in concluding that the two groups did not carry the same name. Eusebius, in his turn, cannot avoid seeing — in his sources, if not also from hearsay — two distinguishable Jewish Christian groups, but he does not succeed very well in discerning the beliefs which separate them. For him there is only one name, Ebionite.

This establishes the continued existence, into the third century at least, if not later, of a Jewish Christian entity whose doctrines tend to distinguish it — in the direction of "orthodoxy" — from the Ebionites. These are the Nazarenes. In the chapters which follow we shall further isolate them and define their doctrines.

35 It is worth noting that only writers who lived and/or worked in the East, and more specifically in the area of Palestine, had any knowledge, however vague, of the Nazarenes. We may list Justin, Origen, Epiphanius, Jerome, and perhaps Hegesippus, Eusebius, and talmudic writings.
36 One should not overlook the fact that Origen several times refers to Ebionite doctrine without giving any hint that there are varying Ebionite opinions; cf, e.g. *in Ep. ad Tit., loc. cit.; hom. in Jer.* XIX 12; *de Princ,* IV 3, 8; *hom. in Luc* XVII.

Chapter Three

Epiphanius

Epiphanius was born about 315 near Eleutheropolis (Beit Guvrin) in Judea and died in 402 or 403 at sea.[1] His native language was Syrian, and besides Greek and Latin he also had limited knowledge of Coptic and Hebrew.[2] He studied in Egypt and then returned home where, in about 335, he set up a monastery which he governed for 30 years. In 367 the bishops of Cyprus elected him Bishop of Constantia (Salamis), which made him effectively the metropolitan of the island. His life was dedicated to the fighting of heresy, particularly Origenism, and in 374 he began writing the *panarion* (generally known as the *Refutation of All Heresies*), which he completed in just over two years. It included some eighty heresies, twenty of them pre-Christian. While the *panarion* preserves for us many traditions that would have otherwise been lost, the work as a whole is tendentious in its use of its sources, citing only what supports his own unbending orthodoxy. This quality, of course, presents the investigator with frequent difficulties and demands extra caution in approaching the facts proffered by Epiphanius.

Before the year 428[3] there appeared a kind of summary of the *panarion*, known as the *anacephalaiosis*. This work is almost certainly not by Epiphanius himself, but it is not impossible that it was compiled by someone not far removed from him.[4] In 382 Epiphanius met Jerome in Rome and from that time the two joined forces against Origenism.[5]

The question of Epiphanius' sources for the *panarion* is an important one in

---

1 For general information see articles in any good Christian encyclopedia or dictionary. For bibliographic information, in particular about Epiphanius' literary works, see Altaner, 315–318; Quasten, *Patrology*, 384–396; Bardenhewer, III, 293–302; M. Geerhard, *Clavis Patrum Graecorum*, II (1974), 3744–3807.

2 Jerome, *adv. Ruf.* 2, 22; 3, 6 (*PL* 23, 445f; 462).

3 Altaner, *loc. cit.*, and "Augustinus und Epiphanius von Salamis," *TU* 83 (1967), 286–296 (=Mélanges J. de Ghellinck, S.J., I (1951), 265–275).

4 K. Holl, "Die handschriftliche Überlieferung des Epiphanius," *TU* 36, 2 (1910), 96–98.

5 *Ep. ad S. Hier.* (*PG* 43, 391–392); Jerome, *Ep.* 51,2 (*PL* 30, 305–306).

our investigation.[6] Generally he was dependent on earlier heresiological lists, notably those of Irenaeus and Hippolytus. However, when we come specifically to his chapter on the Nazarenes, we must start from scratch: the Nazarenes are named in no extant work before Epiphanius. First let us bring the chapter in full.[7]

Panarion 29

|1,1| (K) They are succeeded by the Nazarenes. They lived at the same time, or before them, either with them or after them. In any case they are contemporaries. For I cannot determine who are the successors of whom. For, as I said, they were contemporaries and possessed identical ideas. |1,2| They did not give themselves the name of Christ, or that of Jesus, but they called themselves Nazarenes. |1,3| All Christians were called Nazarenes once. For a short time they were also given the name Iessaians, before the disciples in Antioch began to be called Christians. |1,4| (P) And they were called Iessaians because of Jesse, it seems to me, since David was from Jesse, and by lineage Mary was of the seed of David, fulfilling the holy scriptures according to the Old Testament when the Lord said to David |Ps 131:11 LXX(=132:11)], "From the fruit of your loins will I set upon your throne."

|2,1| But I am afraid that with any proposed interpretation such as that which I have just made, I will be violating the truth if I concentrate too much on the literal meaning, because not much breadth is to be obtained in the construction of the statement. |2,2| For when the Lord said to David 'from the fruit of your loins will I set upon your throne,' clearly the promise of God is unchangeable. |2,3| And what is the primary quality of an oath by God if not 'The Lord says, I have sworn by myself'? 'for God could swear by no one greater.' But even without the divine oath, the word is able to demonstrate its own certainty. For the Lord swore with an oath to David that from the fruit of his loins he would set upon his throne. |2,4| And the apostles bear witness that the Christ had to be born of the seed of David, just as also our Lord and Savior Jesus Christ was born. I will pass over the many testimonies so as not to burden the narrative, as I have already said. |2,5| But someone may perhaps say that after the Christ was born of the seed of David according to the flesh (i.e., from the holy virgin Mary), why is it that he has not been seated on the throne of David? For the gospel says, 'They were going to anoint him king, and when he learned of it, he withdrew' |John 6:15] and 'he hid in Ephraim, a city of the wilderness' |John 11:54]. |2,6| Since we have spoken here about the saying and we may be asked about this testimony and the claim that some of the word regarding the Savior on the physical side was not fulfilled, that he be seated on the throne of David (for it may be thought by some that it was not fulfilled), let us

---

6   The major work on this is still R.A. Lipsius, *Zur Quellenkritik des Epiphanios* (1868), which I have not been able to obtain. However, Lipsius' findings are still reflected in most modern articles on Epiphanius.

7   The text is in Appendix I. Sections marked (K) are the translation of K–R. Those marked (P) are by the present author.

say that it has been fulfilled nonetheless. For not one word of God's holy scripture fails.

[3,1] The throne of David and the royal seat are the priesthood in the holy church, the very royal honor and high priesthood which the Lord gave to his holy church, which he himself united into one. He transferred the throne of David into the church, never to leave her. [3,2] For the throne of David proceeded from that time according to the succession up until Christ himself, not departing from the leaders of Judah until there came 'the one for whom the things were reserved, and he is the expectation of the nations' [Gen. 49:10], as it says. [3,3] With the coming of Christ, the succession of leaders of Judah came to an end. Until him the anointed kings ruled, but the order crumbled and ceased when he was born in Bethlehem of Judaea, in the time of Alexander, who was of priestly and royal stock. [3,4] After Alexander, this office crumbled, from the time of Salina (also called Alexandra), during the years of Herod the king and Augustus the Roman emperor. This same Alexander, one of the anointed rulers, also placed the diadem on himself. [3,5] For joining together the two tribes, both royal and priestly, in other words Judah and Aaron and the whole tribe of Levi, he became king and priest. For not one of the figurative sayings of holy scripture has gone astray. [3,6] Moreover, the foreign king Herod then assumed the diadem, and there were no longer any descendants of David. [3,7] And after the royal seat was changed, the royal honor was transferred in Christ from its fleshly dwelling of Judah and Israel to the Church, and the throne has been established forever in the holy church of God. It holds this honor from two aspects, both royal and high-priestly—[3,8] that is, it holds the *royal* honor from our Lord Jesus Christ according to two ways: both because he is from the seed of King David according to the flesh and because he is the very one who is the greater eternal king by virtue of his divine nature. The *priestly* honor it holds, because he who is high priest and chief of high priests afterward was installed as the first bishop: James, [3,9] called apostle and brother of the Lord. (He was the physical son of Joseph by lineage and called 'the brother of the Lord' because he lived closely together with him.)

[4,1] This James was the son of Joseph from his [first] wife, not from Mary, just as this has also been told to us in many places and very clearly worked out for us. [4,2] We find, on the one hand, that he also was from David because he was the son of Joseph, and he became a Nazirite (because he was the firstborn of Joseph and consecrated [as such to God]). [4,3] Wherefore he was also allowed once a year to enter into the holy of holies, just as the Law commanded the high priests according to the scriptures. So relate many who came before us concerning him, Eusebius and Clement and others. [4,4] On the other hand, he was even allowed to wear the high priest's mitre on his head, just as the aforementioned trustworthy men bear witness in their writings. [4,5] Accordingly, as it says, our Lord Jesus Christ is 'a priest forever after the order of Melchisedek' [Heb. 6:20], and at the same time a king according to heavenly order, so that he might hold the priesthood together with the office of lawgiver. [4,6] Having sat down on the throne of the seed of David through Mary, [the throne remains his] forever, and of his kingdom there shall be no end [Luke 1:33]. Necessarily he also holds the order of the kingship. However, his kingdom is not from the earth, as he said to Pontius Pilate in the gospel, 'My

kingdom is not of this world.' [4,7] For that which was written [ὑποθέσεις] was, to a degree, a figurative anticipation, but now Christ has fulfilled all things. For he did not come to receive the dignified position of kingship, since he is eternally king, but rather he granted the kingdom to those who have been enthroned by him, lest it be thought that he proceeded from the lower estate to the higher. [4,8] For the throne remains his, and of his kingdom there shall be no end, and he is seated on the throne of David, having removed the kingship from David and given it together with the high priesthood to his bondservants, that is, to the high priests of his universal church. [4,9] There is also much to say about this; however, I have come to the passage because of which those who had believed in Christ were called Iessaians before they were called Christians, and because of this I said that Jesse was the father of David; and either on the basis of this Jesse or from the name of Jesus our Lord they were named Iessaians — because they began from Jesus, being his disciples, or because of the etymology of the name of the Lord. For Jesus in the Hebrew dialect means either healer or physician and savior. [4,10] Be that as it may, they acquired this name before they were called by the name Christians. But in the time of Antioch, as if we were named from above and because our way of life had to do with the truth, the disciples and all the church of God began to be called Christians.

[5,1] But you may also find, O Philologist, the way of life of these we are discussing in the writings of Philo, in his book written about the Iessaioi. When he relates in full their custom in words of praise, depicting their monasticism in the area surrounding the Mareotis lake, the man is not telling about Christians. [5,2] For he was in the region [the area is called Mareotis], and staying for a while among them, he was helped in the monasteries of the region. [5,3] And as he was there during the days of Pascha, he even observed their customs, how some extended their fast right through the holy week of Pascha, while others were eating every second day, and still others were eating evening by evening. But, as I said, all of these matters have been worked out by the man in his treatise pertaining to the faith and the practices of the Christians. [5,4] (K) When they were once called Iessaians during a short period, some again withdrew at that time after the ascension of the Lord when Mark preached in the land of Egypt. They were so-called followers of the apostles, but I suppose that they were Nazarenes who are described by me here. By birth they are Jews and they dedicate themselves to the Law and submit to circumcision. [5,5] But as some happen to see a fire but do not understand why they have kindled the fire or for what purpose they did it — whether to get food ready to eat for their subsistence with the help of fire, or because they are used to destroy with the help of fire inflammable wood or firewood — in the same way they have kindled a fire and have set fire to themselves. [5,6] For after having heard the name of Jesus only and having seen the divine signs performed by the hands of the apostles, they also believed in Jesus. When they came to know that he was conceived in Nazareth and had grown up in the house of Joseph and therefore is called Jesus the Nazarene in the Gospel, as also the apostles say: 'Jesus the Nazarene, a man made known by signs and miracles,' etc., they gave themselves this name calling themselves Nazarenes — [5,7] not Naziraeans, which translated means sanctified ones. For this title of honor was borne in the past by the first-born children who were sanctified to

God. Samson belonged to them and others after him and also many before him. But also John the Baptist himself was one of those who were sanctified to God 'for he drank no wine and strong drink.' This way of life has been determined for such people in agreement with their dignity.

[6,1] But they also did not call themselves Nasaraeans, for the heresy of the Nasaraeans existed before Christ and they did not know him. [6,2] However, everyone called the Christians Nazarenes, as I said before. This appears from the accusation against Paul which was as follows: 'We discovered that this man is a pest, somebody disturbing the people, the leader of the heresy of the Nazarenes' [Acts 24:5]. [6,3] The holy apostle did not deny this name although he was not a follower of their heresy, but he gladly accepted the name which was inspired by the malice of his opponents because it had been borne by Christ. [6,4] For he said at the tribunal: 'They did not find me in the temple speaking with somebody or causing a riot. Nothing of what I am accused of did I do. I admit to you that I serve God in that way which they call a heresy, believing everything which is in the Law and the Prophets.' [6,5] For it is no wonder that the Apostle admitted he was a Nazarene because everybody called Christians with that name at that time, because of the city of Nazareth and because at that time there was no other name in use. Therefore persons were called Nazarenes who came to believe in Christ, of whom it is written that 'he will be called a Nazarene' [Matt. 2:23]. [6,6] For also at this time people give all heresies — I mention the Manichaeans, the Marcionites and the Gnostics and all the others — the same name of Christians while they are not Christians. And also every heresy, even if it has a different name, will gladly bear that name because it gives them lustre. For they may suppose that they can be proud of the name of Christ but that does not apply to their beliefs and works. [6,7] Likewise the holy disciples of Christ called themselves disciples of Jesus, which they really were. When they heard the name Nazarenes from others, they did not reject it, because they saw what was meant by those who called them by this name, viz. that they called them by this name because of Christ, since our Lord himself was also called Jesus the Nazarene, as appears from the Gospels and the Acts of the Apostles. [6,8] For he grew up in the city of Nazareth, at the time a village, in the house of Joseph after being born according to the flesh in Bethlehem of Mary, ever virgin, who was betrothed to Joseph. He moved to that same Nazareth when he settled down in Galilee after his departure from Bethlehem.

[7,1] These heresies, just mentioned, of which we here are giving a brief sketch, passing over the name of Jesus, did not call themselves Iessaians and did not keep the name Jews; they did not call themselves Christians, but Nazarenes, taking this name from the place Nazareth. But actually they remained wholly Jewish and nothing else. [7,2] For they use not only the New Testament but also the Old, like the Jews. For the Legislation and the Prophets and the Scriptures, which are called the Bible by the Jews, are not rejected by them as they are by those mentioned above. They are not at all mindful of other things but live according to the preaching of the Law as among Jews: there is no fault to find with them apart from the fact that they have come to believe in Christ. [7,3] For they also accept the resurrection of the dead and that everything has its origin in God. They proclaim one God and his Son Jesus Christ. [7,4] They have a good mastery of the Hebrew

language. For the entire Law and the Prophets and what is called the Scriptures, I mention the poetical books, Kings, Chronicles and Esther and all the others, are read by them in Hebrew as is the case with the Jews, of course. [7,5] Only in this respect they differ from the Jews and Christians: with the Jews they do not agree because of their belief in Christ, with the Christians because they are trained in the Law, in circumcision, the Sabbath and the other things. [7,6] With regard to Christ I cannot say whether, misled by the wickedness of the aforesaid followers of Cerinthus and Merinthus, they believe that he is a mere man or whether, in agreement with the truth, they emphatically declare that he was born of the Holy Spirit from Mary. [7,7] This heresy of the Nazarenes exists in Beroea in the neighborhood of Coele Syria and the Decapolis in the region of Pella and in Basanitis in the so-called Kokabe, Chochabe in Hebrew. [7,8] For from there it took its beginning after the exodus from Jerusalem when all the disciples went to live in Pella because Christ had told them to leave Jerusalem and to go away since it would undergo a siege. Because of this advice they lived in Perea after having moved to that place, as I said. There the Nazarene heresy had its beginning.

[8,1] (P) But these have also erred in boasting of circumcision, and such are still 'under a curse' not being able to fulfill the Law. For how would they be able to keep that which is said in the Law, that 'you shall appear before the Lord your God three times every year' [Exod. 23:17], at the Feast of Unleavened Bread and at Tabernacles and at the Feast of Weeks in Jerusalem? [8,2] Since they have been banned from the region, and the things of the Law cannot be fulfilled, it is clear to all who have any intelligence whatever that Christ came that the Law might be fulfilled; he did not come destroying the Law but rather fulfilling it, and he determined to take away the curse which resulted from transgressing the Law. [8,3] For after the completion of the whole commandment by Moses, when he came to the end of the book, 'he included everyone together under a curse' saying 'cursed is he who does not keep all of the words written in this book to do them [Deut. 27:26]. [8,4] So he [Jesus] came releasing those things chained by the bonds of the curse and instead of the small things which could not be fulfilled, he has granted us greater things which do not conflict with each other for fulfillment as did the former things. [8,5] For thus it is with every heresy, often trying to outdo each other in the matter prescribed concerning the keeping of the Sabbath and circumcision and other things, even though our Lord freely gave us a more perfect way. [8,6] And how can such maintain any argument, when they do not listen to what was said by the Holy Spirit through the apostles to the believers from the Gentiles: 'to lay [on you] no greater burden than these essentials: refrain from blood and from things strangled and from fornication and from things sacrificed to idols'? [8,7] And how will they not fall away from the grace of God when Paul the holy apostle says that 'if you are circumcised Christ will be of no benefit to you,' 'you who boast in the Law, you have fallen from grace'?

[9,1] (K) The brevity of this exposition will also be sufficient for this heresy. For such prople make a fine object to be refuted and are easy to catch, for they are rather Jews and nothing else. [9,2] However, they are very much hated by the

Jews. For not only the Jewish children cherish hate against them but the people also stand up in the morning, at noon, and in the evening, three times a day and they pronounce curses and maledictions over them when they say their prayers in the synagogues. Three times a day they say: 'May God curse the Nazarenes.' [9,3] For they are more hostile against them because they proclaim as Jews that Jesus is the Christ, which runs counter to those who still are Jews who did not accept Jesus. [9,4] They have the entire Gospel of Matthew in Hebrew. It is carefully preserved by them in Hebrew letters, as I wrote in the beginning. But I do not know whether they also have omitted the genealogies from Abraham to Christ. [9,5] (P) But now that we have exposed this heresy as weak and the cause of pain by wasp's poison, and having crushed it with the truth, let us go on to what remains, Beloved, asking help from God.

There is no clear internal evidence as to Epiphanius' source or sources for this information. What is more, there is nothing in this long chapter which gives any clear indication that Epiphanius had any personal contact with the sect against whom he writes. This is particularly surprising, since one often finds it stated that Epiphanius had some personal knowledge of the Nazarenes. As a matter of fact, we may have some evidence that he was *not* personally acquainted with them in his admissions that he cannot determine whether they succeeded the Cerinthians or vice versa (1,1) and that he is unsure about their Christology (7,6). This latter is the one thing we would expect him to discover at the very outset of any direct enounter with them.[8]

We may reserve further assessment of possible sources until we have isolated the facts given peculiar to the sect. They are precious few. We may include here information found elsewhere in the *panarion*.

1. They use both Old and New Testaments (7,2).
2. They have a good knowledge of Hebrew and read the Old Testament and at least one gospel in that language (7,4; 9,4).
3. They believe in the resurrection of the dead (7,3).
4. They believe that God is the creator of all things (7,3).
5. They believe in one God and his son Jesus Christ (7,3).
6. They observe the Law of Moses (7,5; 5,4; 8,1ff).
7. They were joined by Elxai and later adopted his book (19,5,4; 53,1,3 with 19,1,4; 19,3,4ff and 19,4,1).

---

8 We may also see in this lacuna in his knowledge an indication that their Christology was "orthodox." While Epiphanius gives the two familiar choices, it is clear that his sources were silent on the matter. We can be sure that any "orthodox" source would have been quick to attack the smallest deviation in Christology had it been known. The very fact of the silence here may be taken as an indication that there was little or nothing peculiar to draw attention or attack to the Nazarene Christology. On Epiphanius' understanding of "heresy," see F.M. Young, in *Studia Patristica* I (1982), 199–208.

8. Ebion came out of them (30,2,1).

9. Earlier they were called Iessaioi (5,1–4).

10. They had their origin from the Jerusalem congregation which fled to Pella before 70 (7,8).

11. Geographical location in Pella, Kokaba, and Coele Syria (7,7).

12. They are hated and cursed by the Jews (9,2–3).

It will be seen immediately that the bulk of the peculiar data is concentrated in section 7, and one in fact gets the impression that Epiphanius is, in this section, relying on a single source. The confusions here are minor, and the information will be seen to be more reliable than elsewhere. Let us first consider those four items which are not from section 7.

Elxai[9] joined them and later they adopted his book.

It is beyond the scope of the present work to examine in depth Elxai (or Elchasai) and the so-called Eikesaites. Suffice it to say that among scholars there **are those who believe that there was a historical character by that name**, after whom the 'Book of Elxai' was named;[10] and there are those who hold that there was only a Book of Elxai (חיל כסי, 'Hidden Power' — see *pan.* 19, 2,2) which was later attributed to a man invented for the need.[11] According to its own testimony the sect had its origins at the beginning of the second century, during the reign of Trajan.[12] However, there is no external evidence of its existence until about 220, and scholars have often called its early origins into doubt. The Book of Elxai was evidently written in Aramaic and translated into Greek.

Now if there was never a person named Elxai, then Epiphanius has clearly erred in stating that he joined the Nazarenes. In that case, we are left only with the piece of information that the Nazarenes adopted the Book of Elxai. Interestingly enough, for all the lack of unity among scholars on the subject of Elxai and his book, on one thing there is practically universal agreement, that it is extremely unlikely that the Nazarenes really adopted the Book of Elxai as Epiphanius states.[13] We should be able to surmise this when we compare

---

9   The sources for Elchasai (Elxai) and the Elkesaites are Hippolytus, *ref. omn. haer.*, prol. IX 4; IX 13–17; X 29, 1; Epiphanius, *pan.* 19; 53; and Eusebius *HE* VI 38 (quoting Origen). See also W. Brandt, *Elchasai* (1912); H. Waitz, "Das Buch des Elchasai" in *Harnack-Ehrung* (1921), pp. 87–104; G. Strecker, "Elkesai" in *RAC* IV (1959), c. 1171–1186: K. Rudolph, *Die Mandäer*, I (1960), p. 233, n. 4; J. Irmscher in H–S II (1965), 745–750; K–R, 54–67; A. Harnack, *History of Dogma* I (1961), 304–308; *idem., TLZ* 37 (1912), c. 683–685 (review of Brandt); H.J. Schoeps, *Theologie*, 325ff; *idem.*, "Elkesaiten" in *RGG*³ II (1958), 435; G. Bareille, "Elcésaites" in *DTC* 4 (1911), 2233–2239.

10 From the previous note: Harnack, Brandt, Irmscher, and Strecker.

11 Schoeps, Klijn, Bareille, and *ODCC*, s.v.

12 Hippol., *ref. omn. haer.* IX 13, 4.

13 See, e.g., Brandt, *op. cit.*, 61, 116, and Harnack, *Dogma*, 305.

Elkesaite Christology with what we can discern of Nazarene Christology. On this basic, essential point there is a great difference. Hippolytus, who gives us the most complete description of the Elkesaites, tells us that they believed 'that Christ was born a man in the same way common to all and that he was not at this time born for the first time of a virgin but that, having been previously born and being re-born, he thus appeared and exists, undergoing alterations of birth and moving from body to body.'[14] Such a Pythagorean concept (as Hippolytus notes it to be) is quite foreign to Nazarene Christology. Differences exist in other areas, such as the acceptance of Paul and the full Old and New Testament canons,[15] but this matter is enough by itself to assure us that the Nazarene sect as we have thus far understood it would not have been able to accept the Book of Elxai.

Brandt notes that Epiphanius tends to join his heresies together or at least to ascribe to them a kind of line of succession.[16] Each one came out of the one before it and was even worse than the evil which spawned it. Thus we see that the Ossaioi mingled with the Nasaraioi who were later joined by Elxai,[17] and Ebion was a successor of the Nazarenes and generally adopted elements from various other 'Jewish Christian' groups.[18] In fact the impression one gets is that the lines of demarcation are faint to Epiphanius and that he frequently makes generalizations concerning succession or interrelation of heresies that may not have been justified from his sources. This seems to be the case with his statement that the Nazarenes adopted the Book of Elxai.

Ebion came out of them

The problems involved here are similar to those in the case of Elxai, as are the conclusions. First of all, of course, there is serious doubt as to the historicity of a character named Ebion. While there are some scholars who accept that a heresiarch by that name truly existed,[19] most believe that the man was the child of the sect and not vice versa.[20] It is not necessary to explain in depth but only to recall that אביון means poor (πτωχός), and that the group was called "the poor." Irenaeus, who first mentions the sect, knows only the group name.[21] It is

14 Hippol., *ref. omn. haer.* IX 14, 1 (translation by K–R); cf. also X 29, 2.
15 Origen (Eus. *HE* VI 38).
16 *Op. cit.*, 61.
17 *Pan.* 19 1, 1ff; 2, 1. (The word frequently used, as pointed out by Brandt, is συνάπτω. Cf. also 19 5, 4; 30 2, 9; 30 3, 2.)
18 *Pan.* 30 1, 3–4.
19 K–R; Hilgenfeld, *Ketzergeschichte*. 445.
20 Examples are F.X. Murphy, *Cath. Enc.* 5, 28; Bareille, *DTC* 4, 1988f; Strecker, *RAC* 4 488; O. Cullmann, *RGG*³ II, 297.
21 *Adv. haer.* I 26, 2; III 11, 7; 21, 1; IV 33, 4; V 1, 3.

Tertullian (or perhaps Hippolytus — see above chap. 2, n. 28)[22] who first mentions an Ebion, apparently deriving a hypothetical Ebion from the Ebionaioi.

As we have noted for the Elkesaites, it is a literary device of Epiphanius — often supplementary to the evidence of his sources — to state that one heresy grew out of another.[23] While this is probably true in this case also, we may have here a recollection of some split in the Nazarene ranks after the move to Pella. We have little reason to doubt the other statements of Epiphanius which consistently tell us that the Ebionites were later than the Nazarenes.[24] It is reasonable to assume that it was a question of Christology which precipitated the split, although a struggle for leadership is also a possibility. (It is tempting to conjecture that it occurred sometime after the formulation and institution of the birkat ha-mînîm and in some way resulted from it.) Such a split would explain the identical geographical locations of the two groups and why they were so often confused by Christian writers.[25]

We cannot accept, then, that a Nazarene named Ebion developed his own doctrines and gathered a following. But this statement by Epiphanius might preserve a faint recollection that the Ebionite sect had its roots in the remnant of the earliest Jerusalem community. It was, as it were, the grandchild of the first

---

22 Tert. *de praes.* X 8; XXXIII 3–5; 11; *de virg. vel.* 6, 1; *de carne Chr.* 14; 18; 24; Hippol. *ref. omn. haer.* VII 35, 1 (and Ps. Tert. *adv. omn. haer.* 3).

23 Epiphanius did not originate this concept, of course. Besides the fact that it was often true historically, he had literary precedent for it in Irenaeus (Cf. e.g., *adv. haer.* I 28 (Harvey, I, 219): *Ab his autem qui praedicti sunt, eo quod multi ex ipsis, imo omnes velint doctores esse, et abscedere quidem ab haeresi in qua fuerunt; aliud autem dogma ab alia sententia, et deinceps alteram ab altera componentes, nove docere insistunt, semetipso adinventores sententiae, quamcunque compegerint, enarrantes.*) However, the idea that they joined each other seems to be an extrapolation of the Bishop of Constantia. Neither did he find this particular statement, that Ebion came out of the Nazarenes, in Irenaeus.

24 In *pan.* 19 5, 4 there is a textual problem and a seeming contradiction to my statement here. The extant text reads: καὶ κέχρηνται αὐτῷ τέσσαρες αἱρέσεις ἐπειδὴ θέλγονται τῇ αὐτοῦ πλάνῃ. Ἐβιωναίων τε τῶν μετέπειτα Ναζωραίων Ὀσσαίων τε τῶν πρὸ αὐτοῦ καὶ σὺν αὐτῷ καὶ Νασαραίων τῶν ἄνω μοι προδεδηλωμένων (which Petavius [Migne] renders: *eumque sectae quatuor auctorem sibi vindicant, quae illius praestigiis afficiuntur: nimirum Ebionaei, ac posteriores Nazaraei, Osseni qui tam ante illum, quam illo prodierunt, et Nazaraei* [he reads Ναζαραίων, which is not attested], *de quibus antea disputavi*). Holl (*GCS* 25, ad loc. has emended to <ἢ> Ἐβιωναίων τε τῶν μετέπειτα <γεγονότων καὶ> Ναζωραίων κτλ. He also sees the inconsistency (citing Hilgenfeld, *Ketzergeschichte*, p. 426, n. 726, as its prime advocate) and suggests that we should understand μετέπειτα to mean "after Elxai" (or actually, in context, after the Ossaioi). This, though not without its difficulties, is easier to accept than a blatant contradiction.

25 The suggestion is proffered below (chap. 5) that the name of the Nazarenes was left long unattacked, because it was an early one for the Christians. This cannot be said for the name Ebionites, and perhaps it is for this reason (if indeed the Ebionites split off from the Nazarenes) that the two groups were lumped under the latter name rather than the former.

church. Here again one can only speculate as to Epiphanius' source for this information. It seems reasonable to think that a break in the Nazarene ranks would have been more likely remembered in a Nazarene or Ebionite source than in any records of the catholic Church from the Gentiles. However, in light of his general lack of acquaintance with the Nazarenes and their doctrines, it seems safer to say that Epiphanius' knowledge of such a source was only secondary.[26]

They were called *Iessaioi*

This information occupies a sizeable amount of space in the chapter on the Nazarenes (from 4,9 to 5,4 — some 30 lines out of about 266), but does it tell us anything about the sect? Let us begin at the end of the section where Epiphanius states, 'They were so-called followers of the apostles, but I suppose that they were Nazarenes who are described by me here.' Here we learn that he himself has made the equation between Iessaioi and Nazoraioi. He has just cited Philo's description of the Therapeutai in *de vita contemplativa* and expresses his opinion that Philo is referring to none other than Christians (5,1 and 3). This very point causes him some trouble, because on the one hand he wants to see Philo's treatise as an independent description of early Christians, while on the other he has decided that these are Nazarenes, whom he is out to attack.[27] He tries to reconcile the problem in 5,5, but he only resorts to polemic and allegory and not to logic and fact.

Epiphanius takes this idea — that Philo is actually writing about Christians — from Eusebius.[28] In fact, it is evident that the heresiologist is largely dependent on the historian in this whole passage, though he never cites him. But it is too simplistic to say that he is dependent on Eusebius and leave it at that. It would be more accurate to say that Epiphanius is using (or even recalling) Eusebian information and expanding it for his own purposes.

Let us deal with the above-mentioned problem first: 'they were so-called followers of the apostles.' By whom were they so called? Not by Philo certainly, nor does Eusebius ever state this directly. However, the *impression* from Eusebius is exactly that. Compare *HE* II 16, that these were converts of Mark whom Philo describes; 17,2: Philo's description shows that he 'recognized the divine mission of the apostolic men';[29] 17,5–6: their community of property was like that of the Church in the book of Acts; 17,12: their scriptures probably included the Gospels and apostolic writings; and finally this statement at the end of Eusebius' treatment (17,24): 'it is plain to everyone that Philo perceived and

---

26 There may be a hint of this in *pan.* 30 2, 8, where he says that Ebion had first lived in Kokabe; "this is according to the contents of the information which has reached us."

27 Noted by K–R, 44.

28 *HE* II 17.

29 Translations of Eusebius are by Lake in the Loeb series.

described the first heralds of teaching according to the Gospel and the customs handed down from the beginning by the Apostles.' From all of this it is quite reasonable for Epiphanius to refer to 'so-called followers of the apostles.' He is relating the sense of what he has read in Eusebius.

A further look at how he adapts the notice of Eusebius will be useful when we come to the main problem below. In 5,2 Epiphanius relates that Philo 'was helped in the monasteries of the region.' Now as a matter of fact Philo does speak of (*monastēria*),[30] but they are small rooms in the individual houses. Eusebius quotes Philo on this without falling into the anachronism (17,9). But Epiphanius, again probably conflating the general tenor of his source with his recollection that the word *monastēria* is used, develops for the Iessaioi a system of *monastēria*. Not surprising, perhaps, for an old abbot.

Philo does not tell us that he himself had any direct contact with his Therapeutai. Eusebius (17,12) not unreasonably surmises that Philo might have heard some of their expositions of scripture,[31] but Epiphanius (5,2–3) does not hesitate to say that Philo stayed with them and observed their customs, even stating categorically that he was there at Easter (Πάσχα).

This matter of Πάσχα further illustrates his tendency to extrapolation in our passage. Epiphanius describes (5,3) the paschal eating habits of three divisions of these Iessaians, saying that it was all worked out by Philo. This corresponds to *HE* II 17,16–17 (= *de vita* 34–35) in which three levels of abstinence from eating are depicted. But neither Philo nor Eusebius gives any hint that Pascha is intended, and in fact it is clear that no particular time is meant. Now as a matter of fact, in *HE* II 21–22 Eusebius does speak of certain abstinences from food during 'the feast of the Passion of the Savior,' but not in the context of the notice of the three kinds of eating habits. Here, I believe, we have further evidence that Epiphanius is writing from his recollection of Eusebius' account without checking it directly at the time of writing. In so doing he has produced a hybrid which is of little use as a source for the Therapeutai and of no use at all for preserving valid data on the 'Iessaioi.'

But who are the Iessaioi? Epiphanius himself gives two possible etymological derivations of the name. The one he would seem to prefer is that it comes from the name of Jesse (Iessai), David's father. His preference is shown in giving this explanation first and in his repetition of it. I must confess a prejudice toward this explanation myself, because it brings together the two names which appear in juxtaposition in Isaiah 11:1 and increases the likelihood that the name Nazarene

---

30 *De vita cont.* 25; 30. F.H. Colson (Philo [Loeb] IX, 519f), citing Conybeare and Liddell-Scott, notes that this word appears only here in any Greek document until the end of the third century.

31 Cf. *de vita cont.* 75–78. We understand the μαρτυρεῖ of 17, 5 and μαρτυρήσας of 17, 7 to refer to Philo's literary testimony rather than necessarily to an eyewitness account, although there is no reason to eliminate the likelihood that he was in fact describing personal observations.

truly was one of the earliest for the Church in Palestine. It was, therefore, with no little pleasure that I came across the treatment by E.A. Abbott of the name Nazarene.[32] After a thorough survey showing that a connection can be demonstrated in talmudic literature between the name Jesse and the word נצר (netzer), he turns to the *panarion* of Epiphanius and states: 'If there were such sects [Nazoraeans and Nasaraeans], or early traditions mentioning such names, it must occur to everyone that the names had some connection with Isaiah's mention of the *Netzer* of *Jesse*.[33] It may indeed have occurred to everyone, but no one except the distinguished Cambridge don has seen fit to record it.

Epiphanius' alternate suggestion is that the name is derived from the name of Jesus. This is, of course, what we would have expected and of his two choices must be considered *lectio facilior*. However, it is evident that this is a guess by Epiphanius. In fact, in making this suggestion he contradicts his earlier statement (1,2) that the Nazarenes (= Iessaians) did *not* call themselves after Jesus. We would be able to drop this second derivation were it not for Epiphanius' own attempts at working out the etymology: 'for Jesus in the Hebrew dialect means either healer (*therapeutes*) or physician and savior.' This word *therapeutes* seemingly makes the connection to Philo: Epiphanius has simply given us a slightly different form of the name *Essaioi* which, in a momentary oversight, he has inserted in place of the Therapeutai. But solutions are rarely so simple, and this one is no exception.

It is well known that in the *de vita* passage in question neither Philo nor Eusebius makes any reference to Essenes, speaking solely of Therapeutai. In his *praeparatio evangelica*[34] Eusebius does quote two passages from Philo which deal with the Essaioi. In neither one does he try to say that these were actually early Christians, as he says about the Therapeutai, and neither he nor Philo suggests that Therapeutai and Essaioi were the same. Philo, in fact, is careful to tell us that they are distinct (*de vita* I,1).[35] The easiest explanation is that Epiphanius has concluded (with no small number of later scholars) that the Therapeutai and the Essaioi are nonetheless the same and that he has just given us a variation of the name of the latter.[36] Are the Iessaioi Essaioi?

---

32 *The Beginning* (= Vol. II) in *The Fourfold Gospel* (Cambridge, 1914), Appendix I (309–350).

33 *Ibid.*, 318.

34 VIII 11 and 12 (*GCS* 43, 455–461).

35 There is, of course, the often cited phrase θεραπευταὶ θεοῦ in *quod omnis probus liber sit* 75 (cf. e.g., C. Bugge, *ZNTW* 14 [1913], 174) but surely Philo does not intend here to give us a definitive identification of two sects. The wording is too incidental and the idea is in clear contradiction to *de vita* I 1.

36 Bugge, *loc. cit.*: "Dass das 'Jessaioi' nur eine kleine Modification von 'Essaios' ist, geben meines Wissens alle Forscher zu." Cf. Hilgenfeld, *Ketzergeschichte*, p. 427, n. 727; Wirthmüller, *Die Nazoräer*, p. 12; Schoeps, *Theologie*, p. 10. Hilgenfeld (*op. cit.*, pp. 99, 138f; *Judentum u. Judenchristentum* [1886], pp. 27–28) makes much of the mention by Abbot Nilus (d. 430; *de*

The following considerations do not make a negative response mandatory, but they must put a positive one in serious doubt. First, it could have been no 'momentary oversight' which exchanged the two names, as might be claimed for a modern scholar. At the end of the fourth century no scholar had yet concluded that Philo's two monastic sects were one and the same. If Epiphanius is saying as much, then he is the first to do so. Secondly, the form of the name Iessaioi is unique to Epiphanius.[37] It is never a variorum reading for *Essaioi* and must be considered pure invention if he did not, in fact, find the name somewhere for early (Nazarene?) Christians. If he was familiar with the *praep. ev.* quotes of Eusebius, then he surely read *Essaioi*. Why should he change the form? Thirdly, Epiphanius was otherwise familiar with the Essenes.[38] His usual form of the word is *Essenoi*, the normal Greek alternate for *Essaioi*.[39] Did he then invent a name to suit his purposes? And fourth and last, as we have said above, Eusebius never claims for the Essaioi that they are early Christians. If the form *Iessaioi* is a simple alternate spelling for a known sect, would Epiphanius have been so innovative as to come along and claim for the first time that they were actually Christians? It would hardly have been characteristic of this strongly conservative bishop.

There is just enough confusion in Epiphanius' notice to prevent us from drawing any major conclusions about the name Iessaioi, but it may at least be allowed that the solution Iessaioi = Therapeutai-Essaioi is an oversimplification. One would hope that the name Iessaioi may truly have some tradition, that Epiphanius has not simply invented it but may actually have found the name somewhere in reference to early Christians. If so, then his manifold confusions would be the result of an attempt to reconcile the name with the remainder of his data.

The Nazarenes were *hated and cursed by the Jews*

We come to the fourth piece of information which does not fall within section seven. This, of course, refers to the *birkat ha-mînîm* the 'Benediction of the sectarians.' While I shall take this up in full in Chapter Seven below, we may focus on it here for a moment in the course of our quest for Epiphanius' sources.

monastica exercitatione 3) of Ἰεσσαῖοι as proof that Epiphanius is only referring to Ἐσσαῖοι. However, it must be noted that it is not absolutely sure that Nilus' Ἰεσσαῖοι (he says the name means they are λόγιοι) can be unquestionably identified with the Essenes. To my knowledge the name Iessaioi is nowhere else attested. Brandt (*op. cit.*, 48) make the enterprizing suggestion, noting that Epiphanius (*pan.* 29, 5) calls Philo's work ΠΕΡΙΕΣΣΑΙΩΝ, that Epiphanius' source had doubled the iota and the bishop accepted it. This is a neat solution, but it assumes too much ignorance of the part of Epiphanius.

37 Except for the later writer Nilus, cited in the previous note.
38 *Pan.* 10; *rescriptum ad Acacium et Paulum* (PG 41, 169).
39 Compare his own Ὀσσηνοί / Ὀσσαῖοι in *pan.* 19; 30, 1; and 53. Petavius (PG 41, 260), like others, suggested ɪhat Essenes and Ossenes may be the same.

Unlike the previous three points, this fact is well-attested elsewhere, and there is no question of its historicity. But what was the source of this information?

Although Jerome frequently writes of the cursing of the Nazarenes,[40] it is chronologically unlikely that Epiphanius is using him. Jerome's earliest mention of it is about the year 404. Epiphanius wrote this in 375 and did not meet Jerome until 382. We can also eliminate Irenaeus and Hippolytus as possible sources because of their location in the West. Justin must remain a viable candidate here. We know from his *Dialogue with Trypho* (16 and 96) that he was possibly familiar with the Benediction.[41] This leaves the possibility that he mentioned it also in his lost *Syntagma*. In Chapter Five below it is demonstrated to be very unlikely that the Nazarene sect was actually attacked in the *Syntagma*. This, however, does not eliminate the possibility that the name of the sect was mentioned — Justin surely knew the name — and a likely context would be the *birkat ha-mînîm*.

It seems to me that another possible 'source' must be considered. The testimony of Jerome as well as the Geniza fragments show that the curse in question was still part of the synagogue service in the days of Epiphanius.[42] When we consider that the Church was now in government (and had just come through Julian's attempt to rebuild the Temple), it is not unreasonable to assume that the existence of the *birkat ha-mînîm* was fairly common knowledge in Church circles.[43] Epiphanius, born and raised in Palestine, could easily have been familiar personally (or at least from hearsay) with this sentence of the synagogue liturgy.[44]

A brief review, then, of what we have been able to isolate concerning Epiphanius' sources for non-section 7 material shows the following: a. *Elxai* — Epiphanius wrongly grouped the Nazarenes together with other sects. This is his own invention and does not indicate a separate source. b. *Ebion* — generally he has again conflated material from other areas to include Nazarenes. There is a possible echo of a Nazarene (or Ebionite) source dealing with a split in the Nazarene ranks, resulting in the sect of the Ebionites. If such a source ever

---

40 *Ep.* 112; *in Amos* 1, 11–12; *in Is.* 5, 19; 49, 7; 52, 4–6.

41 But see below, chap. 7, n. 51.

42 I would venture to say only in the East.

43 It might be objected that Jerome's letter to Augustine (*ep.* 112, 13) indicates that Augustine was ignorant of the Benediction and that it could not, therefore, have been common knowledge. The words of Jerome give the answer: "Until now a heresy is to be found in all parts *of the East* . . . Minaei . . . Nazaraei." Augustine had never been in the East, and Jerome was right to assume that this might be new to him. The Nazarenes only existed in the East, and it is suggested below, chap. 7, that the addition of Shmuel haKatan adhered only in those areas where there was a present danger.

44 In this regard we may recall that his native language was Syriac, in which all Christians were called "Nazarenes."

existed, Epiphanius knew of it only by secondary sources. c. *Iessaioi* — he uses
Eusebius but not for the essential data. Otherwise there *may* be a vague
recollection of an early name, but the source must remain unknown. d. *Birkat ha-
mînîm* — Justin is speculatively possible as a source; or perhaps Epiphanius' own
general knowledge. One thing is clear from this review: Here is surely no tangible
written source. We see only a collection of strange ideas which reflect
Epiphanius' desire to fill in a sketchy picture. It is only in *pan.* 29,7 that he has
preserved for us the testimony of a knowledgeable source.

Panarion 29,7

The data in this section present us with a body in every way 'orthodox' except for
its adherence to the Law of Moses. If we remember that the Jewish Church of
Jerusalem also kept the Law through the period covered by the book of Acts,
then we have a picture of the earliest Jewish Christian community. Two items
from section 7, the flight to Pella and the geographical data, are dealt with
below.[45]

1. They use both Old and New Testaments. This implies, though it is not
clearly stated, that they make use also of Paul. We know from Jerome[46] that the
Nazarenes respected the Pauline writings, a fact which sets them apart from
other Jewish Christian groups. In fact it is generally a characteristic of the
heresies that they reject some portion of scripture.[47] The very fact that
Epiphanius can credit them with acceptance of canonical scripture is a strong
statement in favor of their 'orthodoxy'. The fact that they read the Old Testament
'and at least one gospel' in Hebrew, which they know well, only serves to confirm
their Jewish background.

2. Section 7,3 gives us three brief pieces of information about the doctrines of
the Nazarenes. One need make only a quick comparison with the opening
chapters of Acts to see that these basic doctrines had a place in the teaching of
the earliest Jerusalem Church: the resurrection of the dead (Acts 2:24,32; 3:15;
4:10); God is the creator of all things (4:24); and belief in one God and his child
(παῖς) Jesus Christ (3:13,26; 4:27,30). To this point we have nothing that would
differentiate the Nazarene sect from the primitive Church. The picture is not full,
certainly, but what we are given in every way confirms the identity of the
Nazarenes as the heirs of the earliest Jerusalem congregation. Even Epiphanius
has nothing condemnatory to say about the data thus far.

3. The parting of the ways is at the Law of Moses. It is their observance of the

---

45 See Appendixes II and III.
46 *In Is.* 9, 1, where he quotes from the Nazarene commentary on Isaiah.
47 Ebionites: Irenaeus, *adv. haer.* I 26, 2; III 11, 7; Origen, *hom, in Jer.* XIX 12; *C. Cels.* V 66;
   and Epiphanius himself in *pan.* 30 16, 8–9; 18, 4f; 18, 7. Cerinthus: Epiph. *pan.* 28 5, 3;
   Filaster, *div. haer. liber* 36. Elxai: Epiph. *pan.* 19 3, 6; 5, 1.

Law — and this alone — which, for Epiphanius, separates the Nazarenes from the main Church. 'Only in this respect they differ from the... Christians.' It is this one thing which so stands out that it is essentially the only thing remembered by subsequent Fathers against the sect, starting with the *anacephalaiosis*.[48] It makes little difference that the first Jewish believers continued to keep the Law (Acts 15; 21:20–26); it is immaterial that the epistle to the Galatians was addressed to Christians from *gentile* background or that Paul perhaps never wrote against *Jewish* Christians keeping the Law. The significance of all of this has long since been lost to men like Epiphanius. The Law is taboo. To attempt to keep it is to put oneself under a curse. If the Nazarenes want to observe parts of the Law, then they are 'Jews and nothing else.' Never mind if the same could be said for James or Peter, or, indeed, Paul. For our purposes, of course, this matter of the Law only reinforces the conviction that we have here a body of Jewish believers who have managed to preserve the very earliest traditions of their forebears.

Nasaraioi

We cannot leave a discussion of Epiphanius and the Nazarenes without dealing with another sect against whom he writes, the Nasaraioi. He is the only Church Father to mention them,[49] telling us that they were a pre-Christian Jewish sect which lived in the area of Galaatides (Gilead), Basanitis (Bashan), and other regions along the Jordan. They accepted the fathers of the Old Testament but rejected the Torah as not given by God. They kept Jewish practices, such as circumcision, the Sabbath, and various feasts, ("being Jews"), but they rejected sacrifices and did not eat meat.

Among scholars the Nasarenes often enjoy the position of a kind of passe-partout. They are an obscure entity with characteristics just non-specific enough to allow them to be called in to solve numerous and varied riddles. Many scholars, of course, simply dismiss them as unhistorical, a confusion of Epiphanius. Among these are some who say that the Bishop of Constantia has simply invented (albeit unwittingly) a pre-Christian sect out of the Nazarenes.[50] Alternately, the Nasarenes existed but Epiphanius has created in them the Jewish Christian sect.[51] A milder corollary to this, of course, is to refrain from denying altogether the existence of the Nazarenes but to say that they were just the continuation of the earlier, pre-Christian sect of Judaism.[52] Having gone this far,

---

48 *Anaceph.* 29; Jerome, *ep.* 112, 13; *in Hiez.* 16, 16; *in Hier.* 3, 14–16; Augustine, *de bapt.* VII 1, 1; *c. Faust.* XIX 4; *de haer.* 9. (From Augustine onward, see chap. 5.)

49 *Pan.* 18; 20, 3; 29, 6, 1; 19, 5.

50 Schoeps, *Theologie,* 14ff; A. Schmidtke, *TU* 37 (1911), 199ff; W. Bousset, *Theol. Rundschau* 14 (1911), 373–385; H. Schaeder in *Theol. Dict. of the NT* 4 (1942), 879; B. Gärtner, *Horae Soederblomianae* 4 (1957), 20.

51 Bugge, *art. cit.,* 174.

52 P. Winter, *NTS* 3 (1956/7), 137.

one must necessarily conclude that Jesus received his title from them.[53] Among this Nazarene-from-Nasarene group there are those who call in the Mandaeans as well, generally equating them with the former.[54]

The majority of scholars, however, seem to accept Epiphanius' notice at more or less face value: there was a pre-Christian Jewish sect of *Nasaraioi* who are not to be identified with the sect of *Nazaraioi*[55] while some connect this sect with the Nazerini of Pliny.[56] This is not impossible, although it does meet with a geographical inconsistency. Epiphanius states that the Nasaraioi were in the areas to the east of the Jordan. This is quite specific enough to make it believable. The notice of Pliny, who is reliable in his geographical details, puts the Nazerini considerably farther north and west. This is a difficulty which should be met by those who would identify the two.

We may limit ourselves here to the question of the identification or non-identification of the Nazarenes with the Nasaraioi. The problem exists mostly, it seems to me, because of the similarity of the names.[57] The earlier group is called Nasaraioi or Nasarenoi and perhaps Nazorei,[58] while the later sect is called (including readings outside of Epiphanius) Nazoraioi,[59] Nazaraei, Nazareni, and — in at least one manuscript — Nazorei.[60] Holl (*GCS* 25, 215) suggests that the name of the Nasaraioi comes from נסר or נשר, 'fallen' or 'fallen away.' He notes that the *anacephalaiosis* gives the meaning of the name as *apheniastes*, 'rebellious.' We have already dealt with the name of the Nazoraioi above. It is at least a possibility that the two names have separate origins.

The other ground for identifying the two sects is geographical. This has been attempted by Gressmann.[61] He equated 'east of Jordan' with Pella, Gilead with Kokabe, and then stretched Bashan to reach Aleppo (Beroea). The first two

53 C. Guignebert, *Jésus* (London, 1935), 79–89.
54 H. Gressmann, *Zeitschrift f. Kirchengeschichte* 41 (1922), 166f; *ZATW* 43 (1925), 24–25.
55 Hilgenfeld, *Ketzergeschichte*, 426; Brandt, *op. cit.*, p. 116; Bacon, *Studies in Matthew* (London, 1930), p. 163; M. Black, *BJRL* 41 (1958/9), 299; M. Simon, *St. Stephen and the Hellenists in the Primitive Church* (London, 1958), pp. 93f; E. Meyer, *Ursprung u. Anfänge des Christentums* II (1921), 409.
56 Brandt, *loc. cit.*; Bacon, *loc. cit.*; see also the discussion of Pliny's Nazerini above, chap. 1.
57 It is probably not lessened any by the tendentious reading of Petavius (Migne), who usually has Ναζαραῖοι for Νασαραῖοι or when he does read a σ persists in transliterating Nazaraei or (20, 3) Nazareni. Since he also transliterates Ναζωραῖοι as Nazaraei, he makes a de facto identification of the two groups. His note on the Nazaraioi (*PG* 41, 257f) confirms his bias. The influence of this anomaly of the Migne text should not be underestimated.
58 If one identifies the Nazorei of Filaster with them: see Petavius, *loc. cit.*, and Lightfoot, *Apostolic Fathers* I, 2, 416, and below.
59 The name Ναζαρηνοι never appears, even though Jesus is called Ναζαρηνός.
60 See Jerome, *de vir. ill.* 3 (Hilberg, *CSEL* 55, 381, 1. 26; cited by Holl, *GCS* 25, 321).
61 *ZATW* 43 (1925), 24–28.

parallels are already general and not very obligating. The third is exaggerated, and here the attempt fails.

When we come to matters of sectarian substance, the similarities cease altogether. The Nasaraioi rejected the books of Moses; the Nazarenes accepted them. The Nazarenes were never accused of being vegetarians, a singular trait of the Nasaraioi. Black suggests they were Samaritans, pointing out the various differences between Nazarenes and Nasaraioi,[62] the possible connection of the latter to the Nazorei of Filaster (who traces them to the Nazirites, the descendants of Jonadab ben Rechab), and the existence of a large group of Jewish, pre-Christian forerunners of the Mandaeans. This group, the Natzoraeans, left Palestine about 37 A.D.[63] There is again a geographical difficulty, but it disappears when we recall that we could be talking of a group which had to pick up and leave, heading east. The more serious objection is the Nasaraean rejection of the Pentateuch, which, of course, is the only part of the Bible accepted by the Samaritans. Black, however, interprets Epiphanius' words, not unreasonably, as meaning that they had their own version of the Torah in place of the one accepted by other Jews.[64] This, indeed, is precisely the case with the Samaritans.

Without going any deeper into the controversy over Mandaean origins, we may conclude here that there is enough evidence in favor of accepting Epiphanius' testimony that there were two distinct and unrelated sects, and that therefore the Nazarenes and Nasaraioi should not be confused with each other. Such confusion is easy and understandable, and Epiphanius himself may have mixed them up at least once.[65]

---

62 *BJRL* 41 (1958/9), 298–303.

63 Black's data on this latter are based on R. Macuch, "Alter und Heimat des Mandäismus nach neuerschlossenen Quellen," *TLZ* 82 (1957), 401–408.

64 Αὐτὴν δὲ οὐ παρεδέχετο τὴν πεντάτευχον, ἀλλὰ ὡμολόγει μὲν τὸν Μωϋσέα καὶ ὅτι ἐδέξατο νομοθεσίαν ἐπίστευεν, οὐ ταύτην δέ, φησίν, ἀλλ᾽ ἑτέραν.

65 In *pan.* 53 1, 3, as suggested by Brandt, *Elchasai*, 116. There is also textual backing for this: Holl, *GCS* 31, 315, 1. 8. Epiphanius is usually careful to keep them distinct; cf. *pan.* 19 5, 4; 29 6, 1.

Chapter Four

Jerome

At least as important for our study as Epiphanius is his younger contemporary Jerome.[1] This most learned and prolific of the Church Fathers has left us fully a third of our testimonies and fragments of the Gospel according to the Hebrews as well as other information about the Nazarenes in some detail and valuable excerpts from one of their own works. However, more than any other of our sources, Jerome is surrounded by controversy. For this reason it will be useful to set the chronology of his life and writings insofar as it touches on the subject of the Nazarenes.

Chronology

Born in the northeastern part of the Italian peninsula in the first half of the fourth century,[2] Jerome stayed in the West until about 372. In that year he journeyed overland to Antioch intending to become an ascetic. After some delay he did go, at the beginning of 375, into the wilderness of Chalcis ad Belum, about 27 kilometers southwest of Beroea. During his sojourn in the desert he studied Greek and, under "A believing brother from among the Hebrews",[3] he learned Hebrew. This desert period is the most likely time when Jerome could have had contact with the Nazarenes of Beroea. Realistically, it is the only time, since he was never again closer than Antioch.[4]

---

1   Major biographical works include G. Grützmacher, *Hieronymus: Eine biographische Studie* (Berlin, 1901, 1906, 1908), 3 Vols.; F. Cavallera, *Saint Jérôme: sa vie et son oeuvre* (Louvain, 1922), 2 Vols.; and more recently J.N.D. Kelly, *Jerome* (London, 1975).

2   Most scholars assign his year of birth somewhere around 341–345 or 347. Kelly (*op. cit.*, pp. 337–339), however, argues for the traditional date of 331, which is derived from Prosper of Aquitaine (*Epitoma chronicon*, *PL* 51, 576 and 592). Kelly also gives a summary of the arguments on both sides.

3   *Ep.* 125, 12 (*PL* 22, 1079).

4   Visits from Antioch are also possible. Cf. Kelly, p. 65. This would extend the period of possible contact from 372 to 380.

The chronology for this time in the East is not completely clear,[5] but it is likely that he returned to Antioch in 377. He stayed there until 380, and during this time he studied Bible under Apollinaris of Laodicea. This is surprising, since the latter had been anathematized in the Synod of Rome in 374, and was again condemned in 378 in Antioch itself[6] while Jerome was present in the city. He was later to write: 'While he instructed me in Scripture, I never accepted his disputable dogma on Christ's human mind.'[7] From Antioch he went to Constantinople and then, in 382, sailed to Rome in the company of Epiphanius.[8] In 385 Jerome returned eastward on his way to Bethlehem and stopped in Cyprus to visit the aging Bishop of Constantia. After an extensive pilgrimage-tour of the Holy Land, including a few weeks in Egypt, Jerome and his party arrived, in the early part of 386, in Bethlehem. He was never again to leave the region of Palestine,[9] and in fact the only travelling we can be sure he did at all were frequent visits to Jerusalem and probably to the library in Caesarea.

Jerome and the Nazarenes

More than any other Church Father, one must analyze not only Jerome's information but also his own relationship to the sect and its writings. This is because of his way of tying himself so inseparably to the facts he relates. In order to do this analysis best, the historian must also play psychoanalyst, because Jerome's personality seems frequently to have colored his claims.

There is only one place where Jerome is usually seen to be claiming that he had personal contact with members of the Nazarene sect. In *de viris illustribus* 3 we read: "The Hebrew itself [of the original Gospel of Matthew] has been preserved until the present day in the library of Caesarea, which Pamphilius the martyr so diligently collected. From the Nazarenes who use this book in Beroea, a city in Syria, I also received the opportunity to copy it."[10] For the moment let us deal only with the matter of his personal contact with the sect. If Jerome did make such contact, the only possible time, as noted above, could have been during the years 372–380, when he was in Antioch and in the desert near Beroea (375–377

---

5 Kelly, pp. 48, 57, whom I generally follow. Depending on just when he went into the desert and when he came out, he was there between two and five years.

6 J.D. Mansi, *Sacrorum conciliorum nova et amplissima collectio* (1901), III, 479 and 486; see A. Fortesque, "Apollinarism" in *ERE* I (1908).

7 *Ep.* 84, 3 (*PL* 22, 745); translation by Kelly, p. 59.

8 *Ep.* 127, 7 (*PL* 22, 1091).

9 Kelly, pp. 134f, and J. Wilkinson, "L'apport de saint Jérôme à la topographie," *RB* 81 (1974), 245–257.

10 *PL* 23, 613: *Porro ipsum Hebraicum habetur usque hodie in Caesariensi bibliotheca, quam Pamphilius martyr studiosissime confecit. Mihi quoque a Nazareis, qui in Beroea urbe Syriae hoc volumine utuntur, describendi facultas fuit.* (Unless otherwise noted, all translations of Jerome are from K-R.)

being the most likely time). But Jerome, in this unique passage, does not specifically say that he had had intercourse with the Nazarene sect. That, indeed, may have been the impression he wanted to give, but all he in fact says is that they made it possible for him to copy their Hebrew gospel. We know that he later was in the habit of borrowing Hebrew manuscripts from synagogues, and that he did this indirectly, not actually taking or returning them in person.[11] For a man committed to live the ascetic life in the desert, it must be considered likely that a loaned copy of the Hebrew gospel was brought to him and not borrowed personally. This passage, then, should not be taken alone as proof that Jerome was personally acquainted with the Nazarenes as a sect.[12] But no other notice corroborates the supposition.

Having taken the narrow view, we may now broaden our vision slightly. In his accounts of his desert sojourn, Jerome never mentions leaving Chalcis, and there is no pressing reason to think that he did. It is not, however, unreasonable to assume that he could have passed through Beroea on his way into and out of his monastic retreat. No one disputes the fact that he did spend several years near Beroea, and few would deny the presence of Nazarenes in that town. Surely, then, Jerome had ample opportunity to ask about them from local Christians and to make himself reasonably informed.[13]

A further context for such familiarization with the sect was suggested by Schmidtke in his pioneering work cited above, in which he tried to show that both Epiphanius and Jerome were primarily dependent on Apollinaris for their knowledge of the Nazarenes and their writings.[14] His conclusions are still generally accepted, although occasionally one hears a dissenting voice.[15] The important point for our investigation is that Jerome *did* study under Apollinaris, an extremely learned and informed man who spent his entire long life in the area

---

11 *Ep.* 36 *ad Damasum* (*PL* 22, 452); and see E.F. Sutcliffe, "St. Jerome's Hebrew Manuscripts," *Biblica* 29 (1948), 195–204.

12 This does not say, of course, that he had not met individual Nazarenes. It seems to me that the believing Jew who taught him Hebrew in Chalcis could easily have been a member of the Beroea Nazarene community (*ep.* 125, 12). But cf. A. Schmidtke, *Neue Fragmente und Untersuchungen zu den judenchristlichen Evangelien* (*TU* 37, 1911), p. 248.

13 We may also remember that Jerome had at least three periods of extended contact with that old heresiologue Epiphanius (382, 385, and 393–4 when the latter visited Jerusalem and Bethlehem during the controversy with John). See Kelly, 197–207. We have seen above (p. 31) that Epiphanius himself probably had no personal contact with them and could only have passed on to Jerome what he knew second hand.

14 *Op. cit.*, pp. 63–94. See also *idem., ZNTW* 35 (1936), 24–44.

15 G. Bardy, "St. Jérôme et l'Évangile selon les Hébreux," *Mélanges de Science Religieuse* 3 (1946), 29–30; P. Vielhauer in H-S I, 134f; M. Lagrange, "Évangile selon les Hébreux," *RB* 31 (1922), 321–349. It will be seen below that while we accept Schmidtke's general hypothesis, we cannot follow the extremes to which he carried it.

of Laodicea and Antioch, that is, in the vicinity of Beroea. The younger scholar was deeply impressed with Apollinaris' erudition, and continues to refer to him with respect long after Apollinarism was a condemned heresy.[16] The potential was there, in those first years after Jerome had started learning Hebrew, for him to learn much orally from Apollinaris. Certainly later, when he was writing his own Bible commentaries, he made extensive use of Apollinaris' voluminous works — notably in those commentaries in which we have references to the Hebrew gospel.[17]

From the foregoing considerations we may conclude that, while Jerome may or may not have made personal contact with the body of Nazarene Christians, he was certainly well enough situated to have learned much about them from contemporaries who did know them well. Not the least important corollary to this is that Jerome may be considered a good witness to their continued existence until at least the end of the fourth century.

Jerome and the Hebrew gospel

While Jerome makes no explicit claim to have known the Nazarene sect personally, he does, however, make two other claims which have frequently been called into question: he copied the Gospel according to the Hebrews (GH), "which is read by the Nazarenes," and he translated it into both Greek and Latin.[18] The parameters of this complicated problem and the limitations of any possible solutions have been well laid down by Vielhauer.[19] His general conclusions were, first, that Jerome was thinking of only one work when he spoke of GH and its various other designations; that this gospel was to be found in Caesarea and was probably the same as the one used by the Nazarenes; and lastly, that Jerome never translated all the gospel. To Vielhauer's article we would add some observations and suggestions.

As we have noted above, it is not *a priori* unlikely that Jerome could have been brought a copy of GH during his stay in Chalcis. As a beginning student of Hebrew, he could have copied it (in whole or in part) as an exercise without actually knowing what he was writing. His first mention of GH is in his commentary on Ephesians (5,4), which he wrote in 386/7. Here he makes no mention of translating it, and it is most likely that he simply found this quotation in an earlier commentary (Origen or perhaps Apollinaris). We must bear in mind that from 386 Jerome had access to the library of Pamphilius in Caesarea to which he made occasional visits.[20] Whether he personally owned a copy of GH or not, he could now use the one in Caesarea (which he believed to be the same

16 *De vir. ill.* 104; *ep.* 84, 3 (written c. 398).
17 See the prologues to *in Eph., comm. in Matth., comm. in Is.*
18 *De vir. ill.* 2 and 3; *in Mic.* 7, 6; *in Matth.* 12, 13.
19 "Jewish Christian Gospels" in H-S I, 126–136.
20 Kelly, p. 135.

and which may indeed have been the same).[21] In 390 he began his project of translating the Old Testament Hebrew into Latin. He began first with the books of Samuel and Kings, perhaps because they could be expected to be easier.[22] He had been preparing himself for this task since his arrival in Bethlehem, and it was during these years that he evidently translated GH, perhaps as a practice exercise before beginning his magnum opus. Therefore, we find his first claims to have translated GH "recently" in about 391 and 392.[23]

But these claims to have translated GH do not oblige us to conclude that he in fact finished the whole gospel. In 392, when he wrote his treatise on *Famous Men*, he claimed for himself that he had translated the Old Testament.[24] In fact he did not complete the translation until 405 or 406. It was a project he had under way, the completion of which was still "only in his intentions." So it may have been also with GH.[25]

At this point we must consider Jerome's personality. It is commonly acknowledged that he was a volatile and gifted man.[26] There can be no doubt that he was extremely learned. But Jerome had a quirk in his personality which seems to have made him claim to be even more learned than he really was. He often exaggerates his achievements in an effort to impress, even on occasion claiming to have read works which we now know never existed.[27] This is germane to our

---

21 Vielhauer, *art. cit.*, p. 132. If these were two distinct gospels, it would still be possible for Jerome to think they were the same if he had only cursory familiarity with each. Some scholars have decided that the two gospels were in different languages (one Hebrew, one Aramaic in Hebrew script) and have concluded that Jerome could not, therefore, have been familiar with them. But could we not, with equal validity, take the fact that he thought them to be the same as proof that they could not have been in different languages?

22 See *Praef. in lib. Sam. et Malachim (PL* 28, 547/558, esp. 555/557) and Kelly, p. 161.

23 *In Micha* 7, 5-7 (*CC* 76, 513): *sed qui legerit . . . credideritque evangelio, quo secundum Hebraeos editum nuper transtulimus*; and *de vir. ill.* 3 (*PL* 23, 611): *et evangelium quoque quod apellatur secundum Hebraeos et a me nuper in graecum sermonem latinumque translatum est . . .* Cf. also *ibid.* 16 (*PL* 23, 653) with *in Is.*, prol. 65 (*CC* 73A, 741).

24 *De vir. ill.* 135 (*PL* 23, 718f): *Novum Testamentum Graece fidei reddidi, Vetus juxta Hebraicum transtuli.*

25 Schmidtke, *TU* 37, 255, who, however, went further to suggest that Jerome only intended to get a copy of GH but never did.

26 This man, who knew plenty of controversy in his own lifetime, has tended to polarize scholars ever since — especially on Catholic-Protestant lines. (See the survey of O. Zöckler, *Hieronymus* [Gotha, 1865], pp. 473-476.) This seems to have begun with Luther himself (Grützmacher, "Jerome," *ERE* VII [1914] 497-500) and manifestly continues until today. On one extreme one may find a doting panegyric such as that of the 16th century Castillian monk, F.J. de Sigüenza; on the other extreme blasts such as those levelled by B.W. Bacon, *Studies in Matthew* (London, 1930), pp. 162, 478-479.

27 Kelly, pp. 65, 302, 334. We need not deal here with the problem of "plagiarism." Jerome frequently lifted long passages from his sources unacknowledged, but that was accepted practice in his day and should not be counted heavily against him.

discussion, because it has often been said against Jerome that he totally fabricated his claim to have translated GH, that in fact he never saw such a gospel but only copied from Origen or Apollinaris and then claimed it as his own.[28] This viewpoint is extreme, often tendentious. In the end, the statements of Jerome may prove to be more reasonable than those of his detractors.

Again in 398, in his commentary on Matthew, he says he recently translated GH.[29] It is significant that we find this claim in this particular commentary. If Jerome did believe GH to be an early (or original) edition of Matthew,[30] then he would naturally consult it at points where he needed help.[31] And, of course, he would make at least cursory translations of those passages which he used. The entire commentary on Matthew was done in about two weeks, and this haste would suggest that once again Jerome did not translate GH in its entirety but only passages from it. While he continues to quote from GH until as late as 415, he never again claims to have translated it — recently or otherwise. We may see this as a plan unfinished, and while there is no way to be sure, we conclude that Jerome did have access to a copy of "the gospel in Hebrew letters which the Nazarenes read" and that on several occasions he translated passages from it without ever completing a systematic translation.

The Nazarenes in Jerome

We may now attempt to isolate and analyze what specifics Jerome gives us about the Nazarene sect and see how it fits in with what we have seen before. We concluded above that it is less than likely that he had personal contact with the sect itself as a group, although he may have encountered individual members of it and he certainly was acquainted — at least in part — with some of their writings. We have also seen that whether he did spend time with the Nazarenes or not, his acquaintance would strongly suggest that his disinterested information be treated as reliable. It is on this assumption that we proceed.

Let us deal first of all with that all-important issue of Christology. The clearest statement comes in Jerome's letter to Augustine, written about 404: "They believe in Christ, the Son of God, born of Mary the Virgin, and they say about him that he suffered under Pontius Pilate and rose again."[32] This statement,

---

28 So Bacon, *loc. cit.*, n. 24.

29 *In Matth* 12, 13 (*CC* 77, 90). The translation "recently" or "lately," while most commonly the meaning of *nuper*, is not the only possibility. Also possible are "in recent years", "formerly", "once" (*Oxford Latin Dictionary* (1976), s.v., 2; Lewis and Short, *A Latin Dictionary* (1969), s.v., IIb).

30 *Ibid.: et quod vocatur a plerisque Mathei authenticum.* Cf. *adv. Pelag.* III 2.

31 Nicholson, 28–77, 104, attempted to show that GH was basically in the same pericope order as Matthew. Cf. *in Matth.* 6, 11, noted by K–R, 48, who also conclude that Jerome must have translated only selected passages.

32 *Ep.* 112, 13: *qui credunt in Christum, Filium Dei, natum de Maria virgine, et eum dicunt esse, qui sub Pontio Pilato passus est, et resurrexit.*

giving the impression almost of an early creedal formula, is corroborated in part in a couple of other places in Jerome's writings. That the Nazarenes believed Christ to be the Son of God we can derive from two citations from their commentary on Isaiah. At 29:17–21 the Nazarenes say against the Pharisees and Scribes that they "made men sin against the Word of God in order that they should deny that Christ was the Son of God."[33] And similarly we read at 31:6–9: "The Nazarenes understand this passage in this way: O sons of Israel, who deny the Son of God with such hurtful resolution."[34] It is possible also that in the same work at 11:1–3 we have a statement of Nazarene belief in the virgin birth, although what appears there may be Jerome's own comment. What we do find in that passage, however, is a clear statement of Christology which Jerome (and perhaps the Nazarenes themselves) connected to Paul's statement in his epistle to the Colossians (Col. 1:19; 2:9): "because in him the whole fulness of the Godhead took pleasure to dwell corporally; not as in the other holy ones moderately, but according to the Gospel read by the Nazarenes which was written in the Hebrew language: 'The whole fountain of the Holy Spirit came upon him'."[35]

It has been objected[36] that Jerome contradicts this statement of Christology (in the letter to Augustine) when he says in his commentary on Matthew, written in 398: "Strange stupidity of the Nazarenes! They wonder whence wisdom possessed wisdom and power possessed powers, but their obvious error is that they looked only at the son of the carpenter."[37] At first glance we would seem to have here evidence of Nazarene Christology, evidence which contradicts what we already know of the sect and which seems to go against what Jerome himself later told Augustine. However, the difficulty is an artificial one. If we look more closely at the context we find that Jerome is commenting on the passage in Matt. 13:53–58 where Jesus goes to visit "his own country" and is rejected. The gospel does not state specifically whether Nazareth or Capernaum or Bethlehem is meant, but Jerome clearly understands the first.[38] It is with this understanding

---

33 CC 73, 380: *qui peccare faciebant homines in Verbo Dei, ut Christum Dei Filium negarent.*

34 CC 73, 404: *Nazarei locum istum sic intellegunt: O filii Israel, qui consilio pessimo Dei filium denegastis....*

35 CC 73, 147f: *quia in ipso complacuit omnem plenitudinem divinitatis habitare corporaliter; nequaquam per partes, ut in ceteres santis, sed iuxta evangelium quod Hebraeo sermone conscriptum legunt Nazaraei: "Descendet super eum omnis fons spiritus sancti."*

36 By A.F.J. Klijn, *RSR* 60 (1972), 242, n. 12; cf. K–R 47. This same mistake was made by K.A. Credner, "Über Essäer und Ebioniten und einen theilweisen Zusammenhang derselben," in *Winers Zeitschrift für Wissenschaftl. Theol.* I, 3 (1829), p. 228, n. 72. See Schmidtke, *TU* 37, 119.

37 13, 53–54: *Mira stultitia Nazarenorum. Mirantur unde habeat sapientiam sapientia et virtutes virtus, sed error in promtu est quod fabri filium suspicabantur.*

38 Cf. Luke 4:24, where the proverb of Matt. 13:57 is repeated and is placed expressly in Nazareth (Luke 4:16).

that he quotes the words of the people in the pericope "where did he get this wisdom and these powers" and calls this *stultitia Nazarenorum* (stupidity of the Nazarenes), i.e., of the citizens of the town of Nazareth. *They* were the ones who had just said "Is this not the son of the carpenter?", and Jerome superficially comments on their query. Nowhere in this passage or near it is he speaking of the sect of the Nazarenes. He has simply given the name Nazareni to the inhabitants of Nazareth. So we have no christological statement and no contradiction in Jerome's notices.

Schmidtke[39] suggested that the christological formula of the letter to Augustine was taken from Epiphanius (*pan.* 30,9)[40] or rather that both had it from the same source, Apollinaris. This cannot be proven. The similarities are certainly striking, but so are the similarities to the various evolving creedal declarations of the early centuries. The formula given by Jerome is just simple enough to suggest that it is earlier than that of Epiphanius, which in any case is not expressly attributed to the Nazarenes.

According to Jerome, then, Nazarene Christology is basically what we have noted previously, a belief in the divine origins and virgin birth of Jesus in accordance with the accepted doctrines of the greater Church. Here we also see an express avowal of Jesus' death and resurrection.

In other matters also Jerome supports what we have found earlier about the sect. He tells us that they are cursed in the synagogues "by the Pharisees,"[41] that they mix faith in Christ with the keeping of the Law,[42] and that they have a gospel in Hebrew.[43] He also tells us that they live in Beroea,[44] but later in that same letter to Augustine he indicates that they are to be found "in all the synagogues of the East among the Jews."[45]

---

39 *TU* 37, 252f.

40 *GCS* 25, 344: ἀπήγγελει λέγων ὅτι "πίστευε <εἰς> ᾽Ιησοῦν, τὸν ἐσταυρωμενὸν ἐπὶ Ποντίου Πιλάτου ἡγεμόνος, υἱὸν θεοῦ προόντα (Schmidtke reads ὄντα) καὶ ἐκ Μαρίας ὕστερον γεγεννημένον, Χριστὸν δὲ ὄντα θεοῦ καὶ ἐκ νεκρῶν ἀναστάντα, καὶ ὅτι αὐτὸς ἔρχεται κρῖναι ζῶντας καὶ νεκρούς."

41 *Ep.* 112, 13; *in Amos* 1:11–12; *in Is.* 5:18–19; 49:7; 52:4–6; *in Hiez.* 16:13. See below, chap. 7.

42 *In Is.* 8:11–15; *in Hiez.* 16:16; *in Jer.* 3:14–16. Cf. also *ep.* 112, 13, which would seem to refer to Ebionites but which Schmidtke (*TU* 37, 247ff) showed to refer to Nazarenes. This statement about the Law-keeping is the only really negative thing Jerome has to say about Nazarenes. Otherwise his references range from neutral to almost respectful.

43 *De vir. ill.* 3; *in Matth.* 12:13; *in Is.* 11:1–3; 40:9–11; prol. 65; *adv. Pelag.* III 2; *in Hiez.* 18:5–9. See chap. 6.

44 *De vir. ill.* 3.

45 *PL* 22, 924: *Usque hodie per totas Orientis synagogas inter Judaeos haeresis est quae dicitur Minaeorum, et a Pharisaeis nunc usque damnatur: quos vulgo Nazaraeos nuncupant ....*

Nazarene Literature: The Jeremiah Apocryphon

Jerome tells us of two pieces of literature which the Nazarenes possessed, and a consideration of these is an issue central to this chapter. In 398 in his rapidly completed commentary on Matthew we read: "Recently I read a certain Hebrew work, which a Hebrew person of the Nazarene sect offered me as the apocryphal book of Jeremiah, in which I found these words literally."[46] The context is an Old Testament citation of Matthew which is wrongly attributed to Jeremiah instead of Zechariah. Jerome in fact decides that the passage should be understood to come from Zechariah, but then he adds the above comment. May we conclude from this that the Nazarenes possessed an apocryphal Jeremiah? It should perhaps first be noted that there is effectively no supporting evidence for Jerome's statement,[47] so our acceptance or rejection will have to depend solely on our analysis of his own words.

In the preface to this commentary, Jerome tells us that he read Origen's commentary (in 25 volumes) on Matthew many years before (*ante annos plurimos*). While it is certainly no proof, it is an indication that he may have consulted his favorite Bible commentator as he wrote his own commentary. At the place in question, Origen deals with the difficulty of Jeremiah/Zechariah, notes that the solution is either an error of Matthew or some apocryphal writing of Jeremiah and offers his opinion that the quote simply came from Zechariah.[48] He then concedes that, if someone is offended by such an idea, it is quite possible that there really was some secret prophecy of Jeremiah.[49] He makes no mention of any known apocryphal book and even says that such a statement of Jeremiah is not to be found "either in those books which are read in the church or in those used by the Jews."

With this background, Schmidtke[50] rejected the claim of Jerome to have seen an apocryphal Jeremiah. Jerome, he said, was simply using Origen's sop and adding a little meat to it and in the process enhancing his own scholarly reputation with regard to Origen. He noted Jerome's well-known tendency to exaggerate and invent and claim knowledge he did not have. Against this judgment of the Lutheran scholar, Fr. M.-J. Lagrange writes: "Schmidtke, who pretends to understand the psychology of Jerome so well, has in fact grasped it quite poorly."[51]

---

46 *In Matth.* 27:9–10 (*CC* 77, 265): *Legi nuper in quodam Hebraico volumine quem Nazarenae sectae mihi Hebraeus obtulit Hieremiae apocryphum in quo haec ad verbum scripta repperi.*

47 Lagrange, *art. cit.* (n. 15), 342, cites Justin's claim (*Dial.* 72) that the Jews omitted three passages from Jeremiah, but under closer scrutiny it is clear that this—even if it is true—can hardly provide corroboration of the existence of an apocryphal Jeremiah.

48 *Comm. in Matth.* 117 (*PG* 13, 1769).

49 *Ibid., Si autem haec dicens aliquis existimat se offendere, videat ne alicubi in secretis Jeremiae hoc prophetatur.*

50 *TU* 37, 253f.

51 *Art. cit.,* 342.

Lagrange acknowledged that Jerome was familiar with Origen's conclusions but suggested that they only served to make Jerome search for the source. Noting that the Nazarenes would have been the most likely to preserve the answer to the Matt. 27:9–10 puzzle because of their polemic with Judaism, Lagrange suggests that Jerome may have sought them out. For him the best guarantee of the accuracy of Jerome's statements is the Bethlehem father's "sincerity." While not wishing to get caught in the crossfire of a holy war, one cannot help but note some weaknesses in Lagrange's stand. He himself[52] reminds us that the scholars of that time had no access to concordances or lexicons or indexes, and we must not forget that Jerome was writing against a deadline and would hardly have had time to search through countless volumes, nor to seek out a Nazarene for the answer.[53]

It is, in fact, difficult not to accept Schmidtke's judgment in this. He points out that where we today read *secretam Jeremiae scripturam*, Jerome probably read Ἰερεμίου ἀπόκρυφον in the original, which he himself then rendered *Hieremiae apocryphum*.[54] We might add one proviso to the words of Schmidtke: "It is not to be credited that the Nazarenes composed a Hebrew Jeremiah writing." He is right. However, there is no reason to prove or disprove that particular idea, because no one — not even Jerome — ever claimed that the Nazarenes themselves *composed* the work. It is in this sense that it is relatively unimportant for our present study if Jerome is accurate or not. The very most his words can tell us is that some individual Nazarene possessed such an apocryphal work. In this light, the "Hebrew of the Nazarene sect" does indeed seem like a literary device to add credibility to Origen's "Apocryphon of Jeremiah."

Nazarene Literature: The Interpretation of Isaiah

Of all the study of the Nazarene sect, perhaps none is more interesting nor potentially more fruitful than five notices which Jerome has left us in his commentary on Isaiah. In these five short passages he quotes from what seems to be a Nazarene work on the prophet.[55] Jerome never specifically identifies the work as to type, but it seems to be some sort of brief commentary or expanded targum.

---

52. p. 343.

53 Lagrange's thesis necessitates either that there were Nazarenes near Bethlehem, an idea for which there would be no proof, or that Jerome sent away for an answer, something impossible in the limited time available and unlikely for the minor problem presented by Matt. 27:9—he could have passed over it as he does with many verses in his commentary—and fraught with much larger difficulties of inter-community relationships.

54 *Loc. cit.*

55 Relatively little scholarly attention seems to have been given to this lost work. See Schmidtke, *op. cit.*, 108–123; F.C. Burkitt, *Christian Beginnings* (London, 1924), pp. 72–75; L. Ginzberg, "Die Haggada bei den Kirchenvätern. VI. Der Kommentar des Hieronymus zu Jesaja" in *Studies in Memory of George A. Kohut* (New York, 1935), pp. 290f; Schoeps, *Theologie*, pp.

On Isaiah 8.14

The Nazarenes, who accept Christ in such a way that they do not cease to observe the old law, explain the two houses as the two families, viz. of Shammai and Hillel, from whom originated the Scribes and the Pharisees. Akiba, who took over their school, is called the master of Aquila the proselyte, and after him came Meir who has been succeeded by Joannes the son of Zakkai and after him Eliezer and further Telphon, and next Joseph Galilaeus and Joshua up to the capture of Jerusalem. Shammai then and Hillel were born not long before the Lord; they originated in Judea. The name of the first means scatterer and of the second unholy, because he scattered and defiled the precepts of the Law by his traditions and δευτερώσεις. And these are the two houses who did not accept the Savior who has become to them destruction and shame.[56]

We may first note the complete lack of condemnation of the Nazarenes by Jerome. They are simply those "who accept Christ in such a way that they do not cease to observe the old Law." True, there are places where he castigates them precisely for that,[57] but the only place where he dwells on and attacks it is in his controversy on the whole matter of Law observance with Augustine (*ep.* 112,13). It would seem that in principle he believed it wrong for even Jewish-born believers to continue to observe the precepts of the Mosaic Law, but this principle did not stop him from using their writings or citing their opinions, nor did it cause him to vent his anger against them as despicable heretics.

Even with its problems, which we shall discuss presently, this is an amazing passage. No less a scholar than F. C. Burkitt was able to say, "I do not think that there is another passage in any of the Church Fathers which betrays so much acquaintance with Talmudic Judaism."[58] Certainly from a *prima facie* view this must tell us something about the continued contact which the Nazarenes maintained with rabbinic Judaism. This is not to say that the passage is free from

214–218; and A.F.J. Klijn, "Jerome's Quotations from a Nazoraean Interpretation of Isaiah," *RSR* 60 (1972), 241–255. Only Schmidtke and Klijn treat all five notices. One would be surprised, given the style of Jerome, if there are not other, unattributed uses of the Nazarene work in his commentary. *In Is.* 59:12–15 (*PL* 24, 581; *CC* 73A, 685f), which speaks of "traditiones Iudaeorum" and expulsion from the synagogue, is one possibility.

56 *CC* 73A, 116 (*PL* 24, 119): *Duas domus Nazaraei, qui ita Christum recipiunt, ut observationes legis veteris non omittant, duas familias interpretantur, Sammai et Hellel, ex quibus orti sunt scribae et pharisaei, quorum suscepit scholam Akibas, quem magistrum Aquilae proselyti autumat et post eum Meir, cui successit Ioannan filius Zachai, et post eum Eliezer, et per ordinem Telphon, et rursum Ioseph Galilaeus, et usque ad captivitatem Hierusalem Iosue. Sammai igitur et Hellel non multo priusquam Dominus nasceretur, orti sunt in Iudaea, quorum prior dissipator interpretatur, sequens profanus; eo quod per traditiones et* δευτερώσεις *suas legis praecepta dissipaverit atque maculaverit. Et has esse duas domus, quae Salvatorem non receperint, qui factus sit eis in ruinam et scandalum.*

57 Cf. *in Hiez.* 16:16; *in Jer.* 3:14–16.

58 *Op. cit.*, p. 73.

difficulties. Far from it. For one thing, the order of succession given seems quite confused. For our analysis we shall assume that Eliezer is Eliezer ben Hyrcanus, that Telphon is Tarphon,[59] and that Iosue is Joshua ben Hananiah, all three of whom, probably (about Tarphon there is some doubt), were students of Yohanan ben Zakkai. The latter established the school in Yavne (Jamnia) after the destruction of the Temple in 70,[60] but he is said here to succeed R. Meir, who was not prominent until after the Bar Kochba revolt (132/135). R. Meir is the latest of the rabbis in our list and takes us perhaps into the second half of the second century. How do we account for the confusion?

Schmidtke has made what seems to be the most plausible suggestion.[61] He thinks that Jerome's source (which he took to be Apollinaris, but which we shall take here to be the Nazarene document itself) spoke of Hillel and Shammai as the forerunners of Akiva (the teacher of Aquila) and his student Meir. Then, having made this broad statement, the source went on to fill in the hundred-year gap between them,[62] naming Yohanan ben Zakkai, his three disciples, and Yosei haGlili (Ioseph Galiliaeus) in an acceptable chronological order. Jerome then copied this passage in the order he found it, said Schmidtke, but failed to notice that the later names should follow Hillel and Shammai instead of Meir. While we must add several provisos to this solution, we may note in its favor that it places the onus of historical confusion on Jerome rather than on the Jewish Christian Nazarenes. This is *a priori* more likely.

First of all, Schmidtke's suggestion makes most sense if we see that the emphasis of the Nazarene comment falls not only on Hillel and Shammai but also on Akiva. Of all the rabbis of the first two centuries the most significant for the Jewish Christians must have been Rabban Gamliel the Elder and Akiva, the former, of course, because of his appearance in the New Testament (Acts 5:34; 22:3), and the latter because of his involvement with the messianic rise of Simon ben Cosiba and the compilation of the earlier Mishnah. The two houses mentioned in Isa. 8:14 naturally would recall the two pharisaic houses, Beit Hillel and Beit Shammai. However, the introduction of the subject of pharisaic leaders led in turn to a mention of Akiva. It was his endorsement of a false messiah (and for Jewish Christians a rival messiah) which was the last straw which broke the ties of the נוצרים with rabbinic Judaism.[63] This provides the natural framework

---

59 See below on this confusion of names.

60 See J. Neusner, *A Life of Rabban Yohanan ben Zakkai* (Leiden, 1970); G. Alon, מחקרים בתולדות ישראל (Tel Aviv, 1957), pp. 219–252 (Eng. trans. in *idem., Jews, Judaism and the Classical World* [Jerusalem, 1977], pp. 269–313.)

61 *Op. cit.*, p. 123.

62 The phrase "ad captivitatem Hierusalem" surely refers to the year 135—not 70 as Ginzberg, *art. cit.*, p. 291, wrongly supposed.

63 Cf. Justin, *First Apology*, 31; Eus., *Chronicon* 283 (*GCS* 77, 201). The famous letter of Bar Kochba about the "Galileans" probably does not deal with Christians; see A. Rubinstein, *JJS* 6

for recalling Aquila, another figure surely known to a Jewish Christian sect of the second century,[64] and R. Meir, disciple of Akiva and perhaps the most important figure in the formation of the Mishnah.[65]

Two noticeable absentees from this list of succession are the first two Gamliels. The omission of the elder Rabban Gamliel is perhaps not too difficult to explain. He is mentioned twice in the book of Acts, both times in a relatively positive light, and he was, indeed, a man noted for this tolerance. Moreover, he held a place of some respect in early Christian literature.[66] Is it too much to suppose that the Nazarenes (remembering that their first leaders were freed on Gamliel's counsel) simply omitted a negative reference to him? The second Gamliel's omission is more difficult. He, after all, was the instigator of the malediction against the sectarians,[67] an act for which he must have been infamous with the Nazarenes. It is tempting to suggest that he was omitted because of his namesake. Or perhaps the very fact of the *birkat ha-mînîm* caused his name and memory to be erased. Perhaps most likely of all is that the Nazarenes did in fact include the name of the younger Gamliel but that Jerome omitted it, confusing him with his more venerable forebear.

This passage and the ones which follow make it difficult to accept Schmidtke's hypothesis that Jerome took all this from a lost work of his master Apollinaris. For one thing, the name Telphon here is a mistake for Tarphon (who is not to be identified with Justin's Tryphon). The mistake is most easily accounted for by a simple orthographical variation, where an elongated *qôz* of the ר (*reš*) has caused it to be read as a ל (*lamed*), i.e., טרפון (*tarfôn*), has become טלפון (*telfôn*).[68] (The

(1955), 26–34, and S. Zeitlin, *JQR* 45 (1954), 11. In favor of the identification are J.L. Teicher, *JJS* 4 (1953), 134; G. Vermes, *Les Manuscrits du Desert de Juda* (1953), p. 201, n. 4; and E. Testa, *Euntes Docete* 10 (1957), 281–284.

64 Epiph., *de mens. et pond.* 14, says that he was a convert to Christianity and then went over to Judaism. The talmuds (Kiddushin 59a; jMegilah 1: 11, 71c) confirm that he was a student of Akiva and—interestingly enough—of Eliezer b. Hyrkanus and Joshua b. Hananiah. His literal Greek translation of the OT was very much in the Akiva exegetical style and became the Bible of Greek-speaking Jews while the LXX had been taken over by the Christians.

65 See A. Oppenheimer, "Meir" in *Encyclopedia Judaica* XI (1971), with accompanying bibliography.

66 In the Clementine *Recognitions* I 65–67 (*PG* 1, 1242ff), a Jewish-Christian (albeit not Nazarene) work, it is said that he became a Christian. Later he is mentioned in *Acta Pilati* 17 (H-S I, 470) and made the author of his own gospel (H-S I, 508–510).

67 TBrach. 28b; see below, chap. 7.

68 It would be possible, of course, to claim that Apollinaris is responsible for all of this and that Jerome has taken it over. But there is little reason to insert a middleman when Jerome himself was quite capable of making the translation. Another explanation for this exchange of ל for ר has been suggested to me by D. Rokeah. The two letters are not infrequently interchanged because of pronunciation similarities. This, however, does not change the likelihood that a text in Hebrew characters was involved, because only in the unpointed Hebrew can we account for the vowel exchange between the two names.

corollary to this is significant: the Nazarene commentary on Isaiah must have been written in Hebrew characters.) Furthermore, at the end of this section we read the definitions of the names Hillel (profanus) and Shammai (dissipator). The first is from הלל (*hillel*) where the ה (*heh*) of הלל (*hillel*) has become a ח (*het*); the second is taken to come from שמם (*šamom*).

G. F Moore[69] suggests that the confusion of הלל (*hillel*) and חלל (*ḥillel*) could not have been that of the Nazarenes and must, therefore, be assigned to Jerome. The Nazarenes, he said, who knew the language and the traditions would not have made such a mistake. Ginzberg[70] disagrees and cites the Jerusalem Talmud (M. Shen. V 56a = Brachot 35a) where חלולים = הלולים (*hillûlîm* = *ḥillûlîm*) and the text goes on to explain that the rabbis do not differentiate between ח and ה.[71] All in all, while we accept here that the basic outline of the latter part of the citation (after "and Joshua up to the capture of Jerusalem") is from the Nazarenes, there are several indications that Jerome has made his own additions.

Here we must take a closer look at his Vulgate. Immediately before, in his translation of Isa. 8:10, he has rendered עצו עצה ותפר (*ʿuzû ʿezah vatufar*) as *inite consilium, et dissipabitur*, a phrase he returns to twice in his commentary on that verse. The word *dissipare*, however, often translates the root שמם (*šamom*) in Jerome's Old Testament, especially in Isaiah,[72] and it is not at all unlikely that the association of the verse immediately preceding this section with the Nazarene mention of Shammai evoked the response שמאי = *dissipator*.

The exchange הלל/חלל could in fact be Jerome's own. If his manuscript was not in fact defective at this point, it was not beyond the Latin Father to make his own equation ה = ח and proceed from there. It would have been reasonably natural in the context before us. The Vulgate at this point speaks twice of holiness: *sanctificate* (v. 13) and *sanctificationem* (v. 14) for תקדישו (*taqdîšû*) and מקדש (*miqdaš*) respectively. The opposites, of course, are *profanus* and חל (*ḥol*) which it sometimes translates.[73] It seems that Jerome himself assigned the meanings to the names,[74] that taking his cue from the names of Hillel and Shammai and the context of the scripture on which he was commenting, he contrived this ingenious etymology. All of this necessitates his using a Latin bible text, which would obviate the involvement of Apollinaris. The last phrase of this

---

69 *Judaism*, III, 56.

70 *Art. cit.*, p. 290.

71 לא מתמנעון רבנין דרשי בין היא לחית.

72 Cf. Isa. 33:8; 42:14; 49:8; 61:4.

73 Cf. Ezek. 48:15 and esp. 22:26 and Lev. 10:10 (ולהבדיל בין הקדש ובין החל).

74 This kind of exercise was surely in Jerome's bag of tricks. Compare his exegesis of the meanings of the letters of the Hebrew alphabet, *ep.* 30 to Paula (*PL* 22, 441–445). We leave aside for the present the word δευτερώσεις. We prefer to think that it goes back to an original Nazarene phrase, for reasons which are discussed below.

passage, *qui factus sit eis in ruinam at scandalum*, also points to Jerome's use of his own Vulgate, where the words *in petram scandali* and *in ruinam* have evoked this independent conclusion.[75]

Allowing for additions by Jerome does not, however, change the fact that this passage from the Nazarene interpretation of Isaiah reveals an antipathy towards the rabbis. The very identification of the two pharisaic houses with the context of Isa. 8:14 is strong enough condemnation. We shall see in the remaining passages that this is a dominant and repeated motif.

It remains then only to see what *terminus ad quem* this portion of the Nazarene work establishes for us. Of the rabbis named, as we have noted, the latest was R. Meir. He was a student of R. Akiva and was not active in Yavne, which ceased to be a center of learning with the end of the Bar Kochba revolt. With the revolt, the Hadrianic government began a persecution of the Jews of Palestine which was stopped only at the command of Antoninus Pius, who succeeded Hadrian in 138. During the persecutions, Meir left the country, returning after the decree of Antoninus. Before he left, he was ordained by R. Judah b. Bava, who was then martyred by the Romans.[76] Subsequently Meir was appointed *ḥakam* at ahe Sanhedrin of Usha, while R. Shimon b. Gamliel was appointed *nasî*. Thus begins the period of Meir's influence, and it was the 'Mishnah of R. Meir' which formed a substantial part of the basis for the compilation of R. Judah the Patriarch. The dates for Meir can only be approximated, but the time of his influence can be set in the middle of the second century. Any non-talmudic reference to him in a context in which he appears along with such rabbis as Yohanan b. Zakkai and Akiva can date from no earlier than the latter half of the second century.

However, there is another observation which should be made. Such a listing of names as we find here draws us to a significant conclusion: The Nazarenes must have remained on such intimate terms with rabbinic Judaism that they were familiar with the names of its leaders into the later second century. This necessitates a familiarity with the mishnaic tradition, which in turn indicates some continuing contact between communities. It is quite possible that the information contained here came from a convert from rabbinic Judaism to the Nazarenes. This would be quite in keeping with the subsequent history of Talmud-trained Christians from Jewish background.

On Isaiah 8:20–21

For the rest the Nazarenes explain the passage in this way: when the Scribes and Pharisees tell you to listen to them, men who do everything for the love of the belly and who hiss during their incantations in the way of magicians in order to deceive

75 Klijn, *art. cit.*, p. 241, while trying to show that Jerome here uses the Targum, concedes that the Vulgate is a possibility.

76 Sanh. 14a.

you, you must answer them like this: "It is not strange if you follow your traditions since every tribe consults its own idols. We must not, therefore, consult your dead about the living ones. On the contrary, God has given us the Law and the testimonies of the scriptures. If you are not willing to follow them you shall not have light, and the darkness will always oppress you. It will cover your earth and your doctrine so that, when you see that they have been deceived by you in error and they feel a longing for the truth, they will then be sad or angry. And let them who believe themselves to be like their own gods and kings curse you. And let them look at the heaven and the earth in vain since they are always in darkness and they can not flee away from your ambushes."[77]

Here again we see the focus of the polemic is the Scribes and Pharisees, that is, presumably, the rabbis. Much of the actual wording of the passage comes directly or indirectly from the Isaiah verses themselves, so the harshness of the attack must be seen in the light of Isaiah's words. At first glance this might seem to indicate some familiarity with synagogue worship, but this cannot be sustained; the hissing and incantations are Isaiah's own words and no clear indication in themselves of Nazarene presence at Jewish ceremonies. The reference to traditions reminds us of the *traditiones et* δευτερώσεις of the previous passage, one which would have almost immediately preceded this one in the original work. The phrase "you must answer them like this" is surely an indication of an ongoing dialogue and polemic, one which we see frequently attested to in the talmudic sources.[78] It is clear that the Nazarenes considered the final authority in any such debate to be the Old Testament and not later rabbinic interpretation, i.e. they rejected the concept of *halakah*. With this one may compare the words of Jesus as recorded in John's gospel near the turn of the first century:[79]

> Search the scriptures, because you think that in them you have eternal life; and it is these that bear witness of me ... Do not think that I will accuse you before the Father; the one who accuses you is Moses, in whom you have set your hope. For if you believed Moses, you would believe me; for he wrote of me. But if you do not believe his writings, how will you believe my words?

77 CC 73, 121 (PL 24, 123f): *Ceterum Nazarei locum istum ita disserunt: Cum dixerint ad vos scribae et pharisaei, ut eos audiatis, qui omnia ventris causa faciunt; et in morem magorum stridunt in incantationibus suis, ut vos decipiant, hoc eis respondere debetis. Non mirum si vos vestras traditiones sequamini, cum unaquaeque gens sua consulat idola. Ergo et nos a vobis mortuis de viventibus consulere non debemus, magis nobis Deus legem dedit, et testimonia scripturarum, quae si sequi nolueritis, non habebitis lucem, sed semper caligo vos opprimet, quae transibit per terram vestram atque doctrinam, ut cum decepti a vobis se in errore perspexerint, et sustinere famem veritatis, tunc contristentur, sive irascantur; et maledicant vobis, quos quasi deos et reges putabant. Et frustra ad caelum terramque respiciant, cum semper in tenebris sint, et non possint de vestris avolare insidiis.*

78 This admittedly depends on allowing that *mînîm* are frequently Jewish Christians.

79 John 5:40, 45–47. Cf. also Acts 17:10–11 and Mark 7:5–9: "Neglecting the commandment of God, you hold to the tradition of men."

This passage reflects more the style of a targum than a commentary. Klijn has shown the possible influence of both the LXX and the Targum, while admitting the possibility that the whole has come in Jerome's own free rendition from the Vulgate.[80] While he would find that the Isaiah commentary had been directly influenced by the Targum, we must remain cautious. It is an attractive suggestion and a not unlikely one. But we would prefer to say that the Nazarene work reflects a knowledge of the targumic tradition.

On Isaiah 9:1–4

The Nazarenes, whose opinion I have set forth above, try to explain this passage in the following way: When Christ came and his preaching shone out, the land of Zebulon and Naphtali first of all were freed from the errors of the Scribes and Pharisees and he shook off their shoulders the very heavy yoke of the Jewish traditions. Later, however, the preaching became more dominant, that means the preaching was multiplied, through the Gospel of the apostle Paul who was the last of all the apostles. And the Gospel of Christ shone to the most distant tribes and the way of the whole sea. Finally the whole world, which earlier walked or sat in darkness and was imprisoned in the bonds of idolatry and death, has seen the clear light of the Gospel.[81]

Let us note once again the polemic against Scribes and Pharisees and the Jewish traditions. The two most significant things about this excerpt from the Nazarene work are its positive view of Paul, and the refusal to bind Gentile Christians to keeping the Law. We see here that the Nazarene view of Paul's mission corresponded very closely to that of Paul himself.[82] In none of the remains of Nazarene doctrine can one find a clear rejection of Paul or his mission or his message. This, of course, is quite the opposite of what we usually hear described as "Jewish Christain," which almost by definition oposses itself to Paul. What we

---

80 *Art. cit.*, pp. 244f. In addition to what he notes on Vulgate influence, we may add the following: v. 19: *cum dixerent ad vos, strident in incantationibus suis, pro vivis a mortuis;* v. 20: *ad legem magis et ad testimonia, non erit eis matutina lux;* v. 22: *ad terram, tenebrae, et non poterit avolare de angustia sua.*

81 *CC* 73, 123f (*PL* 24, 125): *Nazaraei, quorum opinionem supra posui, hunc locum ita explanare conantur: Adveniente Christo et praedicatione illius coruscante, prima terra Zabulon et terra Nephthali scribarum et pharisaeorum est erroribus liberata, et gravissimum traditionum Iudaicarum iugum excussit de cervicibus suis. Postea autem per evangelium apostoli Pauli, qui novissimus apostolorum omnium fuit, ingravata est, id est multiplicata praedicatio; et in terminos gentium et viam universi maris Christi evangelium splenduit. Denique omnis orbis, qui ante ambulabat vel sedebat in tenebris et idololatriae ac mortis vinculis tenebatur, clarum evangelii lumen aspexit.*

82 Cf. Gal. 2:2–9; see also J. Munck, "Primitive Jewish Christianity and Later Jewish Christianity: Continuation or Rupture" in *Aspects du Judéo-Christianisme* (Strasbourg, 1964), pp. 79–81, 87.

have here, then, is an endorsement of Paul's mission to the Gentiles.[83] This spreading of the Gospel to the Gentiles was, according to the Nazarenes, a natural, even a glorious development. One is often led to expect a sort of bitterness on the part of the Jewish Christians that they were swamped, their position usurped by the Gentile Church. But here we find only a positive reaction to the flow of events. As Klijn has pointed out,[84] the land of Zebulon and Naphtali obviously represents the land of the Jews as compared to the rest of the world, and significantly it is this land which was first freed from the yoke of Jewish traditions, the land where Jesus taught.

There is a further indication in this passage that the commentary was in Hebrew letters. The spelling of the name *Nephthali* agrees with the Hebrew text against both the LXX and Matt. 4:15–16.[85] Also, we see here again the targumic form, although our passage adheres far more closely to the Hebrew text of Isaiah than does the Targum. The form here is a bit too loose to be called a targum, yet at the same time too restricted to be called a commentary.

On Isaiah 29:20–21

What we have understood to have been written about the devil and his angels, the Nazarenes believe to have been said against the Scribes and the Pharisees, because the δευτερωταί passed away, who earlier deceived the people with very vicious traditions (and they watch[ed] day and night to deceive the simple ones), who made men sin against the Word of God in order that they should deny that Christ was the Son of God.[86]

It is not clear whence Jerome takes his idea that verses 20 and 21 refer to the devil and his angels (*daemones* just previously in his commentary). The lost commentaries of Origen, Didymus, and Apollinaris are all possibilities, or the idea could have been Jerome's own. The same interpretation does occur earlier in Eusebius' commentary,[87] to which Jerome would surely have had access in the library at Caesarea, and which indeed he cites along with the other three in his prologue to his commentary on Isaiah.[88] However this may be, for the last two verses of his section on verses 17–21 he found the above exegesis in the Nazarene commentary. Again the phrasing is built around the words of the text. In fact the

---

83 Cf. Schmidtke, *TU* 37, 110.

84 *Art. cit.*, p. 251.

85 This and other points are noted by Klijn, *art. cit.*, pp. 245ff.

86 *CC* 73, 379f (*PL* 24, 336): *Quae nos super diabolo et angelis eius intelleximus, Nazaraei contra scribas et pharisaeos dicta arbitrantur, quod defecerint* δευτερωταί, *qui prius illudebant populo traditionibus pessimis; et ad decipiendos simplices die noctuque vigilabant, qui peccare faciebant homines in Verbo Dei, ut Christum Dei Filium negarent.* (I have somewhat altered the punctuation of K–R's translation so as to render the meaning clearer.)

87 *Ad loc.* (*PG* 24, 301–304): λέγω δὴ αὐτὸς ὁ διάβολος.

88 *PL* 24, 21. See also *PL* 24, 154 and 156.

similarity to the Vulgate is marked, but this need mean no more than that the Hebrew texts of Jerome and of the Nazarenes were nearly the same.[89]

This is the fourth of the five citations to stand against the rabbis and their traditions. The significance of this passage hinges on the lone Greek word δευτερωταί, which we saw in its form δευτερώσεις in the first quotation. Schmidtke[90] suggested that its appearance is proof of Jerome's use of a Greek source (i.e. Apollinaris). It stands, he noted, in the place of the Hebrew word עריץ ('arîz), which we saw in other forms also at Isa. 8:12,13. But does the appearance of this word in two of the five pasages necessitate an underlying Greek text?

The word δευτερώσεις and its related forms are the most common LXX rendering of the Hebrew משנה (mišneh).[91] The Hebrew word comes from the root שנה (šanoh) and has the sense of duplicity or repetition.[92] It came early to carry the specific meaning of the teaching handed down from teacher to disciple,[93] even before that body of teaching was actually written down. This repeated teaching was eventually codified and recorded in the work which we now know as the Mishnah. To the Church Fathers it was known as the δευτερώσεις.[94] For them

---

89 Klijn, art. cit., p. 247. There is no need to think that the Vulgate had any influence on the Nazarene work (so Klijn would allow); it is far more likely that Jerome found a known Hebrew text in their commentary and simply rendered it as he already had in his own earlier translation.

90 TU 37, 113, n. 2.

91 Of about 30 appearances of משנה in the OT, the LXX translated it with some form of δευτερ — 17 times with two additional places appearing as alternate readings of Aquila and Symmachus. Of the remaining appearances only διπλοῦς (5 times) is used more than twice for משנה. In two places (2 Chron. 34:22, 2 Kings 22:14) the word is only transliterated.

92 See Brown, Driver, Briggs, Hebrew and English Lexicon of the Old Testament, s.v. שנה, III. Note especially the references to Deut. 17:18 and Josh. 8:32 (D) where משנה speaks of a written copy of Mosaic law.

93 See W. Bacher, Die exegetische Terminologie der jüdischen Traditionsliteratur (Leipzig, 1905), s.v. משנה (pt I, 122f).

94 Or in the plural δευτερώσεις. See Eus. dem. ev. 6, 18 (PG 22, 461); comm. in Is. 1:22 (PG 24, 97); Epiph., pan. 13 (PG 41, 237); 15 (PG 41, 244); 33 (PG 41, 572); Jerome, ep. 121 (PL 22, 1033); ep. 18 ad Damas., 20 (PL 22, 374); in Is. 59:12ff (PL 24, 581); in Ezek. 36:1ff (PL 25, 339); in Hos. 3:1 (PL 25, 842); in Matth. 22:23 (PL 26, 163); Augustine, contra advers. legis et proph. 2, 1, 2 (PL 42, 637); ibid., 2, 2, 6 (642) (His word in both places is deuterosin); Const. Apost. 6, 22 (PG 1, 972); Anastasius Sinaita (PG 89, 105); Olympiodorus, in Eccles. 12:12 (PG 93, 625). The verb δευτερόω appears in Eus., praep. ev. 12, 4 (PG 21, 956); Jerome, Ep. 121, 10 (PL 22, 1034; here Jerome equates δευτερώσεις and traditions: Et si quando certis diebus traditiones suas exponunt, discipulis suis solent dicere, οἱ σοφοὶ δευτερῶσιν id est, sapientes docent traditiones. See also the previous column in Migne.); Const. Apost. 1, 6, 3 (PG 1, 573); ibid., 2, 5, 6 (PG 1, 601). Those who pass on the δευτερώσεις are called, as in our passage, the δευτερωταί: Eus., prep. ev. 11, 5 (PG 21, 852); 12, 1 (PG 21, 952: τούτους δὲ παισὶν Ἑβραίων Δευτερωτὰς φίλον ἦν ὀνομάζειν, ὥσπερ ἑρμηνευτὰς καὶ ἐξηγητὰς ὄντας τῆς τῶν Γραφῶν διανοίας); Epiph., ad Acacium et Paulum (PG 41, 172); pan. 15 (PG 41, 144); Jerome, in Is. 3:14 (PL 24, 67); in Habac. 2:9ff (PL 25, 1297); ibid., 2:15ff (PL 25, 1301); in Is. 10:1ff (PL 24, 133); Procopius, in Is. 22:1 (PG 87, 2176); John Damas., haer. 14 (PG 94, 685).

the term signified either simply "tradition" or the written Mishnah. Evidently the word became very early a *terminus technicus* and does not seem to have been given a Latin translation. As we have seen in the first passage, δευτερώσεις appears together with *traditiones*, so strictly speaking the two should probably not be equated. However, the use of the two words in 29:20–21 shows just how closely they were associated.[95] Jerome may indeed have first heard the Greek word δευτερώσεις for the traditions and secondary writings of the Jews while he was in Antioch learning Greek and studying under Apollinaris, but there is no strong reason to suppose that his use of the word here implies his copying a Greek document. Unless he transcribed the Hebrew itself, he had no other word available — even though he was writing in Latin. And if he *did* have a Hebrew text in front of him, with his knowledge of both the Hebrew and the LXX, the most natural exchange for him to make for משנה, would be δευτέρωσις.

The actual use of the word δευτερωταί in the excerpt before us is not entirely clear. For the Hebrew עריץ (*'arîz*) Jerome's Vulgate has *qui praevalebat* while in the same place in the Nazarene commentary we find δευτερωταί. In his own comments before coming to the Nazarene work, Jerome returns to the *qui praevalebat*, without, however, really touching on the true meaning of עריץ. The only other place where the Vulgate renders עריץ with a form of *praevaleo* is in the fifth verse of this same chapter: *qui... praevaluerunt*. This fact, at least, should assure us that Jerome did read עריץ here. But Jerome is quite inconsistent in his translating of this Hebrew word. Of about 20 instances, he uses no less than eight different words to render it.[96] We must conclude that there is no connection between Jerome's *qui praevalebat* and the δευτερωταί. Since it is most unlikely that the Nazarene document was written in Greek, δευτερωταί must be Jerome's rendition of some Hebrew or Aramaic word. What could it have been? One can only conjecture, but if the basic hypothesis is correct — that δευτερωταί is Jerome's rendering of something he read in the Nazarene work — then the options are limited. The most likely is the word תנאים (*tanna'îm*). This is the Aramaic

In the Novella of Justinian in February 553 (*Novella* 146 1, 2), the reading of the Mishnah by Jews was forbidden under the name of δευτέρωσιν. On this see H. Vogelstein and P. Rieger, *Geschichte der Juden in Rom* (Berlin, 1896), p. 173. They also cite a "Psalmenkatenae" of Jerome (on Ps. 31:7 (I 538) with the statement *Hic Hebraeorum doctissimi qui in deuterosi familiam dicunt.* I have not been able to locate this quotation. Note also (*CC* 73, 116, *var. lec.*) that MS B reads deuterosis at Jerome, *in Is.* 8:14.

95 Citing Jos. *Ant.* 13, 10, 6 (297), which speaks about the Pharisees with the phrase ἐκ παραδόσεως, Juster (*Les Juifs dans l'Empire Romain* [Paris, 1914], I, 375, n. 3) shows that παράδοσις often equals δευτέρωσις. He also notes Eus. *HE* 4, 22, 8; Epiph. *pan.* 13 (*PG* 41, 232), and Jerome, *in Is.* 3:14 (*PL* 24, 67). The word δευτέρωσις and cognates are not used by Josephus.

96 *Fortis* 9x; *robustus* 4x; *qui praeval—* 2x; and once each *crudelissimi, inexpugnabiles, tyrannis, superexaltatem, potentium.*

form from the Hebrew שנה (*šanoh*), which, as we have seen, is the basis for משנה and the most common root to be rendered by some form of δευτερόω.[97]

This conclusion requires us to set a rather later date for the composition of the Nazarene interpretation. The generally accepted period for the transition from Tannaim to Amoraim is with the publication of the Mishnah.[98] We may put this roughly at the beginning of the third century. The statement is that the δευτερωταί (or תנאים, *tanna'îm*) passed away. We must voice some caution, because *defecerint* is only an echo of the Isaiah original. The commentary goes on to say that these "formerly" (*prius*) deceived the people. Here again *illudebant* is the *illusor* of the biblical text. Nonetheless, the use of *prius* and the emphasis on the past would make less sense if the whole comment had been written before, say, 200.[99] One would, in fact, feel safe placing the composition of this targum/commentary in the mid-third century, and at least after 200, when the Mishnah was compiled.[100]

On Isaiah 31:6–9

The Nazarenes understand this passage in this way: O Sons of Israel, who deny the Son of God with a most vicious opinion, turn to him and his apostles. For if you will do this, you will reject all idols which to you were a cause of sin in the past, and the devil will fall before you, not because of your powers, but because of the compassion of God. And his young men, who at a certain time earlier fought for him, will be the tributaries of the church and any of |his| power and stone will pass. Also the philosophers and every perverse dogma will turn their backs to the sign of the cross. Because this is the meaning of the Lord that his will take place, whose fire or light is in Sion and his oven in Jerusalem.[101]

97 It does not have to be inferred from this that the work was in Aramaic. The word תנאים is a common form also in Hebrew documents. Cf. Bacher, *op. cit.,* pt. II, p. 241, s.v. תנ.

98 This distinction is already made early in talmudic literature itself. See Sanh. 33a, a statement which dates from the first half of the 4th century, and earlier (before 279) the statements of Resh Lakish and R. Yoḥanan in Sanh. 63a. Whether the Mishnah was written down at this time is moot. See H. Strack, *Introduction to Talmud and Midrash* (New York, 1978), pp. 12–20, and S. Liebermann, "The Publication of the Mishnah," *Hellenism in Jewish Palestine* (1950), pp. 83–99.

99 It is just possible, of course, that the reference is to none other than the oft-mentioned Scribes and Pharisees of the NT period. The present writer feels, however, that the epithet "Scribes and Pharisees" is being used by the Nazarenes as a derogatory designation of the heirs of the Pharisees, the rabbis.

100 May we voice here the wish that Jerome had quoted the Nazarene treatment (if such existed) of Isa. 29:19 (the verse just before our passage) where we read the phrase ואביוני אדם בקדוש ישראל יגילו. On this whole section see also R. Pritz in *Proceedings*, pp. 125–130.

101 *CC* 73, 404 (=*PL* 24, 357): *Nazaraei locum istum sic intellegunt: O filii Israel, qui consilio pessimo Dei filium denegastis, revertimini ad eum et ad apostolos eius. Si enim hoc feceritis, omnia abiectis idola quae vobis prius fuerant in peccatum, et cadet vobis diabolus, non vestris viribus, sed misericordia Dei. Et iuvenes eius qui quondam pro illo pugnaverant, erunt Ecclesiae vectigales, omnisque fortitudo et petra illius pertransibit; philosophi quoque et omne*

The tenor of this excerpt is different from those we have examined. Here we see no mention of the Scribes and Pharisees nor of the Jewish traditions. Here, rather than simple rejection, we have the proffered hand of reconciliation. The targumic approach is still evident, following the biblical phrasing closely.[102]

Schmidtke, while attempting rather unconvincingly to show references here to specific Pauline verses,[103] did draw attention to the Pauline approach to faith and works and God's mercy.[104] The references mentioned by Schmidtke do indeed show a strong similarity of *outlook*, and this is significant. To be sure, the words in question "not because of human powers but because of God's mercy" are triggered by the text of Isaiah, but the very decision of the Nazarenes to highlight them in such a way must be taken as an indication that they were not disagreeable to Paul's gospel. This confirms what we have seen more explicitly stated above on 9:1.

In fact, we must see the greatest significance of this final passage in the way it relates to the greater Church. The sons of Israel are called to turn to the Son of God and to his apostles. These latter are not limited to James and perhaps Peter, as we might expect, but they seem to be inclusive of the twelve and even of Paul. Then we find the phrase *Ecclesiae vectigales* (tributaries of the church). Jerome is systematic in translating קהל (*qahal*) as *ecclesia*, and we must assume that this is also what he read here.[105] The word קהל generally takes the sense of the larger body or gathering as compared to עדה (*'edah*) which is a word, at least in New Testament times, more specific, tending to signify the local group. If the Nazarenes had developed some sort of exclusivist doctrine, some rejection of the Church from the Gentiles, then we might expect to find here *Synagogae vectigales*[106] (tributaries of the synagogue). The expression as it stands—taken together with the other hints we have seen—may serve as testimony to a rather ecumenical ecclesiology among the Nazarenes. This, we admit, is tenuous, but the evidence can bear that interpretation. The statement itself speaks of the fall of the

---

dogma perversum ad crucis signum terga convertent. Domini quippe sententia est, ut hoc fiat, cuius ignis sive lumen est in Sion et clibanus in Hierusalem.

102 Cf. from the Vulgate: *filii Israel; convertimini; abiiciet ... Idola; quae fecerunt vobis ... in peccatum; et cadet (Assur in gladio) non viri; et iuvenes eius; vectigales erunt; et fortitudo ... transibit; cuius ignis est in Sion et caminus eius in Ierusalem.* Klijn, *art. cit.,* p. 247, states incorrectly that the vocative *O filii Israel* is not found in the Hebrew text.

103 *Op. cit.,* p. 117: Eph. 2:2, 4; Rom. 16:20.

104 One might refer to Rom. 9:16, which reads in the Vulgate *Igitur non volentis, neque currentis, sed miserentis est Dei.*

105 The other candidate would be עדע, but Jerome is equally faithful in rendering this word as *synagoga.* Cf. Prov. 5:14.

106 This, of course, might not have suited Jerome, and he might then have omitted quoting the passage altogether.

devil and the turning of young men from supporting him to supporting the Church.[107] This is more than tolerant; it is positive.

Summary

As we noted at the outset, these passages are very important, perhaps as informative as anything we will consider in this study. We have been able to trace through them an active Nazarene presence well into the third century. The sect which produced this document was actively engaged in a dialogue—heated, no doubt—with rabbinic Judaism. It was familiar with the developments within Judaism and rejected the authority of the pharisaic scholars to interpret scripture definitively. The Nazarenes of this work may themselves have continued to keep the Law of the Pentateuch, but they did not see it as binding on those who believed from among the Gentiles. Nor did they accept as binding on themselves (or on any Jews) the Oral Law as embodied in the Mishnah. These Jewish Christians viewed Paul and his mission favorably and evidently even accepted—in theory at least—the unity of the Church as composed of both Jewish and Gentile believers in Christ. Their Christology too called Christ the Son of God. The document itself displays an active familiarity with the Hebrew language and must have been written in either Hebrew or Aramaic.[108] It seems to betray a knowledge of the targumic tradition. And finally, this group had not lost hope that the Jewish people might yet turn to accept Jesus as the Messiah.

107 One is also reminded of that rare synoptic appearance of ἐκκλησία in Matt. 16:18: "I will build my church and the gates of Hades shall not overpower it."

108 Hebrew seems more to fit the evidence. If it was written in Hebrew, then it would be wrong, of course, to call the work a *targum*.

Chapter Five

Patristic Evidence after Jerome

While it is true that Epiphanius and Jerome form the core of our study, useful information about the Nazarenes, and particularly about their place in early Church thought, can be gained from a consideration of their treatment by later Christian writers. We shall be led into a valuable path of investigation if we move chronologically and first consider a heresiogragher who made no mention of the sect.

Filaster

Filaster,[1] Bishop of Brescia, was a contemporary of Epiphanius (d.397). His *diversarum haereseon liber*[2] was written in 385 (also possible are 380 and 390)—about five or ten years after Epiphanius' *panarion*—and covered 156 heresies or heretical teachings. The Jewish Christian Nazarene sect is not mentioned by Filaster. This fact naturally causes one to wonder why the Nazarenes were omitted from so extensive a work when Filaster went so far as to condemn even those who differed from the Church only in their belief that the stars occupied fixed positions in the heavens (as against the then-current teaching that God set them in place every evening).[3] It is often held that Filaster drew from Epiphanius, but we have seen that the Bishop of Salamis quite roundly condemned the Nazarenes. Why did Filaster omit them? Was he at this point using a source other than Epiphanius?

The treatment of this question by Bishop Lightfoot[4] is most instructive. First of all, it had been commonly assumed that the work of Hippolytus against the heresies had given both Epiphanius and Filaster their material. For a long time this work, mentioned by Eusebius and Jerome,[5] had been lost, but with the

---

1 Also commonly spelled Philaster with several rarer variations. Bardy, *DTC* 12 (1935), 1398f; J. Kraus, *Lexikon f. Theol. u Kirche* 4 (1960), p. 124f; M. Pellegrino, *Enciclopedia Cattolica* V (1950), 1291f; Bardenhewer, III, 481–485.

2 *PL* 12, 1111–1302.

3 *ODCC* "Philaster," 1079.

4 J.B. Lightfoot, *The Apostolic Fathers* 1, 2, 413ff.

5 Eus. *HE* VI 22; Jerome *de vir. ill.* 61 (*PL* 23, 671).

discovery and publication in 1851 of the so-called *Philosophumena* by E. Miller (who wrongly attributed the work to Origen), scholars at last had an anti-heretical work whose author was Hippolytus, as was demonstrated by J.J.I. Döllinger.[6] Numerous scholars at the time also wanted to identify the *Philosophumena* (or, more correctly, *Refutation of All Heresies*) with a treatise described in some detail by Photius.[7] Photius gave a rather full description of this work, which he calls a *syntagma*, or compendium. It contained 32 heresies, beginning from the Dositheans and ending with Noetus and the Noetians, and he calls it a βιβλιδάριον, *libellus*, a little book. It was founded on some lectures by Irenaeus (Hippolytus' teacher) and was brief[8] (ἀπέριττος) in its style. But this description does not fit the *Philosophumena*, which is not a short work at all,[9] does not contain 32 heresies, and neither begins nor ends as Photius described. As it happens, the *Philosophumena* itself describes just such a work, the author stating that he had long ago written against these heresies roughly, not in detail, but that since they had not been shamed by what he wrote then, he would now reveal their secret mysteries.[10]

Lightfoot went on to point out, like others before him,[11] that the short appendix to Tertullian's *Praes. haer.* (=Ps. Tertullian) is a brief summary of heresies which fits Photius' description (as well as that of Hippolytus himself just mentioned) in almost every detail. This most assuredly is the work described by Photius, not the *Philosophumena*, and the author of both was Hippolytus. If we then list the heresies of Ps. Tertullian synoptically with those of Epiphanius and Filaster (see Table I), we find that those of Ps. Tert., in the words of Lightfoot, "run like a backbone" through the works of the later heresiographers. However, when we remove this framework, we find almost no correspondence at all between Epiphanius and Filaster.[12] From these facts we may draw two inescapable

---

6   *Hippolytus und Kallistus* (1853).

7   *Myriobiblon sive Bibliotheca* CXXI (*PG* 103, 401f).

8   This is Lightfoot's translation. The lexicons give "plain, simple." The discrepancy does not, however, affect his argument.

9   Comprising over 200 columns in Migne, who follows Miller in ascribing it to Origen.

10 Hipp., *Refutation of all Heresies* I 1: ὧν καὶ πάλαι μετρίως τὰ δόγματα ἐξεθέμεθα, οὐ κατὰ λεπτὸν ἐπιδείξαντες, ἀλλ᾽ ἀδρωμερῶς ἐλέγξαντες, κτλ. ("We have likewise, on a former occasion, expounded the doctrines of these briefly, not illustrating them with any degree of minuteness, but refuting them in coarse digest....") (Salmond's translation in ANCL VI).

11 He mentions Allix, Waterland, and especially Lipsius, *Quellenkritik*.

12 The point of correspondence which interests us here is the sect which Epiphanius calls the Nasararioi and Filaster the Nazorei. (Alternate spellings — for Epiphanius Nazaraioi [see *PG* 41, 257] and for Filaster Nazarei [*CSEL* 38, 4] — make it at least possible that the two men gave equivalent names for the sect.) As no sect by this name appears in Ps. Tert., we may justifiably wonder a) What was Epiphanius' source? And b) Did Filaster use Epiphanius, or did both use some third (i.e. fourth) source? The first question has been treated above, chap. 3. The sect described in this short notice of Filaster (chap. VIII) is clearly not our Nazarene sect. The

conclusions: both Epiphanius and Filaster made use of Ps. Tert. (i.e. Hippolytus) as a basis for their works against heresies; and the two fourth-century works are independent of each other.

It hardly needs more than a synoptic look at the lists to show that the first conclusion is correct. In a few places (designated by Lightfoot with brackets) there are slight variations in order. Without exception the variation is on the part of Epiphanius, while Filaster follows the order of Ps. Tert. faithfully. This would seem to strengthen the conclusion that Filaster is not using Epiphanius (but see note 12 above). If we now turn to the question of why Filaster omitted mention of the Nazarenes, we must direct the question in turn at Hippolytus. It is generally recognized that Hippolytus drew from his master Irenaeus for his information on the heresies, both from the latter's verbal instruction, and from his written works, which Hippolytus quotes frequently.[13] Irenaeus' work *adversus omnes haereses* (*Against all Hereses*),[14] written in the latter part of the second century, is the earliest major heresiological treatise of its kind still extant.[15] In the first book he deals with about 21 heresies, placing most of his emphasis on Valentinus (an older contemporary) and Gnosticism. Of these 21 heresies, no less than 18 form the core of the Ps. Tert. list, often appearing in the same order.

Irenaeus' sources were Justin and Theophilus of Antioch.[16] We have analyzed above the places in Justin's extant writings in which he may have been referring to the Nazarene sect. All in all, we can hardly say that he considered them "heretical" enough to be included in his *Syntagma*, and *a priori* we should not be risking too much in suggesting that Irenaeus would not have found Nazarenes in

---

difficulty arises, however, when we decide that Nasaraioi correspond to Nazorei. A comparison of the two notices shows that one could not have been taken from the other; neither could they both derive from a common source. They share only a similarity of name and relative placement in the two contemporary heresy lists. (See the note by Migne in *PG* 41, 257f.) The sect of Filaster derives somehow from the Nazirites and accepts the Law and prophets. Epiphanius' Nasaraioi reject parts of the OT and do not offer sacrifice. I would suggest that Filaster used the outline (but generally not the facts) provided by Ps. Tert. and at the same time had Epiphanius before him (perhaps only in outline form). Where Epiphanius varied from Ps. Tert. in order, Filaster remained loyal to the older document. But when Epiphanius took a natural break between Pharisees and Herodians to add other Jewish sects, Filaster took the opportunity to follow his own program of 28 Jewish sects. Under Epiphanius' influence (for outline, but evidently not for facts) he inserted Samaritans, Essenes, and Nazarenes before taking off on his own unique list of strange sects. Note that in keeping with his plan to group all of the "Jewish" heresies together at the beginning, he could not follow the order of either Ps. Tert. or Epiphanius as regards the Ophites, Cainites, and Sethites. So he simply transposed them to the head of his list.

13 Photius, *loc. cit.* (n. 7 above); Altaner, 164.

14 *PG* 7, 438–1224.

15 The earliest was Justin Martyr's *Syntagma* (which he mentions in *1 Apol.* 26, 8).

16 *ODCC*, s.v. "Irenaeus".

EPIPHANIUS	PSEUDO-TERTULLIAN	PHILASTER
Hellenism:—		
Platonists		
Pythagoreans		
Stoics		
Epicureans		
Samaritans:—		
Gortheni		
Sebuaei		
Essenes		
Dositheus	Dositheus	Dositheus
Judaism:—		
Scribes		
Pharisees	Sadducees {	Sadducees {
Sadducees {	Pharisees	Pharisees {
Hemerobaptists		Samaritans
Oseenes		Nazarenes (Nazaraei)
Nazarenes (Νασαραίοι)		Essenes
		Heliognosti
		Frog-worshippers (Ranarum cultores)
		Musorites
		Musca-accaronites
		Troglodytes
		De Fortuna Caeli
		Baalites
		Astarites
		Moloch-worshippers
		De Ara Tophet
		Puteorites
		Worshippers of the Brazen Serpent
		Worshippers in subterranean caves
		Thamnuz-mourners
		Baalites (or Belites)
		Baal-worshippers
		Astar and Astaroth-worshippers de Pythonissa
Herodians	Herodians	Herodians
Simon Magus	Simon Magus	Simon Magus
Menander	Menander	Menander
Saturninus	Saturninus	Saturninus
Basilides	Basilides	Basilides
Nicolaitans	Nicolaitans	Nicolaitans
Gnostici		(isti Barbelo venerantur)
Borborians (Barbelitae)		
		Judaites
Ophites	Ophites	
Cainites	Cainites	
Sethites	Sethites	
Carpocrates	Carpocrates	Carpocrates
Cerinthus	Cerinthus	Cerinthus
Nazarenes (Ναζωραίοι)		
Ebionites	Ebionites	Ebionites

EPIPHANIUS	PSEUDO-TERTULLIAN	PHILASTER
Valentinus	Valentinus	Valentinus
Secundus	Ptolemaeus	Ptolemaeus
Ptolemaeus	Secundus	Secundus
Marcosians	Heracleon	Heracleon
Colarbasus	Marcus	Marcus
Heracleon	Colarbasus {	Colarbasus {
Ophites		
Caians		
Sethites		
Archontici		
Cerdon	Cerdon	Cerdon
Marcion	Marcion	Marcion
Apelles {	Lucan	Lucan
Lucian	Apelles {	Apelles {
Severians		
Tatian	Tatian	Tatian
Encratites		
Cataphrygians:—	Cataphrygians:— secundum Proclum secundum Aeschinem	Cataphrygians
Montanists		
Tascodrugites		
Pepuzians		
Quintillians		
Artoyrites		
Quartodecimans		
Alogi		
Adamians		
Sampsaeans (Elkesaeans)		
Theodotus	Theodotus	Theodotus De Patre et Filii substantia
	Blastus	
	Theodotus	
Melchizedekites	Melchizedekites (Theodotus II)	Melchizedekites
Bardesanes		
Noetians	Praxeas (end)	Noetians
	Noetians	
Valesians		Sabellians (Praxeans)
Cathari		(Hermogenians)
Angelici		Seleucus
Apostolici		Hermias
Sabellians		Proclianites (Hermeonites)
Origeneans		Florians (Carpocratians)
Paul of Samosata		Quartodecimans
Manichaeans		Chilionetites
Hierakites		Alogi
Meletians		Manichaeans
		Patricians
		Symmachians
		Paul of Samosata
		Photinus
		Arians

a heresy list of Justin. But what of Theophilus of Antioch? What remains to us of his writings is relatively scant.[17] Most recently his work has been edited[18] and analyzed[19] by R.M. Grant. At the end of his analysis, Grant found strong Ebionite leanings in Theophilus, that this Bishop of Antioch was "following a Jewish or Jewish-Christian source" and that "in spirit and in content he is very close to Judaism."[20] He goes on to note "that there is no mention of a bishop of Antioch among those who opposed Jewish Quartodecimanism in the East (Eusebius, *HE* V,23)."[21] We may recall at this point that Irenaeus himself wrote in 190 to Pope Victor supporting the Quartodecimans.[22] Clearly, one would scarcely expect to find much of a polemic against Jewish Christians in a writer such as Theophilus. So, whether Irenaeus used Justin or Theophilus or both, we must conclude that he would not have found material to warrant special attention to the Nazarene sect.

Where does all this leave us? In tracing Filaster's literary heritage back to near its beginnings, we may at least hazard the suggestion that the earliest heresiographers did not include the Nazarenes for the simple reason that they did not consider them heretics. This, of course, was not true of the offshoot Ebionites, who even by the time of Irenaeus (and earlier Justin, who, however, does not mention them by name) had been recognized as heretics. If we extend this logic into the late fourth century, we arrive at this important conclusion: the lack of polemic against the Nazarenes until the fourth century does not show that they were a late phenomenon;[23] rather, it shows that no one until Epiphanius considered them heretical enough to add them to older catalogues. The very existence of Filaster's contemporary anti-heretical work with its omission of the Nazarenes in accord with his inherited tradition lends weight to the suggestion that Epiphanius is solely responsible for their inclusion in his own heresiography, and this despite the fact that he could not deny their ancient beginnings. While each author used the lists of his predecessors and added to them where he saw fit, no one until Epiphanius felt it necessary to include the Nazarenes, even though they had existed from the earliest times and their gospel was known. As a final

17 *PG* 6, 1023–1168; Altaner, 75–77; Bardenhewer, I, 302–315; F. Loofs, *Theophilus von Antioch und die anderen theologischen Quellen bei Irenäeus* (*TU* 46, 2, 1930).
18 *Oxford Early Christian Texts* (1970), with English translation.
19 In a series of six articles: *HTR* 40 (1947), 1–17, 227–256; *JBL* 66 (1947), 173–199; *Angl. Theol. Rev.* 30 (1948), 91–94; *HTR* 42 (1949), 41–51; *HTR* 43 (1950), 176–196.
20 *HTR* 43 (1950), 192f.
21 *Ibid.*, 195.
22 *PG* 7, 1228–1232.
23 Against J. Munck, *Aspects du Judéo-Christianisme* (1964), pp. 77–91.
24 τὸν Ματθαῖον δοκεῖ ἐν τῷ κατὰ Λουκᾶν Λευὶν ὀνομάζειν. οὐκ ἔστιν δὲ αὐτός, ἀλλὰ ὁ καταστασθεὶς ἀντὶ τοῦ Ἰούδα ὁ Ματθίας καὶ ὁ Λευὶς εἰς διώνυμοι εἰσιν. ἐν τῷ καθ᾽ Ἑβραίους εὐαγγελίῳ τοῦτο φαίνεται. Translation by K–R, 199.

argument in favor of this view, we may mention again the ambivalence of Jerome toward the sect, sometimes treating them with respect, sometimes attacking them. After Augustine, such indecision would be unthinkable.

Didymus the Blind

Didymus the Blind (313-398) was an older contemporary and teacher of Jerome. In his commentary on the Psalms[24] he mentions the Gospel according to the Hebrews once: "It seems that Matthew is named Levi in the Gospel according to Luke. But they are not the same, but Mathias who replaced Judas and Levi are the same with a double name. This appears from the Gospel according to the Hebrews." This particular quotation from GH appears nowhere else. It is not impossible that Didymus himself saw the Gospel (or rather had it read to him, since he was blind almost from birth). As an Alexandrian and one who was greatly influenced by Origen, we must also consider that he may have found this citation in some lost work of Origen, who frequently used the Hebrew gospel.

The passage itself is not without interest. The mention of Mathias would seem to indicate that GH contained information on events subsequent to Jesus' ascension.[25] Especially noteworthy is the way in which Didymus refers to GH. He seems to treat it as having no less authority than the canonical Gospel of Luke and even used it to correct a false impression gained from Luke. This fact in itself, though hardly decisive, may weigh in favor of Didymus' personal use of GH rather than his extracting here from Origen, who frequently adds some hesitant proviso such as "if one is willing to accept the Gospel of the Hebrews."[26] Nevertheless, because the possibility remains that Didymus may have used Origen, we cannot assert that he had any direct knowledge of the sect. In fact, his location in Alexandria in the fourth century makes this highly unlikely.

Augustine

Augustine of Hippo (354-430) marks a decisive point in the history of the Church's view of the Nazarenes. While Epiphanius was the first to brand them clearly as heretical, it was the authority of Augustine's acceptance of this judgment which seems to have fixed their fate and led to their final rejection by the Church. As we shall see, later Christian writers generally followed Epiphanius' statements about the sect, but theirs was only a reflection or echo of the definitive stamp of authority which permeates so much of what Augustine wrote.

He mentions the Nazarenes in five places in his writings, always in a negative tone, and, as if to complete their rejection, he never once quotes from or even mentions the Gospel acording to the Hebrews. In his treatise *de baptismo contra*

---

25 Other post-resurrection material appears in Jerome *de vir. ill.* 2.
26 Origen, *in Joh.* II 12; also *hom. in Jer.* XV 4; *in Matth.* XV 14.

Donatistas[27] he says, "just as they persist to the present day who call themselves Nazarene Christians and circumcise the carnal foreskins in a Jewish way, are born heretics in that error into which Peter drifted and from which he was called back by Paul." This would seem to indicate that Augustine was personally aware of their continued existence. However, in *contra Faustum*, written at about the same time, or perhaps even three or four years earlier,[28] he seems less sure, when he says "they exist until the present day or at least until recently."[29] While it is true that he writes in 405/6 "now there are some heretics who call themselves Nazarenes",[30] this is hardly as strong as "who persist until now" or "up until our own time." Augustine never travelled outside the Italy–North Africa axis, and this in itself is enough to suggest that he had no first-hand knowledge of Nazarenes.

We have a strengthening of this suggestion in his repeated identification of the Nazarenes with Symmachians.[31] In fact there is little reason to brand Nazarenes as Symmachians, and had he had any personal contact with these sects (if indeed the Symmachians still existed in his time), he would not have committed such an error. It is generally stated that Augustine had his information on heresies from either Filaster or Epiphanius. However, the former never mentions the sect, as we have seen above, and the latter does not mention the Symmachians; so he could not have found this identification of the two sects in either author. It is equally unlikely that he himself made a synthesis of the two authors: The notice of Filaster on the Symmachians is short and bears no resemblance to Epiphanius' Nazarenes.[32]

In all likelihood we need search no farther for the source of this confused identification than the words of Augustine himself: "these are those whom

27 VII 1, 1 (*PL* 43, 225; *CSEL* 51, 342), written in 400/1: *sicut illi, qui se Christianos Nazarenos vocant et more Iudaico carnalia praeputia circumcidunt, nati haeretici ex illo errore, in quem Petrus devians a Paulo revocatus est, in hoc adhuc usque persistunt.* (Translations from Augustine by K–R.)

28 For the relative dating of all of Augustine's known writings, see the list, of O.J.–B. DuRoy in *Catholic Encyclopedia* 1 (1967), 1049–1051.

29 XIX 17 (*PL* 42, 359; *CSEL* 25, 516): *qui usque ad nostra tempora iam quidem in exigua ... perdurant.* The "in exigua" could also carry the meaning "in small numbers," but this would make the latter half of the sentence redundant (*sed adhuc tamen vel in ipsa paucitate perdurant*).

30 *Contra Crescionum* I 31, 36 (*PL* 43, 465; *CSEL* 52, 355); for non-temporal use of *nunc*, cf. *Oxford Latin Dictionary*, Fasc. V (1976), s.v. "nunc", 9c.

31 *C. Cresc., loc. cit.; c. Faust.* XIX 4;17. See also the comments below on Theodoret *haer. fab.* II 1. Cf. the comments of K–R, 50f.

32 *Div. haer. liber* 63 (*PL* 12, 1122; *CSEL* 63, 33): *Symmachiani alii discipuli istius (Patricius) eadem sentientes in omnibus, non sperantes iudicium, vitiis saecularibus et carnalibus concupiscentiis praedicant serviendum.*

Faustus recalls by the name of Symmachians or Nazarenes."[33] Before his conversion, Augustine adhered for some years to Manichaean philosophy. In 383 Faustus of Milevis, a Manichaean propagandist, visited nearby Carthage and taught for a short time. Augustine's keen intellect had raised certain questions, and he began to study under Faustus. However, Faustus was unable to satisfy Augustine, and thence began his turn to Christianity, completed some three years later. So it is not unlikely that he heard this identification from Faustus. This would also explain that hesitating statement in the treatise against Faustus that "they exist until the present day or at least until recently"; it could be information heard from the Manichaean some fifteen years before but unconfirmed by any later witness.[34]

In addition to this second-hand information, that the Nazarenes still existed in his day, Augustine supplies us with the following information about the sect: 1) they profess to be Christians and confess that Christ is the Son of God; 2) they practice baptism; 3) they keep the old law, specifically including a) circumcision, b) Sabbath observance, and c) food restrictions such as abstinence from swine; and 4) they are few in number. Of these eight items, five are clearly stated by Epiphanius and the *anacephalaiosis*,[35] and in fact elsewhere he clearly admits using Epiphanius.[36] The statement that they are few in number, coming as it does after Augustine's uncertainty as to whether they still exist, gives the impression that it is not so much a statement of known fact as it is a reasonable assumption based on their obscurity. He himself has not encountered them and knows very few who have, therefore they cannot be (or ever have been) a very populous group. Likewise the assertion (3c) that they abstain from eating swine's flesh could well be a conclusion Augustine has drawn on his own. He knows that they keep the Law and are "Jews and nothing else," as Epiphanius says.[37] He may logically infer that these Jewish Christians will not eat swine. It should be remembered that neither Epiphanius nor Jerome nor indeed any other writer brings this charge against the sect. Epiphanius does state that the Ebionites abstain from all flesh,[38] and this may have influenced Augustine. Similarly, the statement

---

33 *C. Faust.* XIX 17.

34 This was written before the well-known correspondence with Jerome, to which we have referred above. The *contra Crescionum* with its "et nunc" seems to have been written after receipt of Jerome's testimony and could reflect this affirmation of continued Nazarene existence.

35 1) *anaceph.* 29: *de bapt.* VII 1, 1; *c. Faust.* XIX 4; *de haer.* 9. 3) *anaceph.* 29: *de haer.* 9. 3a) *pan.* 29 5, 4: *c. Cresc.* I 31, 36; *c. Faust.* XIX 4; 17. 3b) *pan.* 29 7, 5: *c. Faust.* XIX 4.

36 *De haer.*, praef. 6 (*PL* 42, 23; *CC* 46, 288), and passim (see *CC* 46, index, s.v. Epiphanius). Altaner, "Augustinus und Epiphanius von Salamis," *TU* 83 (1967), 286–296.

37 Note that in this context he classes Nazarenes and Jews together quite purposely: "Do you too, like a Jew or a Nazarene . . . congratulate yourself on being conscientious regarding the abstinence from swine's meat?" (*c. Faust.* XIX 4).

38 *Pan.* 30 15, 3; *anaceph.* 30, 3.

that the Nazarenes "have Christian baptism," while not having a direct counterpart in Augustine's known sources, could have been prompted by Epiphanius' testimonies about other Jewish Christian sects.[39] In sum, there is no obligation to conclude that Augustine had any personal knowledge of the Nazarenes, nor even that he has any new material to contribute. His primary, if not sole source of information about a named sect of Nazarenes (before his correspondence with Jerome) was Epiphanius.

Theodoret of Cyrrhus

We may safely pass by a short notice in the treatise entitled *Praedestinatus*.[40] The work is nothing more than a plagiarism of Augustine's *de haeresibus* (wich it was written to refute).

Theodoret, Bishop of Cyrrhus (c. 393–c.466) has left us a short notice on the Nazarenes in his *haereticorum fabularum compendium*,[41] composed about 453: "The Nazarenes are Jews. They honor Christ as a righteous man and use the Gospel according to Peter. Eusebius said that these heresies originated during the time of the emperor Domitian. Against those Justin the philosopher and martyr has written, as also Irenaeus, the successor of the apostles, and Origen." He offers us two clear bits of information about the Nazarenes: They honor Christ as a righteous man, and they use the Gospel according to Peter. The first statement has no precise parallel in extant patristic literature, and we need not understand it as any definitive christological statement, no more at least than such New Testament statements as Luke 23:47 or 1 John 2:1, 2:29 and 3:7.[42] The most likely source of this statement would seem to be the *Ecclesiastical History* (III 27,2) of Eusebius: "for they considered him a plain and common man who was justified only because of his progress in virtue, born of the intercourse of a man and Mary."[43] If this indeed be the source of Theodoret's statement, we must first note that he has confused the Nazarenes with the Ebionites. In fact, if we look at the immediately preceding paragraph about the Ebionites, we find that he may have given us more information about the Nazarenes here than in the paragraph under their name. In any case, he has clearly mixed them together.

In II,1 he tells us of two groups, both known as Ebionites, who are different in

---

39 *Pan.* 30 16, 1.

40 *PL* 53, 587–672 (590 on Nazarenes). It was composed during the papacy of Sixtus III (432–440).

41 II 2 (*PG* 83, 389): Οἱ δὲ Ναζωραῖοι Ἰουδαῖοί εἰσι, τὸν Χριστὸν τιμῶντες ὡς ἄνθρωπον δίκαιον, καὶ τῷ καλουμένῳ κατὰ Πέτρον Εὐαγγελίῳ κεχρημένοι. Ταύτας συστῆναι τὰς αἱρέσεις Δομετιανοῦ βασιλεύοντος ὁ Εὐσέβιος εἴρηκε. Κατὰ τούτων συνέγραψεν Ἰουστῖνος ὁ φιλόσοφος καὶ μάρτυς, καὶ Εἰρηναῖος ὁ τῶν ἀποστόλων διάδοχος, καὶ Ὡριγένης.

42 These 1 John references should be considered in the context of the antidocetic flavor of the entire epistle with its affirmation that Christ has come in the flesh.

43 *PG* 20, 274. Cf. also Hippolytus, *ref. omn. haer.* VII 33, 1 (Ebion) and X 21, 2 (Cerinthus).

several ways. One does not accept the virgin birth, one does. One uses the Gospel according to the Hebrews, the other the Gospel according to Matthew. To the first group belongs Symmachus, and these reject Paul. The second group honors the Sabbath and "the Lord's day." The general run of this information comes from the above-mentioned passage of Eusebius, but Theodoret seems to have combined it with a second passage on the Ebionites (*HE* VI 17), which brings in the Symmachus connection and opposes the Gospel of Matthew.[44] We need look no further for Theodoret's source for the Ebionites; it is a synthesis of information given by Eusebius in his Church History. It is in this light that we should read the statement in *haer. fab.* II 2 that "'Eusebius stated that these heresies arose during the reign of Domitian. Justin, the philosopher and martyr, Irenaeus the successor of the apostles, and Origen wrote against them." He is not stating that his information about the Nazarenes is taken from Eusebius, Justin, Origen, and Irenaeus, but rather that he has consulted all of these for his data on the Jewish Christian sects generally. At this point we may recall that three of the four mention the existence of two kinds of Ebionites (above, chap. 2) while Irenaeus, who does not make that distinction, does speak of a sect which reads only Matthew.

The opening statement, that "the Nazarenes are Jews", may give us the hint that Theodoret has taken the name of the sect from Epiphanius, who says "they are rather Jews and nothing else."[45]

Finally it remains for us to consider Theodoret's curious reference to the Gospel according to Peter. Here again is a unique claim with no confirmation in any other known literature. Both Eusebius (*HE* III 23) and Origen (*Comm. in Matth.* X 17) mention the Gospel of Peter. In about the year 200 Serapion saw a copy of it and decided that it was inadmissable on the grounds that it was docetic.[46] If Serapion was correct, then this Gospel does not coincide with what we know of Nazarene doctrine, and we are safe in assuming that Theodoret has erred. How the error came about is a matter of conjecture.[47]

---

44 K–R have omitted this passage from their collection. See also *dem. evang.* VII 1. That is a negative about Matthew's gospel. The positive side of it may be found in Irenaeus (whom Theodoret also cites) *adv. haer.* I 26, 2, and III 11, 7, where it is stated that the Ebionites use only Matthew.

45 *Pan.* 29 9, 1.

46 Eusebius *HE* VI 12, 2–6, but not extremely docetic, as Serapion admitted. Two examples which may have influenced his decision (from H–S, *ad loc.*): 4 (10) "As if he felt no pain" (on the cross); 5 (19) "And the Lord called out and cried 'My power, O Power, thou hast forsaken me!' And having said this he *was taken up.*"

47 The most plausible explanation is that of Schmidtke (*TU* 37, 119f) who finds that Theodoret confused the words of Origen's commentary on Matthew at 13:54 (*PG* 13, 876). Just after mentioning the inhabitants of Nazareth, Origen speaks of the Gospel of Peter. It is from this same misassociation that Theodoret has concluded that the Nazarenes deny the divine birth of Jesus. See also our discussion above, in chap. 4 on "The Nazarenes in Jerome," and notes.

Later Writers

With one exception later fathers quote some early predecessor directly without expansion. Eugippius Abbas Africanus (c. 455-535) extracted from Augustine's writings and in his *thesaurus ex s. Augustini operibus* he quotes directly from the passage in *de baptismo* VII 1,1.[48]

Isidorus, Archbishop of Seville (c. 560-636) twice mentions the Nazarenes, once in *etymologiarum libri xx* (VIII 6,9) and once in *de haeresibus* (X).[49] In both cases he gives a close paraphrase of *anacephalaiosis* 29. Isidorus is followed or even quoted verbatim by Honorius Augustodunensis (*de haeresibus libellus*, XXIV) and Paulus (*de haer. libell.*, V).[50] Also directly dependent on the *anacephalaiosis* are John Damascene (*de haer.* 29) and Theodor Bar Khonai (*liber scholiorum*).[51]

The single exception to this tradition of plagiarism of the ancients is Paschasius Radbertus (790-865) in his *expositio in Mattheum* II 2.[52] This abbot of Corbie (near Amiens) is noted for his critical and extensive use of the fathers in his writings.[53] The passage cited would seem to depend primarily on Jerome[54] for such information as the earliest name of Christians, the holiness of the sect, the reference to the root, and even the name *evangelium Nazarenorum* ("Gospel of the Nazarenes"). This is in fact the first time that this name appears, although it is clearly a natural progression from the words of Jerome in several places.[55] It is worth noting here that Isidorus is the first writer to refer to the Nazarenes in the past tense, even though the sect must have ceased to exist as a recognizable entity centuries before.[56]

We need only briefly summarize our findings. No author after Jerome seems to have had any direct knowledge of the Nazarene sect, and only one (Didymus) even so much as quotes from the gospel they used. When exactly the sect passed

---

48 226 (*PL* 62, 888).

49 *PL* 82, 299, and K–R, 260.

50 *PL* 172, 236 (Honorius); K–R, 274 (Paulus).

51 K–R, 266.

52 On Matt. 2:23 = *PL* 120, 149.

53 E. Choisy, *Paschase Radbert* (1888); H. Peltier in *DTC* 13 (1937), c. 1628–1639 (s.v. "Radbert, Paschase"); *idem., Paschase Radbert* (1938).

54 *In Is.* 11, 1–3; *de situ* 143; *comm. in Matth.* I (on Matt. 2:23).

55 E.g. *de vir. ill.* 3; *in Matth.* 12, 13; 23, 35; 29, 9–10; but most probably from the same *in Is.* 11, 1–3 passage. At about the same time was the use of the same title by Haimo. This is taken up in the next chapter.

56 It is also possible that Epiphanius (in Latin translation?) had some influence on this whole passage of Isidore. Cf. *pan.* 29 5, 7, where he also makes mention of both John the Baptist and Samson. See also Isidore's *Expositio in Lamentationes* (on 4:7, *PL* 120, 1214f), where he speaks of Nazarei and Nazareni (for "nazır," but he is clearly reading only the Latin of the Vulgate), referring only to Christians and the Church with no mention of any heresy.

out of existence is impossible to determine. If we give a measure of credence to Jerome's claims to their presence in his time, then we must conclude that they survived into the early fifth century. But if we accept the judgment of certain scholars in denying Jerome's credibility and refusing his testimony, then there is little to force us to continue their existence even to the end of the fourth century. As we have noted above, it is not likely that Epiphanius knew them personally. Nonetheless, the attestations of extant Nazarene literature at the end of the fourth century may allow us to see their final demise somewhere around that time.

The most important conclusion of this chapter is that the Nazarenes were not mentioned by earlier fathers *not* because they did not exist but rather because they were still generally considered to be acceptably orthodox. The history of the Nazarene sect must be clearly distinguished from that of the Ebionites. Once Epiphanius failed to do so, he introduced a confusion which continues until today. The Bishop of Salamis did us the service of preserving certain data on a sect about which we would have been otherwise ignorant. But he did us the disservice of overreacting and misinterpreting his sources.

Chapter Six

The Gospel According to the Hebrews

There can be no doubt that the story of Jesus was early commited to writing in the Semitic language of his followers. First of all, the nature of the case makes this likely. Secondly, we have numerous testimonies to the existence of such a gospel and a few fragments from it, albeit not in the original language. In the preceding chapters we saw that the Nazarenes themselves were reported to be in possession of a gospel written in Hebrew. This Hebrew gospel is generally said to be the Gospel of Matthew but with some differences. It is clear that such a gospel, were it to come into our possession, would be a valuable tool in gaining additional knowledge of the Nazarene sect. Unfortunately, no Hebrew gospel exists today for scholars to examine, although archeologists could conceivably discover one in some place such as Pella, Jerusalem, Galilee, or Aleppo.

Until that awaited find occurs, we must content ourselves with examining existing fragments of the gospel used by the Nazarenes and gleaning what information we may from them. This is not as easy as it may seem, because there are many complications and uncertainties. It must be stated at the outset that it is not our intent in this chapter to make another exhaustive study of all fragments of the Jewish Christian gospels nor even of the "Gospel according to the Hebrews."[1] The scope of the present chapter remains within the limits of the overall study: to extract whatever information is possible on the history and doctrines of the Nazarene sect. The extremely complex problem of the Jewish Christian gospels has been so complicated by the speculations of investigators that it is difficult to cut one's way through the jungle of suggestions and proofs. This chapter deals only with those fragments where doubt as to provenance is at a minimum.

The earliest indication we have of the existence of a Hebrew written account

---

1 Collections of the fragments can be found in Nicholson; R. Handmann, *TU* 5, 3 (1888), 66–103; M.R. James, *The Apocryphal New Testament* (1903), pp. 1–8; A. Schmidtke, *TU* 37, 1 (1911); M.-J. Lagrange, *RB* 31 (1922), 161–181, 321–349; J.T. Dodd, *The Gospel according to the Hebrews* (1933); P. Vielhauer, "Jewish-Christian Gospels" in H–S I, 117–165; R. Cameron, ed., *The Other Gospels: Non-Canonical Gospel Texts* (1982).

for some of Jesus' life comes to us from Papias.[2] He speaks of a collection of logia of Jesus made by Matthew in the "Hebrew language." He also knew of a story of a woman accused of many sins, which, Eusebius tells us, was to be found in the Gospel according to the Hebrews. Hegesippus also knew the Gospel according to the Hebrews (GH), this again from Eusebius.[3] The first writer in whose extant works we actually have mention of the name of the gospel is Clement of Alexandria[4] and soon after him Origen.[5] Although Eusebius does mention GH by name, it is a moot point whether he actually saw the gospel.[6] Epiphanius only once (*pan.* 30 3,7) gives us the name κατὰ Ἐβραίους ("according to the Hebrews"), as does Didymus the Blind.[7] This takes us up to Jerome, who mentions GH (*secundum* or *juxta Hebraeos*) frequently.[8] If he saw it, he was the only Latin writer to have done so.

We have focused here on specific mentions of the "Gospel according to the Hebrews" for two reasons which will serve to highlight the complications involved. First of all, let us note that while the gospel may have been recorded in a Semitic language even before the end of the first century, we do not find the name "Gospel according to the Hebrews" until the third century, and before Jerome at the end of the fourth century it is mentioned by name less than ten times. Elsewhere we find references to a nameless gospel written in Hebrew characters. The general impression is that this gospel did not have a specific, known name until fairly late, and that this name designated its users rather than its author. However—and this is our second point—the period during which the designation appeared was a time, as we have seen, when there was general unfamiliarity in the Gentile Church with the finer distinctions existing in Jewish Christianity. The name "Ebionite" was used for Nazarenes as well as for Ebionites, and more generally, they were all thought of as those Christians from among the Jews or Hebrews who still adhered to the Law and read the Bible in Hebrew. If there were few Christians from among the Gentiles who had actually seen a gospel written in

---

2   Eus. *HE* III 39, 16. Papias, a companion of Polycarp and disciple of a "John," is quoting "the Elder" for this information.

3   *HE* IV 22, 8.

4   *Stromateis* II ix 45, 5 (*GCS*, 137).

5   *Comm. on John* II 12 (*GCS* 10, 67); *in Matth.* XV 14 (*GCS* 40, 389).

6   He never directly quotes from it, but see the Syriac *theophania* 4, 12 (*GCS* 11, 183; cited by K-R, 148, and James, *op. cit.*, p. 2). The *HE* III 39, 16 reference may only be from Papias. There is a mention in Klostermann's edition of the *theophania* (not in Gressmann's *GCS* edition) of a "gospel in Hebrew letters which has come to us," τὸ εἰς ἡμᾶς ἧκον (James, 3; H-S GN 18; *PG* 24, 685f). Jerome indicates that GH was to be found in the Caesarea library (*de vir. ill.* 3), where Eusebius would certainly have seen it. Some have argued, however, that had Eusebius been in possession of such a treasure he would have said so.

7   Epiph.: *GCS* 25, 337f; Didymus, *comm. in Ps.*, K-R, 198.

8   See chap. 4, n. 18.

Hebrew letters, they were even fewer who would have been able to tell if it was in Hebrew or Aramaic much less to discern textual and doctrinal differences between two such gospels.

For indeed it is clear that there was not just one "authorized version" of GH. The fragments which have come to us ascribed to some Hebrew gospel will not all fit neatly into one consistent, contiguous work. All of this is significant for our study of the Nazarenes and their doctrines. No writer before Epiphanius mentions the Nazarenes by name, but Epiphanius, by his own admission (*pan.* 29 9,4), never saw a copy of their gospel, and so could not have compared it with that used by the Ebionites, from which he quotes. There is, therefore, no reason for us to assume that every patristic reference to a gospel written in Hebrew letters speaks of the same gospel. Nor should we be too quick to take all such references and use them as pieces in the Nazarene puzzle.

It is our position, then, that the one earliest *Urschrift* (if there was only one) or collection of logia was variously adapted, expanded, edited, and used by the different streams of Jewish Christianity.[9] By this view there was only one so-called GH, but it made its appearance as the GH of the Ebionites, the GH of the Nazarenes, and perhaps the GH used by Egyptian Jewish Christians, called "the Gospel according to the Egyptians." From the earliest times the name assigned to the basic writing was Matthew's, and it was probably by that name that each group knew its own recension of GH, if they did not simply call it "the gospel." Some groups had their gospel in a Greek translation, and it would seem that additions to the basic translation may have been made in Greek.

Here we must make some observations on the name "The Gospel of the Nazarenes." In most dictionaries and encyclopedias of Christianity, as well as in other scholarly work, th s gospel is presented as an attested title for a known ancient work. The fact is that the eariest appearances of the name "Gospel of the Nazarenes" are in the ninth century, within a very few years of each other. Haimo of Auxerre (d. 855) in his commentary on Isaiah[10] makes an indirect quotation from an *evangelium Nazarenorum*. Whether he actually saw a manuscript with that title we cannot say for sure, but it seems most likely that he was influenced in his use of the name by Jerome.[11] As we have noted, Jerome

9   Cf. A.A.T. Ehrhardt in *Studia Evangelica* III (=*TU* 88 [1964]), 361.
10 On 53:12 (*PL* 116, 994): *"et pro transgressoribus" Judaeis, sive persecutoribus "rogavit" dicens, dum penderet in cruce: "Pater, ignosce illis." Sicut enim in Evangelio Nazarenorum habetur, ad hanc vocem Domini multa millia Judaeorum astantium circa crucem crediderunt.* This work, like all of Haimo's writings, was wrongly ascribed to Haimo of Halberstadt.
11 Haimo had Jerome's Isaiah commentary before him when he wrote his own. Cf. Is 48 (*PL* 116, 960); 49:7 (965), where he uses Jerome on *birkat ha-mînîm* without citing him; 52:4 (983). Also here at 53:12 Haimo quotes the same verse from Luke (23:34) on which Jerome ends his treatment of Is 53.

repeatedly mentions the Gospel of (or according to) the Hebrews "which is read by the Nazarenes." While he himself never uses the title *evangelium Nazarenorum*, it is a natural step from his words, a step that Haimo evidently took.

The other ninth-century appearance of this derived name we have already seen in the previous chapter. It is by Paschasius Radbertus around the year 860.[12] We have already noted his dependence on Jerome. There is no reason to look for any connection between these two medieval authors in this matter; the derivation of the name "Gospel of the Nazarenes" from Jerome's words is so natural that many have done it and are doing it even until today.[13]

The name "Gospel of the Nazarenes"(GN), then, is a later hybrid, derived from Jerome. Jerome himself only knew the name "Gospel according to the Hebrews" or "Matthew." However, as Vielhauer has observed, Jerome had only one work in mind when he wrote of this Hebrew gospel.[14] The designations GH and GN may be only a convenient way of differentiating recensions of the same basic work. But if we are to use them in that way, let us be clear that we are doing so and not think that we are speaking of two works independent of each other, composed separately and in different languages.

The Nazarenes and the Gospel according to the Hebrews

Hebrew." When writing about the Ebionites (*pan.* 30 3,7), he also credits them with accepting Matthew, which they call κατὰ Ἐβραίους ("according to the Hebrews"). However, this cannot be equated with the canonical Matthew, both because it omitted the opening two chapters and because quotations from it which Epiphanius does preserve for us are not found in Matthew. Moreover, he is not sure that the Nazarenes omitted the first two chapters, thus leaving us in doubt whether the versions used by the two sects were the same. So on the one hand we find both Nazarenes and Ebionites calling their gospels "Matthew," while on the other the works are demonstrably not the same. We may recall that

---

12 *Expos. in ev. Matt.* II 2 (*PL* 120, 149). See above, chap. 5, on "Later Writers."

13 Schmidtke, *TU* 37, 282f, notes Petrus Comestor (d. 1179) and Hugh of St. Cher (d. 1263); Vielhauer in H–S I, 152f, cites six uses of the name in the "Historia passionis Domini" of the 14th century. According to J.A. Fabricius (1703, cited by J.B. Wirthmüller, *Die Nazoräer* [Regensburg, 1864], pp. 48), J. Drusius (d. 1616) and M. Sandaeus (d. 1656) both claimed that copies of *evangelium Nazarenorum* were extant in their time. We may also add H. Grotius, *Annotationes in quatuor Evangelia et Acta Apostolorum* (in *Operum Theologicorum*, Tomi II, Vol. I) (London, 1679), pp. 4–5, 7; R. Simon, *Histoire Critique des principaux commentateurs du Nouveau Testament . . . ,* (Rotterdam, 1693), p. 49; G.E. Lessing, "Neue Hypothese über die Evangelisten, als bloss menschliche Geschichtschreiber betrachtet" in *Theologischer Nachlass* (1778), no. 22ff.

14 H–S, 132.

it is Epiphanius who tells us that the Ebionites arose out of (or split off from) the Nazarenes. In such a split it would be natural that the dissenters take with them the gospel they had used. But if the split arose as a result of christological differences, then we might expect that the basic document would be revised, deletions made (like the genealogies), and appropriate phrases added.[15]

Among ancient writers the only Church Father specifically to connect the Nazarene sect to GH is Jerome. This he does in eight places: *de vir. ill.* 3; *in Matt.* 12,13; 23,35; *in Is.* 40,9-11 (= *in Ez.* 16,13); prol. 65; *in Ez.* 18,5-9; and *adv. Pelag.* III 2. One other passage, *in Is.* 11,2, mentions a "gospel written in Hebrew which the Nazarenes read"; this we will take to be the same work. The passage *in Matt.* 12,13 is one of the three which support Epiphanius in calling this gospel by Matthew's name (also the *de vir. ill.* and *adv. Pelag.* passages). In another respect this passage is unique when it says that both Nazarenes and Ebionites use this gospel. Although it is most likely that Jerome is simply making a generalization based on Epiphanius, if there is any factual basis to what he says, it can only support our hypothesis that both sects made use of gospels which were commonly thought to be the same work and which were in fact of the same family.

It must be pointed out that the situation we have surmised—two related gospels, both called Matthew by their users and GH by outsiders but diverging to a greater or lesser degree from each other—such a state of affairs must cause grave difficulties to one who would collect the fragments of one or the other. Let us say that fragment A is said to come from GH as used by Nazarenes. Then we find fragment A elsewhere, also assigned to GH but without mention of the Nazarenes. We cannot automatically conclude that both quotations were taken from the Nazarene version of GH. The gospel tradition for GH may have left fragment A synoptically in both Nazarene and Ebionite versions of GH (see note 37 below). Thus, Origen or Clement of Alexandria quotes a fragment from GH, and it is clear that he found it in Greek. Then Jerome comes along, quotes the same saying, also assigns it to GH, but tells us that it was in Hebrew. Do we have a contradiction? Not necessarily. Jerome is using the version of the Nazarenes, which he first translated to Greek and Latin. The Egyptian authors had the Ebionite version, already in Greek. Now to be sure, Jerome thought his was the same as theirs, but may not that be because he knew the Ebionite (Greek) version only through their citations?

One more limiting proviso must be made before extracting from GH fragments

---

15 Cf. Epiph. *pan.* 30 13, 7, the addition of ἐγὼ σήμερον γεγέννηκά σε at the story of the baptism of Jesus and the descent of the Holy Spirit — clearly an addition and one which made a basic difference between Nazarene and Ebionite. Cf. G. Quispel, *VC* 11 (1957), 140, n. 5. Could the very split in Jewish Christianity at this early stage have been over the compilation of their gospel?

what data we can about the Nazarenes. Even if we manage successfully to select fragments only from the Nazarene recension of GH, we must beware of putting our own interpretation on a particular pericope and then making far-reaching conclusions based on that exegesis. Our information is limited at best, and one spotlighted phrase may give a distorted picture of their doctrines, especially if we begin to extrapolate from that one saying. Nicholson[16] demonstrated the potential hazards of such extrapolation from verses out of context. He proposed an exercise in which we imagine that only three canonical gospels had come to us and that the fourth had been preserved—in fragments—by the Nazarenes.[17] Selecting material peculiar to Matthew, such as Matt. 5:17, 10:5,6, and 15:24 would show the extreme Judaizing views of this Matthean sect. "Or let us suppose Mark to have been the Nazarene Gospel. From the fact that it began with the Baptism, we should forthwith conclude that it was designed to support the heresy that Jesus was mere man until the divine Christ descended into him in 'the shape of a dove.'" Let us recall that the Nazarenes, unlike the Ebionites, used New Testament material in addition to GH.[18] By now we have seen enough of their general "orthodoxy" to prevent us from "discoveries" of aberrent Christology.

Information on the Nazarenes derivable from the Gospel according to the Hebrews

The foregoing considerations will seriously limit the number of fragments which we may allow ourselves to use with reasonable certainty that they have something reliable to tell us about the Nazarene sect. This is no bad thing, however, because the very purpose of this study limits the selection even more. Let us reiterate: We are not attempting here a new analysis or compilation of GH. Rather our purpose is to derive all information possible about the history and beliefs of the Nazarenes. With our self-imposed limitation of avoiding speculative extrapolation from doubtful fragments, we have to consider only a handful of passages.

1.   According to the Gospel written in Hebrew speech, which the Nazarenes read, the whole fount of the Holy Spirit shall descend upon him . . . Further in the Gospel which we have just mentioned we find the following written: And it came to pass when the Lord was come up out of the water, the whole fount of the Holy Spirit descended upon him and rested on him and said to him: My Son, in all the prophets was I waiting for thee that thou shouldest come and I might rest in thee. For thou art my rest; thou art my first-begotten Son that reignest for ever.

                                                                      (Jerome, *in Is.* 11,2)[19]

---

16 *Op. cit.*, pp. 82 ff.

17 We may add to Nicholson's exercise the assumption that these fragments were quoted only by Church Fathers and were selected because they somehow *differed* from the three "canonical" gospels. This assumption gives us an exact parallel to the GH case.

18 Epiph. *pan.* 29 7, 2.

19 The translation is from H–S, 163f. *PL*, 144f: *Evangelium quod Hebraeo sermone conscriptum legunt Nazaraei: Descendet super eum omnis fons Spiritus sancti . . . Porro in Evangelio, cujus*

We may first of all note the difference between this account of Jesus' baptism and the account given by Epiphanius (*pan.* 30 13,7–8), which may also come from a work called GH.[20] It is clear that our gospel here is different from the one which the old heresiologue assigns to the Ebionites.

This passage contains a strong affirmation of that Christology of Jesus' sonship which we have seen elsewhere,[21] without necessarily falling into the Cerinthian heresy that he was somehow adopted at his baptism.[22] We also note here a strong resemblance to the canonical Epistle to the Hebrews with its emphasis on the sonship and the culmination of prophetic word in the Messiah.[23]

2. But in that Gospel written according to the Hebrews, which is read by the Nazarenes, the Lord says: "A moment ago my mother, the Holy spirit, took me up."

(Jerome, *in Is.* 40,9)[24]

This quotation is repeated by Jerome in his commentary on Ezekiel 16:13 and earliest in Micah 7:6, where he adds the phrase *in uno capillorum meorum*. The earliest appearance of this saying is in Origen's *Commentary on John* II 12, repeated by him (without the hair) in his homily on Jeremiah XV 4; he adds that the Holy Spirit took Jesus to Mount Tabor. The possibility cannot be discounted that Jerome simply took this quotation from Origen's *Commentary*, where it is specifically attributed to GH. This cannot be taken for granted, however, as Jerome goes on in his own comments on the logion to note that the unfamiliar

---

supra fecimus mentionem, haec scripta reperimus: Factum est autem cum ascendisset Dominus de aqua, descendit fons omnis Spiritus sancti, et requievit super eum, et dixit illi: Fili mi, in omnibus prophetis expectabam te, ut venires, et requiescerem in te. Tu es enim requies mea, tu es filius meus primogenitus, qui regnas in sempiternum.

20 The text possibly reads Ἑβραϊκὸν δὲ τοῦτο καλοῦσιν, but it is not clear at this point. See the comments of Holl, *GCS* 25, *ad loc.* K–R render *pan.* 30 13, 7–8 as follows: "And after much is said in the Gospel it continues: 'After the people had been baptized Jesus also came and was baptized by John. And when he ascended from the water the heavens opened and he saw the Holy Spirit in the form of a dove descending and coming to him. And a voice from heaven said: "Thou art my beloved Son, in thee I am well pleased," and next: "This day I have generated thee." And suddenly a great light shone about that place. When John saw it, they say, he said to him: "Who art thou Lord?" And again a voice came from heaven which said to him: "This is my beloved Son, in whom I am well pleased." After this, it says, John fell down before him and said: "I pray thee, Lord, baptize thou me." But he withstood him and said: "Let it be, since so it is necessary that everything will be fulfilled"'".

21 Epiph. *pan.* 29 7, 3; Jerome, *ep.* 112, 13; *in Is.* 31, 6–9.

22 See Nicholson, 83.

23 See O. Cullmann, *The Christology of the New Testament* (London, 1959), pp. 16, 38–40 and 89–104. Note also this implied endorsement of the OT prophets.

24 Translation of K–R, 225. *PL* 24, 405: *Sed et in Evangelio quod juxta Hebraeos scriptum, Nazaraei lectitant, Dominus loquitur: modo me tulit mater mea, Spiritus sanctus.*

reference to the Spirit as Jesus' mother is attributable to the feminine gender of the Hebrew word. This is an observation which Origen (who, as we have suggested, only knew GH in Greek) never makes and one which would seem to reinforce the chance that Jerome was actually using the Hebrew version of GH. (He makes a similar comment at Micah 7:6.)

But we have brought this passage only on the chance that it has something to tell us of Nazarene Christology. What is this reference by Jesus to the Holy Spirit as his mother? The explanation of Jerome is ingenious and not wholly unsatisfying: "No one need be scandalized by this, since in Hebrew spirit is in the feminine gender, while in our language it is masculine and in Greek it is neuter. There is no gender in the godhead." We must add to this the observation that the most likely setting for this saying is when the Spirit took Jesus into the wilderness to be tempted (Matt. 4:1). This follows the story of Jesus' baptism where, in the verses immediately preceding, the Spirit descends on him and a voice declares "this is my son."[25]

In the canonical account the voice comes "out of heaven," from which the Spirit is descending. Even this could easily enough be understood as the Spirit speaking; passage 1 above is simply more explicit in having the Spirit say "My Son." The doctrine of the Holy Spirit was the slowest to develop in the doctrine of the trinity in the Church catholic, and there is no reason to assume that it was otherwise among the Nazarenes. This passage reveals a primitive pneumatology but not some developed heretical view of the Holy Spirit.[26] In the last analysis it only confirms Nazarene belief in the divine sonship of Jesus.

3.   The Gospel called according to the Hebrews which was recently translated by me into Greek and Latin, which Origen frequently uses, records after the resurrection of the Savior: And when the Lord had given the linen cloth to the servant of the priest, he went to James and appeared to him. For James had sworn that he would not eat bread from that hour in which he had drunk the cup of the Lord until he should see him risen from among them that sleep. And shortly thereafter the Lord said: Bring a table and bread! And immediately it is added: he took bread, blessed

---

25 See the comments of Martian in *PL* 24, *ad loc.*

26 One must draw attention to the fragment said to be from GH in a Coptic translation of a discourse by Cyril of Jerusalem (d. 386) (H–S GH 1): "When Christ wished to come upon the earth to men, the good Father summoned a mighty power in heaven, which was called Michael, and entrusted Christ to the care thereof. And the power came into the world and it was called Mary, and Christ was in her womb seven months." This passage was advocated as truly from GH by V. Burch in *JTS* 21 (1920), 310–315, but he was adequately refuted by M.R. James in the following issue of the same journal (pp. 160–161). See also Vielhauer in H–S I, 137, who noted that its doctrine of the Holy Spirit is inconsistent with that of the authentic passages given by Jerome (1 and 2 in our treatment above).

it and brake it and gave it to James the Just and said to him: My brother, eat thy bread, for the Son of Man is risen from among them that sleep.

(Jerome, *de vir. ill.* 2)[27]

Even though we are working from the hypothesis that Jerome knew only the Nazarene version of GH, we can further confirm it as the provenance for this fragment from the next chapter (3) of *de vir. ill.*, in which he specifically identifies the work as that used by the sect. We may first note that this entire pericope takes place after the resurrection of Jesus and strongly affirms Nazarene belief in that event. As we have seen in Chapter 3, Epiphanius (*pan.* 29 7,3) tells us that they believed in the resurrection of the dead. The present passage connects that belief specifically to Jesus.[28]

Of no less significance is the honor with which this fragment treats James, vouchsafing him this personal visit and endorsement by Jesus. The chronology would seem to differ from that of the canonical gospels, but the tradition of a Christophany to James is as old as Paul's first epistle to the Corinthians (15:7). This expanded account of that appearance, whenever it took place, recalls the respectful treatment of James by Epiphanius in his chapter on the Nazarenes. While he specifically refers (*pan.* 29 4,3) to Eusebius and Clement (for which we should read Hegesippus), it is not unlikely that this association is a reflection of what he found in his source for the Nazarenes.

4.   For since the apostles believed him to be spirit according to the Gospel which is of the Hebrews and is read by the Nazarenes, a demon without a body, he said to them (Luke 24:38f). . .

(Jerome, *in Is.*, prol. 65)[29]

Rather than being a full passage, this is more like a variorum reading, where Jerome found *incorporale daemonium* (bodiless spirit) in place of the *spiritum* of Luke 24:39. If this is authentically from the GH used by the Nazarenes, then it

---

27 Translation from H–S I, 165. *PL* 23, 611f: *Evangelium quoque quod appellatur secundum Hebraeos et a me nuper in graecum sermonem latinumque translatum est, quo et Adamantius saepe utitur, post resurrectionem Salvatoris refert: Dominus autem cum dedisset, sindonem servo sacerdotis, iit ad Iacobum et apparuit ei (iuraverat enim Iacobus se non comesurum panem ab illa hora qua biberat calicem Domini, donec videret eum resurgentem a dormientibus) rursumque post paululum: Adferte, ait Dominus, mensam et panem. Statimque additur: Tulit panem et benedixit et fregit et dedit Iacobo Iusto et dixit ei: Frater mi, comede panem tuum, quia resurrexit Filius hominis a dormientibus.* (The translation "Origen" for Adamantius is correct in Jerome; cf. *ep.* 33 [*ad Paulam, PL* 22, 447].) For a full commentary on this passage, see Nicholson, 62–68.

28 Jerome also refers, in *ep.* 112, 13, to their belief in the resurrection of Jesus.

29 Translation from K–R, 227. *PL* 24, 628: *Cum enim Apostoli eum putarent spiritum, vel juxta Evangelium, quod Hebraeorum lectitant Nazaraei, incorporale daemonium, dixit eis* (Luke 24:38f).

gives further evidence of Nazarene belief in the resurrection of Jesus. But there
must be some doubt as to its authenticity, or at least as to its provenance. The
Vulgate *spiritum* and the GH *daemonium* are both valid translations of πνεῦμα.[30]
However, the word *incorporale* is from the Greek ασώματον and cannot have
come from a Hebrew original.[31] Some years before writing the above, Jerome
quoted this same fragment, saying that it was "from the Gospel which was
recently translated by me," that is, GH.[32] He was, he said, quoting Ignatius, but
he wrongly attributed the saying to the Epistle to Polycarp. (It is in the Epistle to
the Smyrnaeans, 3.) Vielhauer points out that Jerome was not using GH nor even
Ignatius but rather Eusebius' report of what Ignatius said.[33] However, Eusebius,
in his reference to this logion, confesses that he does not know where it originated
(*HE* III 36), even though he himself seems to have had access to GH in the
Caesarea library. As we have seen above (no. 3), Jerome first uses the phrase "the
Gospel which was recently translated by me" in the second chapter of *de vir. ill.*,
where he went on to say "of which also Origen often makes use." Now in fact
Origen once gives us the same logion,[34] but he ascribes it to a different work, the
Doctrina Petri. Lightfoot[35] delineated two possible conclusions: either Jerome
had a lapse of memory when quoting Origen, or his copy of GH was a different
recension from that known to Eusebius and Origen. We would combine his con-
clusions, agreeing that Jerome's GH was not the same as Origen's and that
Jerome, misunderstanding his Eusebius, recalled the same logion from Origen but
mistakenly remembered it as coming from GH (which Origen frequently quoted).
In other words, we cannot accept it as coming from a gospel used by the
Nazarenes.

5.   In the Gospel according to the Hebrews which is indeed in the Chaldaean and
        Syrian speech but is written in Hebrew letters, which the Nazarenes use to this day
        . . . the story tells us: Behold, the mother of the Lord and his brethren said unto
        him: John the Baptist baptizeth unto the remission of sins; let us go and be bap-
        tized of him. But he said unto them: Wherein have I sinned, that I should go and be
        baptized of him? Unless peradventure this very thing that I have said is [a sin of]
        ignorance.
            And in the same book: If thy brother (saith he) have sinned by a word and made
        thee amends, seven times in a day receive thou him. Simon his disciple said unto

---

30 See Nicholson, 74.
31 Vielhauer, H–S I, 129. On this word see also J.B. Lightfoot, *The Apostolic Fathers* II 2, 294;
    296f.
32 *De vir. ill.* 16.
33 *Art. cit.*, p. 129. Cf. Schmidtke, *TU* 37, 256f; 62.
34 *De princ.* I, praef. 8 (*PG* 11, 119): *Si vero quis velit nobis proferre ex illo libello qui Petri
    Doctrina appellatur, ubi salvator videtur ad discipulos dicere, Non sum daemonium
    incorporeum . . ..*
35 *Op. cit.*, pp. 295f.

him: Seven times in a day? The Lord answered and said unto him: Yea, I say unto thee, seventy times seven times. For in the prophets also, after they were anointed by the Holy Spirit, the word of sin was found.

(Jerome, *adv. Pelag.* 3,2)[36]

We may comment on several points from this long fragment. First of all we should note Jesus' own awareness of his sinlessness as compared to the sinful natures of the prophets.[37] This is more than just the "progress in righteousness" of Ebionite doctrine; it may even point, as Dodd has suggested, to a self-awareness of divinity.[38] On the other hand, this Nazarene fragment has Jesus admitting to the possibility of ignorance. This Christology, Nicholson has suggested, may have its canonical parallels in passages such as Luke 2:52 and Mark 13:32, which indicate a partial knowledge in Jesus.[39] The same writer has also noted that here we have a clear endorsement of the divine inspiration of the prophets.[40] This opposes Ebionite doctrine, which did not accept the Old Testament prophets.[41]

Let us bundle our gleanings. This purposely limited analysis of five fragments from GH has yielded a picture of a group distinctive from the Ebionites in its

---

36 Translation from M.R. James, *op. cit.*, p. 6. *PL* 23, 570f: *"Ex Evangelio juxta Hebraeos". — In Evangelio "juxta Hebraeos", quod Chaldaico quidem Syroque sermone, sed Hebraicis litteris scriptum est, quo utuntur usque hodie Nazareni, . . . narrat historia: Ecce mater Domini et fratres ejus dicebant ei: Joannes Baptista baptizat in remissionem peccatorum: eamus et baptizemur ab eo. Dixit autem eis: Quid peccavi, ut vadam et baptizer ab eo? Nisi forte hoc ipsum quod dixi, ignorantia est.*

  Et in eodem volumine: Si peccaverit, inquit, frater tuus in verbo, et satis tibi fecerit, septies in die suscipe eum. Dixit illi Simon discipulus ejus: Septies in die? Respondit Dominus, et dixit ei: Etiam ego dico tibi, usque septuagies septies. Etenim in prophetis quoque postquam uncti sunt Spiritu sancto, inventus est sermo peccati.

37 The expression "sermo peccati' does not necessarily have to mean a *word* of sin. The Hebrew or Aramaic word translated by sermo can as well carry the meaning "something", "a matter of sin" (דבר חטא ,דבר עברה ,דבר), i.e. even the prophets continued to sin after they had prophesied. On this fragment see J.B. Bauer, "Sermo Peccati. Hieronymous und das Nazaräerevangelium," *BZ* 4 (1960), 122 128. The latter half of our fragment has a parallel in the Judaikon at Matt. 18:22, a fact which James, *op. cit.*, p. 7, says "shows the identity of the 'Jewish' with Jerome's gospel." With such logic we may take isolated parallels and prove Matthew, Mark, and Luke to be identical.

38 J.T. Dodd, *The Gospel according to the Hebrews* (London, 1933), p. 34f.

39 *Op. cit.*, p. 38.

40 *Op. cit.*, p. 81.

41 Epiph., *pan.* 30 18, 4 and 5. Cf. *ibid.*, 29 7, 2. Vielhauer (*art. cit.*, p. 145) nicely summarized the data from this fragment thus: "The conversation of Jesus with His mother and His brethren is a variant of the conversation with the Baptist [cf. Matt. 3.13–15] and is determined by the dogmatic idea of the sinlessness of Jesus."

doctrine of the divine sonship of Jesus and its acceptance of the Old Testament prophets. The Nazarenes who used this gospel clearly affirmed the resurrection of Jesus from the dead but may have had (at least at the time when the gospel was composed) an incomplete doctrine of the Holy Spirit. The recension of GH which we have examined may have revealed a balance between Jesus' humanity and his divinity, and especially of his own self-awareness of a "dual nature." One fragment shows a sect which afforded James the Just a place of special honor in its records. This in itself may be taken as another difference from Ebionite tradition, which tended to honor Peter, while not, however, belittling James. Finally, we note that all these data are consistent with what we have already learned elsewhere about the Nazarenes. Along the way (and incidentally) we have perhaps seen that Jerome is not to be trusted in everything that he says, but neither is he to be rejected out of hand as unreliable.

Chapter Seven

Jewish Sources

No investigation of the history of a phenomenon as Jewish as early Jewish Christianity can safely ignore the wealth of potential data available in Jewish written sources. Any wide study of Jewish Christianity will find much that is useful there, and indeed the renewed interest in the field in the last generation of scholarship has only lately begun to tap this well. In a work as narrowly defined as the present one, however, we shall find the talmudic material of only small help. We have chosen to restrict this study to that which can be identified as "Nazarene" with a minimum of speculation, because a structure built on a foundation of speculation and guesswork will be easily undermined. Hence we have kept our focus only on those places where the name Nazarene specifically appears, or where the sect can with reasonable certainty be identified from descriptions of its peculiar doctrines.

With this limitation, we may note that the name Nazarene(s) (נוצרי, נוצרים *nôẓrî, nôẓrîm*) appears only some dozen times in all extant talmudic literature.[1] In all but two of these cases it is found in the name of ישו הנוצרי (*yešû ha-nôẓrî*), Jesus the Nazarene. It must be noted that half of these passages were censored during the Middle Ages, either by Christian censors or by Jewish editors in fear of them.[2] Almost certainly, numerous other mentions of *yešû ha-nôẓrî* or *nôẓrîm* were cut out of our extant texts and remain unrestorable, replaced in centuries past by אפיקורסין (*'epiqôrsîn*) or צדוקים (*ẓdûqîm*) or similar harmless substitutes, or simply omitted altogether.

To take up an earlier matter, in the few appearences of (ם)נוצרי, there are no etymological data given. The town of Nazareth never appears in talmudic

---

1 These have been compiled by Herford (see below, n. 3) and others: Sanh. 107b (2x); 43a (4x); Sota 47a; Av. Zar. 16b–17a (2x); Taanit 27b.

2 The censored passages were restored from older MSS and editions by R.N.N. Rabbinovicz, דקדוקי סופרים. See also G. Dalman in the appendix to H. Laible, *Jesus Christus im Talmud* (Berlin, 1891).

3 The first five in note 1 above. See T. Herford, *Christianity in Talmud and Midrash* (New York, 1975 [1903]), pp. 50f, 56f, 83, 97, 138f and texts in his appendix.

literature, and Jewish sources have nothing to tell us of the provenance of the name Nazarene.

Yeshu Ha-nôẓrî

Jesus the *nôẓrî* is mentioned in five places in the Babylonian Talmud only.[3] The earliest is that in Avodah Zarah 16b–17a,[4] where the name appears twice and seems to have escaped the eye of the censor.

> Our Rabbis teach, When R. Eliezer was arrested for Minut they took him up to the tribunal to be judged. The governor said to him, "Will an old man such as thou busy himself about these vain things?" He said "Faithful is the judge concerning me." The governor supposed he said this in reference to him; but he only said it in regard to his Father in Heaven. He (the governor) said, "Since I am trusted concerning thee, Dimissus, thou art released." When he came to his house his disciples came in to comfort him, but he would not take comfort. R. Akiva said to him. "Rabbi, suffer me to say something of what thou hast taught me." He said to him, "Say on." He said to him, "Rabbi, perhaps there has come Minut into thy hand and it has pleased thee, and on account of that thou hast been arrested for Minut." He said to him, "Akiva, thou hast reminded me. Once I was walking in the upper street of Sepphoris, and I found a man of the disciples of Jeshu the Nazarene, and Jacob of Kfar Sechania was his name. He said to me, 'It is written in your Torah, "Thou shalt not bring the hire of a harlot," etc. What may be done with it? Latrinae for the high priest.' And I answered him nothing. He said to me, 'Thus hath Jeshu the Nazarene taught me, "For the hire of a harlot hath she gathered them, and unto the hire of a harlot shall they return." From the place of filth they come, and unto the place of filth they shall go.' And the saying pleased me, and because of this I was arrested for Minut; and I transgressed against what is written in the Torah, 'Keep thy way far from her,' this is Minut; 'and come not nigh the door of her house,' this is the Government."

We have quoted this passage in full because it is probably quite early and because it raises a number of questions. The *terminus ad quem*, given the appearance of Eliezer b. Hyrkanos, must be about 130. However, as Herford has pointed out, the arrest of R. Eliezer for *minut* indicates a Roman persecution of Christians

---

4 ת״ר כשנתפס ר״א למינות העלוהו לגרדום לידון אמר לו אותו הגמון זקן שכמותך יעשוק בדברים בטלים הללו אמר לו נאמן עלי הדיין כסבור אותו הגמון עליו הוא אומר והוא לא אמר אלא כנגד אביו שבשמים אמר לו הואיל והאמנתי עליך דימוס פטור אתה כשבא לביתו נכנסו תלמידיו אצלו לנחמו ולא קיבל עליו תנחומין אמר לו ר״ע רבי תרשיני לומר דבר אחד ממה שלימדתני אמר לו אמור אמר לו רבי שמא דבר מינות בא לידך והנאך ועליו נתפסת (למינות) אמר לו עקיבא הזכרתני פעם אחת הייתי מהלך בשוק העליון של ציפורי ומצאתי אדם אחד (מתלמידי ישו הנוצרי) ויעקב איש כפר סכניא שמו אמר לי כתוב בתורתכם לא תביא אתנן זונה וגו׳ מהו לעשות הימנו בהכ״ג לכ״ג ולא אמרתי לא כלום אמר לי כך לימדני (ישו הנוצרי) מאתנן זונה קבצה ועד אתנן זונה ישובו ממקום הטנופה באו למקום הטנופה ילכו והנאני הדבר ועל ידי זה נתפסתי למינות ועברתי על מה שכתוב הרחק מעליה דרכך זו מינות ואל תקרב אל פתח ביתה זו רשות The additions are those of Rabbinovicz from the Munich codex.

and may be placed about 109.[5] Additionally, one must remember that the conversation in question happened long enough before that R. Eliezer had forgotten it.
This may have been a long time previously, but since he is called an old man and
his memory may not have been what it once was, the time lapse need not have
been extremely long. We may be justified in pushing the event itself back, say, ten
years, to the turn of the century.

But on what basis may we assert that Jacob was a member of the Nazarene
sect? The appearance of the name *nôẓrî* in itself is not decisive, since it is applied
to Jesus, not to Jacob.[6] However, if we consider that Jacob was likely born before
70, that his name indicates that he was Jewish, that his town makes him a local,
and that before 70 *all* Jewish Christians were Nazarenes, then we may conclude
that Jacob was indeed a member of the sect. Of course, we do not need the name
ha-nôẓrî to arrive at this. If Jacob was a Jew and a Christian and flourished in the
Galilee at the time of R. Eliezer, then our options are limited. Most likely he was a
descendant of the first Jewish (Nazarene) Christians.[7] Less likely is the possibility
that he was a product of the Ebionite split, a gnostic Christian (Jewish), or just a
Jewish adherent to the main Church.[8] We shall return to Jacob later.

It must be noted that there is an earlier version of the same incident,[9] parallel in
most aspects with one significant difference: The name is Yeshu ben Pantiri instead of Yeshu *ha-nôẓrî*.[10] This in fact may be the earlier reading of the text;
every other reference to the name (נוצרי(ם) in Talmud (which can with some certainty be dated) is from the third century, a fact which must weigh in favor of the
Tosefta reading here.

The other appearances of the name ישו הנוצרי add nothing to our discussion. In
these, mostly from the latter part of the third century, no disciple appears, only
Jesus. Even the use of the name "Nazarene" in these passages is of no more
significance (nor less) than it is in the New Testament. We can assume from the
gospels that Jesus was called *ha-nôẓrî* from early in his ministry. The meaning of
the name—as we have seen above—is obscure. It should not be a surprise that it is
preserved in the rabbinic tradition. But we find it etymologically no less enigmatic
there.

5 *Op. cit.*, pp. 140–142. He cites Hegesippus (Eus., *HE* III, 32) on a general persecution in which
   Simon b. Clopas was martyred.
6 The talmudic language here would seem to indicate that Jacob was one who had personally
   heard Jesus teach. See, however, n. 22 below. The word תלמיד can indicate a more distant
   student or follower of someone; cf. Sanh. 11a, where Hillel is called תלמידו של עזרא.
7 Herford, *op. cit.*, pp. 106, 143; see below, and notes, esp. n. 25.
8 Cf. J. Jocz, *The Jewish People and Jesus Christ* (Grand Rapids, 1979), p. 191. This view
   seems to me least tenable at this early date.
9 THull. 2, 24.
10 See D. Rokeah, "Ben Stara is Ben Pantera," *Tarbiz* 39 (1969), 9–18, in Hebrew.

Ha-nôẓrîm

In two passages we find the sect title *ha-nôẓrîm*.[11] Avodah Zarah 6a: "R. Taḥlifa bar Abdimi said that Shmuel said 'The *nôẓrî* day is forbidden forever, according to R. Ishmael'."[12] The question here is on the extent of business-dealings allowed with idol worshippers (literally star worshippers) before their feasts. The ruling of the rabbis is that business is forbidden on the feast day and the three days preceding. R. Ishmael gave his own opinion that the prohibition should include also the three days following an idolatrous holiday, thus a total of seven days. Logically then business should always be forbidden with the Christians, who have Sunday as a weekly holiday. There are difficulties here. It is clear from both extant readings that Christians are intended (and the censoring of the text bears this out). What is not clear is who is intended by נוצרים, and who made the statement, R. Ishmael or R. Shmuel? If Shmuel is the one introducing the *yôm nôẓrî*, then he is most likely referring to catholic Christianity. The simple sense of this sentence is that Shmuel is basing a statement on the broader opinion of Ishmael under discussion.[13] This would place the saying in the first half of the third century in Babylonia.[14]

Taanit 27b: "On Sabbath eve it was customary not to fast out of respect for the Sabbath; of course the same was true on the Sabbath itself. Why did they not fast on Sunday? R. Yohanan said, because of the *nôẓrîm*."[15] The context for this passage is one of the custom of אנשי מעמד (*'anšeî ma'amad*)—those who prayed while sacrifices were being offered—to fast four days a week, Monday through Thursday. The reason for the fast (and the subject of their prayers) is given for each of these four days. There is no fasting on Friday or Saturday, and all agree that it is out of respect for the Sabbath. But the original reason for refraining from fasting on Sunday seems to have been forgotten, and three rabbis each give their opinions, but no concensus is given. The three, Yohanan, Shmuel b. Naḥmani, and Resh Lakish, were all contemporary in Eretz Israel in the latter half of the third century. At first glance, R. Yohanan's reason seems a bit strange. If Friday and Saturday are avoided out of respect, consistency would dictate that avoidance of fasting on Sunday somehow also indicated a respect for the day. This is, in fact, the sense given by R. Shmuel ("because it is the third day after the creation of man"). But this cannot be the sense intended by R. Yohanan. There would have been no respectful treatment of the holy day of either Nazarenes or

---

11 Av. Zar. 6a; Taanit 27b.

12 דאמר רב תחליפא בר אבדימי אמר שמואל יום נוצרי לדברי רבי ישמעאל לעולם אסור. The present text reads .... אמר שמואל יום א' לדברי רבי ישמעאל לעולם אסור

13 See Herford, *op. cit.*, p. 172.

14 Shmuel was born, lived and died in Nehardea.

15 בערב שבת לא היו מתענין מפני כבוד השבת ק"ו בשבת עצמה באחד בשבת מ"ט לא אמר ר' יוחנן מפני הנוצרים.

catholic Christians.[16] R. Yoḥanan died over thirty years before the Edict of Milan and would have had nothing to fear from a persecuted Christianity. Indeed the very introduction of the *nôzrîm* into the discussion is rather strange. R. Yoḥanan is answering a question of why something was done (or not done) while the Temple stood, at a time effectively before the *nôzrîm* were any factor. Or conversely, he is speaking about *nôzrîm* in a Temple activity long after the Temple was destroyed.[17] Hereford's assessment seems valid: R. Yoḥanan has simply introduced an anachroism into the time of the Temple Service, although even so it is not easy to understand his reasoning.[18] Be that as it may, the *nôzrîm* of this passage are most likely catholic Christians of the mid-third century and not only the almost-extinct Jewish Christian Nazarenes.

A third passage which we must consider is found in Gittin 57a:

> Once when R. Manyumi b. Ḥelkiah and R. Ḥelkiah b. Tobiah and R. Huna b. Ḥiyya were sitting together they said: If anyone knows anything about Kfar Sechania of Egypt, let him say. One of them thereupon said: Once a betrothed couple (from there) were carried off by heathens who married them to one another. The woman said: I beg of you not to touch me, as I have no Ketubah from you. So he did not touch her until his dying day. When he died, she said: Mourn for this man who has kept his passions in check more than Joseph, because Joseph was exposed to temptation only a short time, but this man every day. Joseph was not in one bed with the woman but this man was; in Joseph's case she was not his wife, but here she was. The next began and said: On one occasion forty bushels (of corn) were selling for a dinar, and the number went down one, and they investigated and found that a man and his son had had intercourse with a betrothed maiden on the Day of Atonement, so they brought them to the Beth Din and they stoned them, and the original price was restored. The third then began and said: There was a man who wanted to divorce his wife, but he hesitated because she had a big marriage settlement. He accordingly invited his friends and gave them a good feast and made them drunk and put them all in one bed. He then brought the white of an egg and scattered it among them and brought witnesses and appealed to the Beth Din. There was a certain elder there of the disciples of Shammai the Elder, named Baba b. Buta, who said: This is what I have been taught by Shammai the Elder, that the white of an egg contracts when brought near the fire, but semen becomes faint from the fire. They tested it and found that it was so, and they brought the man to the Beth Din and flogged him and made him pay her Ketubah. Said Abaye to R. Joseph: Since they were so virtuous, why were they punished?—He replied:

---

16 This is the view of Rabbenu Gershom, introducing, it would seem, a 10th-century anachronism: ‏ואם היו ישראל מתענין היו כועסין‎.

17 If we possessed some evidence of an early Christian Sunday fast, this might be seen as a pre-70 Sadducean reaction to Christian priests. But there is no evidence of a Sunday fast unless, doubtfully, it might be 1 Cor. 11:33–34.

18 *Op. cit.,* p. 172.

Because they did not mourn for Jerusalem, as it is written: Rejoice ye with Jerusalem, and be glad for her, all ye that love her, rejoice for joy with her all ye that mourn over her. (Ps. 60.12).[19]

Samuel Klein has suggested a minor and plausible emendation here, reading נוצרים (or נצרים) for מצרים (*miẓraîm*).[20] This would give us "Kfar Sechania of the Nazarenes" and would line up well with the town of the same name which was notorious as the home of Jacob the Min, the disciple of Yeshu *ha-nôẓrî*.[21] The passage can be set sometime in the first quarter of the fourth century in Babylonia, more specifically in Pumbedita. The three stories give every indication of being authentically early: the fact that it was considered exceptional and unacceptable that the value of the dinar should drop shows that the second story took place before the inflation of the third century; the appearance of Baba b. Buta limits the third story to a period before 70 (see n. 20); the final reference to the destruction of Jerusalem, if it is not simply a didactic addition of R. Joseph, gives us a *terminus ad quem* of 70 A.D.; and the reference in the second story to the imposition of the death penalty would also require a pre-70 dating, since capital punishment was said to have ceased with the destruction of the Temple (Ketubah 30a).[22]

So Kfar Sechania was noted for its adherence to *halakah* before 70 but was "punished" after the fall of Jerusalem. What was its punishment? Perhaps it was

---

19 רב מניומי בר חלקיה ורב חלקיה בר טוביה ורב הונא בר חייא הוו יתבי גבי הדדי אמרי אי איכא דשמיע ליה
מילתא מכפר סכניא של מצרים לימא פתח חד מינייהו ואמר מעשה כארוס וארוסתו שנשבו לבין העובדי
כוכבים והשיאום זה לזה אמרה לו בבקשה ממך אל תגע בי שאין לי כתובה ממך ולא נגע בה עד יום מותו
וכשמת אמרה להן סיפדו לזה שפטפט ביצרו יותר מיוסף דאילו ביוסף לא הוה אלא חדא שעתא והאי כל
יומא ויומא ואילו יוסף לאו בחדא מטה והאי בחדא מטה ואילו יוסף לאו אשתו והא אשתו פתח אידך ואמר
מעשה ועמדו ארבעים מודיות בדינר נחסר השער השער למקומו ואמר מעשה באדם אחד שנתן עיניו
ביום הכפורים הביאום לבית דין וסקלום וחזר השער למקומו פתח אידך ואמר מעשה הלך חימן את שושביניו והאכילן והשקן שיכרן והשכיבם על
מיטה אחת והביא לובן ביצה והטיל ביניהן והעמיד להן עדים ובא לבית דין היה שם זקן אחד מתלמידי שמאי
הזקן ובבא בן בוטא שמו אמר להן כך מקובלני משמאי הזקן לובן ביצה סולד מן האור ושכבת זרע דוחה מן
האור בדקו ומצאו כדבריו והביאוהו לב"ד והלקוהו והגבוהו כתובתה ממנו א"ל אביי לרב יוסף ומאחר דהוו
צדיקים כולי האי מאי טעמא איענוש א"ל משום דלא איאבול על ירושלים דכתיב שמחו את ירושלים וגילו בה
כל אוהביה שישו אתה משוש כל המתאבלים עליה: The translation is that of the Soncino Press
edition of the Talmud.

20 *Beiträge zur Geschichte u. Geographie Galiläas* (Leipzig, 1909), p. 29, n. 4. Are there any geographical indicators to support Klein's emendation? I think there is at least one. Baba b. Buta was a resident of Jerusalem in the generation before 70 or even a bit earlier. He may have been contemporary with Herod the Great (see B.B. 3b–4a). Margoliot, in his *Encyclopedia of Talmudic Sages and Geonim*, s.v. Baba b. Buta, suggests that these Egyptians sailed all the way to Eretz Israel to seek out his opinion. It is easier to believe that they came only from Galilee.

21 Av. Zar. 27b; 16b–17a; THull. 2, 24; Kohelet Rabba on 1:8; Yalk. Sh. on Mic 1 and Prov. 5:8. Cf. also jAv. Zar. 40d–41a and A. Neubauer, *La Géographie du Talmud* (Paris, 1868), pp. 234f.

22 In jSanh. 7 2, 24b the date is set at forty years *before* the destruction.

some unrecorded destruction of the village. Or just maybe the hint is to be found in the epithet "Kfar Sechania of the Nazarenes"; the appearance there of the Nazarene sect is the punishment—the village has become somehow spiritually משומד (*mešûmad*). If this latter suggestion has some validity, then R. Joseph's explanation of why this "punishment" came about takes on extra meaning: because they did not mourn for Jerusalem. This, it seems to me, is a reminder of the events immediately following the loss of the capital: the work of Rabban Yohanan ben Zakkai and his colleagues at Yavne. With the destruction of Jerusalem the Pharisees went west and the Nazarenes went east. The separation was more than just one of geography. With Yavne began the consolidation of Judaism. In the post–70 crisis, there was no place for the diversity which had so characterized the later Second Temple period.[23] The Sadducees, of course, were out. But so, soon, was the school of Shammai after the well-known voice from heaven (*bat qôl*) declared all rulings to be according to Bet Hillel. Now a centrally recognized authority was paramount, and a refusal by any group or locality to accept that authority could only result in its isolation. This is not to say that R. Yohanan b. Zakkai advocated a Judaism which only mourned over Jerusalem; far from it. But the picture of collective mourning in the words of R. Joseph speaks of joining the national attempt to adjust to the new status quo without forgetting the old ways. One can see that the loss of the Temple did not hit the Jewish Christians quite as hard as it did their compatriots, and if the village of Kfar Sechania accepted their interpretation of events, then they could easily be accused of failing to mourn over Jerusalem.

With this identification of Kfar Sechania as a town "of the Nazarenes," we are led to reconsider the town's best-known citizen, Jacob. Herford[24] concluded that Jacob flourished in Galilee in the early part of the second century,[25] and that he is

---

23 Cf. S. Safrai, "The Pluralism in Judaism of the Yavne Period," *Deot* 48 (1980), 166–170, in Hebrew.

24 *Op. cit.*, pp. 103–108, 144f.

25 Cf. M. Goldstein, *Jesus in the Jewish Tradition* (New York, 1950), 33f, who follows D. Chwolson, *Das letzte Passamahl Christi u. der Tag seines Todes* (Leipzig, 1908), pp. 99f, n. 3, in dating Jacob's meeting with R. Ishmael's nephew Ben Dama in 116 or perhaps even a bit earlier. But see J. Gutmann, *Encyclopedia Judaica* VIII (Berlin, 1931), 837f, who, while denying that Jacob could be either James the brother of Jesus or James the brother of John, suggests either James the Less (Mark 15:4) or James the son of Alphaeus (Mark 3:18). Klausner, *Jesus of Nazareth* (New York, 1929), pp. 37–42, attempted to prove that this Jacob was to be identified with the brother of Jesus who died in 62. The solution to the problem depends on whether this Jacob the healer of Kfar Sechania is the same as the Jacob the healer of Kfar Sama (Sechania also attested, but later, Av. Zar. 27b.). This latter appears in context with R. Ishmael (see n. 28 below), when he was an ordained rabbi with a grown, ordained nephew. However, we know that Ishmael was taken captive as a child (תינוק, i.e. below the age of 12 at least) to Rome, where he was redeemed by R. Joshua b. Hanania (Gittin 58a). Ishmael must have been born, then, no earlier than about 60, and Jacob's encounter with Ben Dama can hardly have been

not, therefore, to be identified with any known New Testament figure.[26] The time and place of his activity should come as no surprise to us, although we can see here at least a confirmation of the continued existence and activity of the Nazarenes in the second century. We know that Jacob recalled an apocryphal saying of Jesus.[27] What is perhaps of more interest for our purposes is what we learn of the relations between rabbinic Judaism and the Nazarenes at this time. On the one hand, there seems to have been a fair amount of contact and intercourse. R. Eliezer meets Jacob on a street of Sepphoris and not only exchanges views with him but is even pleased with what Jacob says in the name of Jesus. This happens before Bar Kochba but after the time when the atmosphere was right for the introduction of the *birkat ha-mînîm*, if not after it had already been composed. The separation process was no sudden tear but a slow parting of company. Nevertheless, we see on the other hand that even here, before 135, there was no small opposition by some to this contact. Between the time of R. Eliezer's conversation with Jacob and the reminder of it by Akiva, attitudes were changing. R. Ishmael prefers the death of his nephew to his healing in the name of Jesus.[28]

Birkat ha-mînîm

There remains one important aspect of talmudic tradition to consider. This is the enigma of the *mînîm* and their inclusion in the twelfth Benediction of the ʿamîdah prayer.

Numerous studies, few of them comprehensive, most of them tendentious, have been done on the question of who the *mînîm* are in talmudic literature. Some have decided that the term refers to Christians, either Pauline Christians[29] or, more often, Jewish Christians.[30] Others, on the other hand, have asserted that the *mînîm* are never Christians in the Talmud,[31] and Friedländer tried to prove that they were always pre-Christian anti-nomistic Gnostics.[32] Most scholars, however,

---

before 90; in fact, on this reasoning there is a good correspondence in dates of Jacob's activities with respect to both Ben Dama and R. Eliezer. We must decide that there was only one Jacob and agree with Herford that a known NT Jacob (James) is precluded.

26 Also against E.K. Winter, *Judaica* 9 (1953), 17.

27 THull. 2, 24; Av. Zar. 16b–17a.

28 THull. 2, 22f; Av. Zar. 27b; jAv. Zar. 2, 2, 40d.

29 H. Hirschberg, *JBL* 62 (1943), 73–87; *JBL* 67 (1948), 305–318.

30 H. Graetz, *Geschichte der Juden* (Leipzig, 1908 [1893]), IV, 85, 94ff; Herford, *op. cit.*, passim; M.-J. Lagrange, *Le Messianisme chez les Juifs* (Paris, 1909), p. 292; K.L. Carroll, *BJRL* 40 (1957/8), 20; G.F. Moore, *Judaism* III, 67f; J. Neusner, *A History of the Jews in Babylonia* (Leiden, 1968), III, 12–16.

31 F.C. Grant, *The Earliest Gospel* (New York, 1943), p. 92f; F.W. Beare, *JBL* 63 (1944), 315.

32 M. Friedländer, *Der vorchristliche jüdische Gnosticismus* (Göttingen, 1898); *REJ* 38 (1899), 194–203; *Der Antichrist in den vorchristlichen jüdischen Quellen* (Göttingen, 1901), pp. 78ff; *Synagoge u. Kirche in ihren Anfängen* (Berlin, 1908), pp. 124ff.

agree that the term has a variety of applications,[33] and even most of those who opt for Jewish Christians make this concession. A survey of the term reveals *mînîm* who clearly lived before Christianity,[34] *mînîm* who reject the resurrection from the dead and therefore cannot be Christians,[35] etc. However, one will also see many places where the *mînîm* clearly are Christians and most likely *Jewish Christians*.[36] Generally, it is safe to say that *mînîm* are Jews who reckon themselves to be Jews but who are excluded by the rabbis.[37]

As was stated at the beginning of this chapter, we cannot allow ourselves to speculate that the *mînîm* might be Nazarenes in places where a variety of interpretations is possible. There is one event, however, which promises a positive contribution to our survey, the *birkat ha-mînîm*. Brach. 28b: "Said R. Gamaliel to the Sages: Can anyone among you frame a benediction relating to the *mînîm*?[38] Samuel the Lesser arose and composed it."[39] The time of this event falls somewhere between 80, when R. Gamaliel became *nasî*, and the death of Shmuel *ha-qatan*. Herford[40] has shown, and most scholars agree, that it is more likely soon after 80 rather than much later.[41] Almost no one would date it after 95. The matter in question is the formulation (or perhaps more precisely the revision)[42] of the twelfth Benediction in the *šemôneh-ʿesreh* prayer of the daily *ʿamîdah*. In its present form in all Ashkenazi liturgies there is no mention of *mînîm*, although the term is preserved in Sephardi rites[43] (where censorship did not interfere). The very

33 Bacher, *art. cit.*; H.L. Strack, *Jesus, die Häretiker u. die Christen nach den ältesten jüdischen Angaben* (Leipzig, 1910), pp. 47–80; A. Büchler in *Judaica* (Festschrift für Hermann Cohen) (Berlin, 1912), pp. 272ff; I. Broyde, "Min," *Jewish Encyclopedia* VII (1904), 594ff; J. Jocz, *op. cit.*, pp. 174–190; C.M.I. Gevaryahu, *Sinai* 44 (1958/9), 367–376; K.G. Kuhn in *Judentum, Urchristentum, Kirche*, pp. 24–61; D. Sperber, "Min," *Encycl. Judaica* XII (1971), 1–3; M. Simon, *Verus Israel* (Paris, 1948), pp. 214–238.

34 Midrash Leviticus 13, 5.

35 MBrach. 9, 5. The statement of R. Yoḥanan in jSanh. 10, 6, 29c further indicates a great variety of minim: מינים של כיתות וארבע עשרים שנעשו עד ישראל גלו לא יוחנן רבי אמר. See also Strack, *Jesus*, pp. 50–56.

36 See the oft-cited work of Herford, the most comprehensive on the thesis that *mînîm* are usually Jewish Christians.

37 THull. 2, 20; TShabb. 13, 5; Brach. 29a; cf. Kuhn, *art. cit.*, 36ff.

38 This is restored from older versions. The censor has Sadducees. See also jBrach. 4, 8a; TBrach. 3, 25.

39 ותקנה הקטן שמואל עמד [הצדוקים] המינים ברכת לתקן שיודע אדם יש כלום לחכמי ר"ג להם אמר.

40 *Op. cit.*, pp. 125–135.

41 Dating it between 80 and 90 are Lagrange, Parkes, E.K. Winter, Davies, Carroll, Jocz.

42 See Herford, *op. cit.*, p. 127; J. Heinemann, *Prayer in the Talmud* (New York, 1977), p. 225; K. Kohler, *HUCA* 1 (1924), 401f. One reason for the change may well have been the aversion of the Pharisees to the former reading in the Benediction, פרושי, meaning the "separatists"; cf. S. Liebermann, *Tosefta Ki-Fshutah* I (New York, 1955), pp. 53f.

43 See L. Finkelstein, "The Development of the Amidah," *JQR* 16 (NS) (1925/6), 156.

reference in our passage and parallels to *birkat ha-mînîm* indicates that the original version included the word *mînîm*. But this is not the limit of its significance.

Following an analysis primarily of the patristic evidence (see below) Krauss, in a remarkable piece of scholarship,[44] concluded in 1892 that the actual wording of the original formula must have been something like וכל הנוצרים כרגע יאבדו ("may all the *nôzrîm* perish in a moment".) The yields of the Cairo Geniza soon began to vindicate his assertion. In 1898 Schechter published the first of several fragments of the *šemôneh-'esreh* from the Geniza.[45] The twelfth Benediction includes the words והנוצרים והמינים כרגע יאבדו ("may the *nôzrîm* and the *mînîm* [sectarians] perish in a moment".) In subsequent years further manuscripts came to light from widely scattered provenances which would seem to prove conclusively that a very early version of the *birkat ha-mînîm* (if not the original of Shmuel *ha-qaṭan*) contained the words *nôzrîm* and *mînîm*. In 1907 Marx published a text of the Siddur of R. Amram Gaon.[46] The manuscript dates from 1426 and reads והנוצרים והמינים יכלו כרגע ("may the *nôzrîm* and *mînîm* be destroyed in a moment".) In 1925 another Geniza fragment was published with exactly the same words at the point in question as Schechter's fragment.[47] In the first Venice printing of the Talmud we find this comment by Rashi (missing in later, censored editions) at Brachot 30a (=28b in today's pagination):[48] "They revised it at Yavne after a long time in the vicinity of the teaching of the *nôzrî*, who taught to overturn the ways of the living God."

Recently Schäfer[49] has compared numerous versions of the twelfth Benediction and reached a conclusion to which the present writer would subscribe. He noted that another version of Amram reads only *mînîm*; a version of Saadya has neither *mînîm* nor *nôzrîm*; and the Old Yemenite version has *mînîm* and *mosarîm*. Schäfer compares all of this with a passage from the Tosefta,[50] a parallel to the *birkat ha-mînîm* which reads:

44 S. Krauss, *JQR* 5 (1892/3), 131–134.

45 S. Schechter, *JQR* 10 (1897/8), 657.

46 A. Marx, *Jahrbuch der jüdisch-literarischen Gesellschaft* 5 (1907), 5 (in the Hebrew section). See also D. Hedegård, *Seder R. Amram Gaon* (Lund, 1951), p. 37 (ל"ז).

47 J. Mann, *HUCA* 2 (1925), 306.

48 ביבנה תקנוה לאחר זמן מרובה קרוב לתרבותו של הנוצרי שלמד להפוך דרכי אלהי' חיי': The text on which he is commenting, omitted in later editions, reads ביבנה תקנוה. אמר רבי לוי ברכת המינים ביבנה תקנוה. כנגד מי תקנוה אמר רבי לוי בריה דרבי שמואל בר נחמני לרבי הלל כנגד אל הכבוד הרעים לרב יוסף כנגד אחר שבקרית שמע לרבי תנחום אמר רבי יהושע בן לוי כנגד חוליא קטנה שבשדרה. Further comment is made on this note of Rashi in n. 53 below.

49 P. Schäfer, "Die sogenannte Synode von Jabne. Zur trennung von Juden und Christen im ersten/zweiten Jh. n. Chr.," *Judaica* 31 (1975), 54–64.

50 TShabb. 13, 4f. Cf. Rosh Hashana 17a. Herford, *op. cit.*, pp. 118–123, comments on the passage at length, although he does not connect it to *birkat ha-mînîm*. I use his translation.

but the minim, and the apostates (משומדים) and the betrayers (מסורות) and the
'epiqursîn, and those who have lied concerning the resurrection of the dead, and
everyone who has sinned and caused the multitude to sin, after the manner of
Jeroboam and Ahab, and those 'who have set their fear in the land of the living'
[Ezek. 32:24], and have stretched forth their hand against Zebul, Gehinnom is
shut in their faces and they are judged there for generations of generations. . . .

This is a list of heresies, many of which appear in the various versions of the
twelfth Benediction. One of the heresies was the nôzrîm, but we cannot say for
sure whether it was part of the original of Shmuel. Schäfer concludes that the
actual wording at the critical point varied according to the local situation.

The patristic evidence provides an interesting corollary to Schäfer's conclusion.
We find clear references to the synagogue curse in Epiphanius and Jerome.[51]
Epiphanius (pan. 29 9,2) states:

> However, they are very much hated by the Jews. For not only the Jewish children
> cherish hate against them, but the people also stand up in the morning, at noon and
> in the evening, three times a day, and they pronounce curses and maledictions over
> them when they say their prayers in the synagogues. Three times a day they say:
> "May God curse the Nazarenes."[52]

Jerome wrote to Augustine (ep. 112,13): "Until now a heresy is to be found in all
of the synagogues of the East among the Jews; it is called 'of the Minaeans' and is
cursed by the Pharisees until now. Usually they are called Nazarenes." In Amos
1.11–12: "until today they blaspheme the Christian people in their synagogues
under the name of Nazarenes." In Is. 5.18–19: "Three times each day they
anathematize the Christian name in every synagogue under the name of
Nazarenes." In Is. 49.7: "They curse him [Christ] three times a day in their
synagogues under the name of Nazarenes." In Is. 52.4–6 adds nothing different
to the above.

---

51 Justin Martyr, Dial. 137, says to Trypho and his friends: "Assent, therefore, and pour no
ridicule on the Son of God; obey not the pharisaic teachers, and scoff not at the King of Israel,
as the rulers of your synagogues teach you to do after your prayers"; 96: "For you curse in
your synagogues all those who are called from Him Christians." Cf. also ibid., 108. G. Alon has
pointed out (The Jews in their Land in the Talmudic Age [Jerusalem, 1980] I, 289) that these
statements of Justin are general, about all Christians, and cannot with certainty be equated with
the birkat ha-mînîm. Krauss, art. cit., p. 131, would include also Origen, Hom. in Jer. 18, 12
(καὶ μέχρι νῦν, ὑπὸ παρανόμου ἀρχιερέως λόγου προστασσόμενοι Ἐβιωναῖοι τύπτουσι τὸν
Ἀπόστολον Ἰησοῦ Χριστοῦ λόγοις δυσθήμοις), but nothing obligates us to accept his
reasoning that what applies to the Ebionites applies also to the Jews. More likely, but still
general, is the statement in the same passage Εἴσελθε εἰς τὰς τῶν Ἰουδαίων συναγωγὰς καὶ ἴδε
τὸν Ἰησοῦν καθ᾽ ἡμέραν ὑπ᾽ αὐτῶν τῇ γλώσσῃ τῆς βλασφημίας μαστιγούμενοι. But here again
Origen is not clearly referring to the formulated curse of the mînîm and nôzrîm.

52 Translation of K–R; text in Appendix I.

It was from these clear statements with their inclusion of the name Nazarenes that Krauss concluded that the word נוצרים must have figured in the original of the twelfth Benediction, as indeed it did. We note here that any knowledge of the cursing of Christ or Christians is only to be found among Christian writers who had spent time in the East. This observation is highlighted by the fact that Jerome in the East found it necessary to explain the whole matter to his younger western contemporary Augustine. The suggestion is that western fathers knew nothing of a synagogue cursing because in fact such a curse was not uttered in the synagogues of the West. Thus Jerome's words *per totas* Orientis *synagogas inter Iudaeos* ("among the Jews in all the synagogues of the *East*"). Jerome evidently took it for granted that Augustine would not know about this curse, which he himself only discovered since moving eastward. Add this to Schäfer's suggestion that the wording of the twelfth Benediction varied according to locality, and we may conclude that the name *nôzrîm* appeared only in places where there were (or had been) Nazarenes threatening synagogue life.[53]

The wording of Jerome's letter to Augustine raises one further question. He seems to equate the names *minaei* (*mînîm*) with *Nazaraei* (*nôzrîm*). In the Geniza fragment the wording is והנצרים והמינים. Are the two names equivalent in the benediction? In other words, is this a tautology or are the two specifically separated by the original wording? Jerome would seem to be the first scholar to decide that they are tautologous. He has been followed by most investigators,[54] although acceptance of this idea has not been universal.[55] We would suggest a slight modification to the tautology approach. As we noted above, the term *mînîm* in talmudic literature frequently refers to Jewish Christians. It is feasible that there was a transition in the meaning of *mînîm*, so that whereas it began as a general term for Jewish heretics, it gradually came to be understood as Jewish Christians primarily, and later occasionally may have included Gentile Christians. So not all *mînîm* are always Jewish Christians, and neither are all Jewish Christians Nazarenes. Therefore, all Nazarenes are *mînîm*, but not all *mînîm* are Nazarenes. And this would have been truer, of course, at the time the Benediction was formulated than, say, at the time of Jerome's letter to Augustine. So we would suggest that the formula והנצרים והמינים is a kind of refining or

---

53 We need not accept Krauss's conclusion from Rashi's notice (above n. 48) that still in Rashi's day (and presumably in his locale) the *birkat ha-mînîm* mentioned *nôzrîm*. Rashi is more likely preserving what he has learned of an eastern tradition. Similarly, Agobard, Bishop of Lyon (d. 840), knows of the Nazarene curse, citing Jerome (*de insolentia Judaeorum* 4 [*PL* 104, 73]).

54 E.g., Alon, *op. cit.*, p. 290; Kuhn, *art. cit.*; Gevaryahu, *art. cit.*; Herford, *op. cit.*, pp. 378f.

55 Hirschberg, *JBL* 62 (1943), 77f, took it as self-evident that the appearance of both names means they cannot be the same.

narrowing of terms: "the sectarians, including the *nôẓrîm*," or "the sectarians and especially the *nôẓrîm*."[56]

By way of summary for this chapter we may compare what we have found with corresponding findings in the patristic sources. We find in the Jewish sources nothing of any clarity about the Christology of the Nazarenes. Neither, of course, do we have any real information about their relations with the non-Jewish Church, acceptance of Paul, etc. In four areas, however, we find useful corroborating data. First of all, the talmudic writings provide us with a reasonably certain continuity of the existence of Jewish Christian Nazarenes after 70. How long after 70 is difficult to say, perhaps impossible; but in combination with the patristic evidence, these sources make it clear that there was a continuation of the sect. Secondly, the geographical picture is filled in somewhat by the clear references to Jacob of Kfar Sechania and his activities in the Galilee. Thirdly, the study of the *birkat ha-mînîm* from Jewish documents provides an excellent example of how the two sides can complement and confirm each other. Finally, and here again we must call Jacob to witness, we see further evidence of the ongoing attempt of these Jewish believers in Jesus to win over their brothers. In this light Jacob may be seen as more that just an isolated individual; he is representative, a type of Jewish Christian evangelist-healer which post–70 Jewish communities in Palestine may have encountered frequently.

56 The recent study by W. Horbury in *JTS* 33 (1982), 19–61, contains excellent overviews both of the history of the 12th Benediction and of modern scholarship on the subject. See also the recent article by S.T. Katz (*JBL* 103, 1 [1984], 43–76) who denies that the *birkat ha-mînîm* included the name *nôẓrîm*. His argument is weakened if, as I have suggested, the name was not universally included in the Benediction but only in those places where Nazarenes were to be found.

Summary and Conclusions

There emerges from our considerations an entity, a viable entity of Law-keeping Christians of Jewish background. These were direct descendants of the first Jewish believers in Jesus. They survived the destruction of Jerusalem in part because they fled successfully to Pella of the Decapolis, and in part because they had roots also in the Galilee. These Jewish Christians were called Nazarenes after Jesus, and probably received the title on the basis of early Christian interpretation of certain Old Testament passages (e.g. Isa.11:1) as referring to the Messiah and specifically to Jesus himself. The Nazarenes were distinct from the Ebionites and prior to them. In fact, we have found that it is possible that there was a split in Nazarene ranks around the turn of the first century. This split was either over a matter of christological doctrine or over leadership of the community. Out of this split came the Ebionites, who can scarcely be separated from the Nazarenes on the basis of geography, but who can be easily distinguished from the standpoint of Christology.

The continued existence of this Nazarene entity can be traced with reasonable certainty through the fourth century, contingent upon the credence we give to the evidence of Epiphanius and Jerome at the end of that century. While their corroborating testimonies cannot fairly be dismissed, even without them we must allow for the continuation of the Nazarenes at least to the third century. The sect numbered only a few members, no doubt. Geographically they were limited to pockets of settlement along the eastern shore of the Mediterranean, mostly just east of the Jordan rift. They were to be found in the Galilee and probably in Jerusalem until 135, when all Jews were expelled from the city. It would seem that members of the sect moved northward at a somewhat later date and were to be found also in the area of Beroea of Coele Syria near the end of the fourth century. There is no firm evidence of any Nazarene presence in the West, in Africa, or even further to the East. Their numbers stayed as limited as their geographical presence.

What we have seen of their doctrines lines up well with the developing christological doctrines of the greater catholic Church. The sect seems to have been basically trinitarian. They accepted the virgin birth and affirmed the deity of

Jesus. They also seem to have had an embryonic, developing doctrine of the Holy Spirit, one which was no more nor indeed less developed than that of the greater Church at a comparable stage. Contrary to other Jewish Christian groups of the time (and also to current scholarly opinion) they did not reject the apostleship of Paul. They recognized his commission from God to preach to the gentiles, and they seem fully to have accepted the fruit of his labors: the "Church from the Gentiles." Those fathers of the fourth century who wrote against them could find nothing in their beliefs to condemn; their objections were to matters of praxis. The Nazarenes, as Jews, continued to observe certain aspects of Mosaic Law, including circumcision and the Sabbath, and it was this which brought about their exclusion from the Church. This rejection and exclusion was, however, gradual. For this reason—and because Nazarene numbers remained small throughout—Church writers do not mention Nazarenes by name until such a time as the Church was free from persecution and began to refine its own narrowed orthodoxy. The Nazarenes were not included in the earlier heresy lists because they were simply not considered heretical enough or a threat to "orthodoxy." While there may have been very little intercommunal contact, individual Nazarenes seem to have had sporadic visits with certain Church leaders. We have found it unlikely that either Epiphanius or Jerome had any direct contact with the community of the Nazarenes, although the latter may just possibly have met individuals from the sect.

On the Jewish side, the exclusion of the Nazarenes was not nearly so gradual. At the end of the first century, the *birkat ha-mînîm* was formulated with the sect specifically named. This is recorded in both patristic and Jewish sources. Nonetheless, we have found it possible that there was some limited synagogue attendance by Nazarenes into the early decades of the second century. In addition to this, we find continued contact between the two communities in the form of a polemic or dialogue. Such contact should not surprise us, since the Nazarenes lived in the same geographical areas with predominantly Jewish communities. However, as the polemic and distrust grew, the separation and isolation from the Jewish community were increased. Different steps along the way effected this separation: the flight to Pella, the *birkat ha-mînîm*, the refusal of the Nazarenes to recognize and support Bar Kochba. By the middle of the second century, the rift was probably complete.

The sectarians themselves kept up their knowledge of Hebrew, and in this we may perhaps see an indication that they maintained (as one would expect) some internal system of education. They read the Old Testament and at least one gospel in Hebrew. What we can clearly isolate from this gospel as being appropriate to the Nazarene sect confirms what we find elsewhere about their doctrines, although the inherently uncertain nature of fragment isolation and gospel exegesis yields relatively little by way of fresh information about the group.

Of particular interest is the Nazarene commentary on Isaiah. This work shows clearly that the rejection was not solely from the Jewish side. The Nazarenes refused to accept the authority established by the Pharisaic camp after the destruction of Jerusalem, and in so refusing they adjudicated their own isolation from the converging flow of what we call Judaism. Just as they rejected the Church's setting aside of the Law of Moses, so also they refused the rabbis' expansive interpretations of it. In other words, they rejected *halakah* as it was developing in rabbinic Judaism. It is not far wrong to say that the demise of the Nazarenes resulted from their own restrictive approach to the Law. Such a spurning of rabbinic authority could not, of course, be tolerated by that authority.

There is another factor in this separation from Judaism, one of perhaps greater importance than the rejection of *halakah*. It is the person of Jesus. With their acceptance and proclamation of the deity of Jesus, the Nazarenes went beyond allowable limits for a Judaism of ever stricter monotheism. Either one of these—their non-acceptance of rabbinic *halakah* and even more their belief in Jesus—would have been sufficient to consign them to the category of apostates. From talmudic sources we have seen that the Nazarenes may have conducted an active program of evangelism among Jews. The Isaiah commentary confirms that they never relinquished hope that Jews would one day turn away from tradition and towards Jesus: "O Sons of Israel, who deny the Son of God with such hurtful resolution, return to him and to his apostles."

APPENDIXES

Appendix I

Κατὰ Ναζωραίων

1. Ναζωραῖοι καθεξῆς τούτοις ἕπονται, ἅμα τε αὐτοῖς ὄντες ἢ **1,1**
καὶ πρὸ αὐτῶν ἢ σὺν αὐτοῖς ἢ μετ᾽ αὐτούς, ὅμως σύγχρονοι· οὐ γὰρ
ἀκριβέστερον δύναμαι ἐξειπεῖν τίνες τίνας | διεδέξαντο. καθὰ γὰρ
ἔφην, σύγχρονοι ἦσαν ἀλλήλοις καὶ ὅμοια ἀλλήλοις κέκτηνται τὰ
φρονήματα.   οὗτοι γὰρ ἑαυτοῖς ὄνομα ἐπέθεντο οὐχὶ Χριστοῦ οὔτε **2**
αὐτὸ τὸ ὄνομα τοῦ Ἰησοῦ, ἀλλὰ Ναζωραίων. πάντες δὲ Χριστιανοὶ **3**
Ναζωραῖοι τότε ὡσαύτως ἐκαλοῦντο· γέγονε δὲ ἐπ᾽ ὀλίγῳ χρόνῳ
καλεῖσθαι αὐτοὺς καὶ Ἰεσσαίους, πρὶν ἢ ἐπὶ τῆς Ἀντιοχείας ἀρχὴν
λάβωσιν οἱ μαθηταὶ καλεῖσθαι Χριστιανοί. ἐκαλοῦντο δὲ Ἰεσσαῖοι **4**
διὰ τὸν Ἰεσσαί, οἶμαι, ἐπειδήπερ ὁ Δαυὶδ ἐξ Ἰεσσαί, ἐκ δὲ τοῦ Δαυὶδ
κατὰ διαδοχὴν σπέρματος ἡ Μαρία, πληρουμένης τῆς θείας γραφῆς,
κατὰ τὴν παλαιὰν διαθήκην τοῦ κυρίου λέγοντος πρὸς τὸν Δαυὶδ
»ἐκ καρποῦ τῆς κοιλίας σου θήσομαι ἐπὶ τὸν θρόνον σου«.

2. Δέδια δὲ καθ᾽ ἑκάστην ὑπόθεσιν λέξεως, † ὡς ταύτην τὴν **2,1**
† ὑπόθεσιν ποιοῦμαι, παρακινούσης με τῆς ἀληθείας τὰς ἐν αὐτῇ τῇ
λέξει θεωρίας ὑποφαίνειν, διὰ τὸ μὴ πολὺ πλάτος περιποιήσασθαι
τῇ συντάξει τῆς διηγήσεως. τοῦ γὰρ κυρίου φήσαντος τῷ Δαυὶδ »ἐκ **2**
καρποῦ τῆς κοιλίας σου θήσομαι ἐπὶ τὸν θρόνον σου« καὶ ὅτι »ὤμοσε
κύριος τῷ Δαυὶδ καὶ οὐ μεταμεληθήσεται« δῆλον ὡς ἡ τοῦ θεοῦ ἀμε-
τάθετός ἐστιν ἐπαγγελία. καὶ πρῶτον μὲν ὅτι ὅρκος παρὰ θεῷ τί **3**
ἐστιν ἀλλ᾽ ἢ τό »κατ᾽ ἐμαυτοῦ ὤμοσα λέγει κύριος«; »οὐ γὰρ κατὰ
μείζονος ἔχει ὅρκον ὁ θεός«· ἀλλὰ οὐδὲ ὄμνυσι τὸ θεῖον, εἰς παρά-
στασιν δὲ βεβαιώσεως ὁ λόγος ἔχει τὴν δύναμιν. μεθ᾽ ὅρκου γὰρ
ὤμοσε κύριος τῷ Δαυὶδ ἐκ | καρποῦ τῆς κοιλίας θήσειν ἐπὶ τὸν θρό-
νον αὐτοῦ. μαρτυροῦσι δὲ οἱ ἀπόστολοι ὅτι ἐκ σπέρματος τοῦ Δαυὶδ **4**
ἔδει τὸν Χριστὸν γεννηθῆναι, ὡς καὶ ἐγεννήθη ὁ κύριος ἡμῶν καὶ
σωτὴρ Ἰησοῦς Χριστός· παρήσω δὲ τὸ πλῆθος τῶν μαρτυριῶν, ἵνα
μὴ εἰς πολὺν ὄγκον ἀγάγω τὸν λόγον, ὥς γε προεῖπον. εἴποι δ᾽ **5**
ἄν τις ἴσως· τοῦ Χριστοῦ γεννηθέντος ἐκ σπέρματος Δαυὶδ κατὰ
σάρκα τουτέστιν ἀπὸ τῆς ἁγίας παρθένου Μαρίας, τίνι τῷ λόγῳ ἐπὶ

τοῦ θρόνου Δαυὶδ οὐ καθέζεται; »ἦλθον« γάρ φησι τὸ εὐαγγέλιον
»χρῖσαι αὐτὸν εἰς βασιλέα, καὶ γνοὺς ἀνεχώρησε« »καὶ ἐκρύβη ἐν
Ἐφραῒμ πόλει τῆς ἐρήμου«. φθάσαντες δὲ ἐπὶ τὸν τόπον τοῦ ῥητοῦ 6
τούτου καὶ ἐρωτώμενοι περὶ τῆς μαρτυρίας ταύτης καὶ τῆς ὑποθέ-
σεως, ὅτι τίνι τῷ λόγῳ κατὰ | τὸ σαρχικὸν οὐ πεπλήρωται ἐπὶ τὸν
σωτῆρα τὸ καθίσαι ἐπὶ θρόνον Δαυὶδ | (ἐνομίσθη γὰρ τοῦτό τισι μὴ
πεπληρῶσθαι), ὅμως ὡς ἔστιν ἐροῦμεν. οὐδεμία γὰρ λέξις τῆς ἁγίας
τοῦ θεοῦ γραφῆς διαπίπτει.

3. Θρόνος γὰρ Δαυὶδ καὶ βασιλικὴ ἕδρα ἐστὶν ἡ ἐν τῇ ἁγίᾳ ἐκ- 3,1
κλησίᾳ ἱερωσύνη, ὅπερ ἀξίωμα βασιλικόν τε καὶ ἀρχιερατικὸν ὁμοῦ
ἐπὶ τὸ αὐτὸ συνάψας ὁ κύριος δεδώρηται τῇ ἁγίᾳ αὐτοῦ ἐκκλησίᾳ,
θρόνον μεταγαγὼν ἐν αὐτῇ τὸν τοῦ Δαυίδ, μὴ διαλείποντα εἰς τὸν
αἰῶνα. ἐκεῖσε γὰρ κατὰ διαδοχὴν διήρκεσεν ὁ θρόνος Δαυὶδ ἕως αὐ- 2
τοῦ τοῦ Χριστοῦ, μὴ διαλειπόντων τῶν ἐξ Ἰούδα ἀρχόντων ἕως ἦλθεν
»ᾧ τὰ ἀποκείμενα ἦν καὶ αὐτὸς προσδοκία ἐθνῶν« ⟨ὥς⟩ φησιν.
ἔληξαν γὰρ ἐν τῇ τοῦ Χριστοῦ παρουσίᾳ οἱ κατὰ διαδοχὴν ἐξ Ἰούδα 3
ἄρχοντες. ἕως γὰρ αὐτοῦ * ἡγούμενοι, διέπεσε δὲ ἡ τάξις καὶ
⟨μετ⟩έστη ἐξότε αὐτὸς γεννᾶται ἐν Βηθλεὲμ τῆς Ἰουδαίας, ἐπὶ Ἀλεξάνδρου τοῦ ἀπὸ γένους ἱερατικοῦ καὶ βασιλικοῦ. ἀφ᾽ οὗ Ἀλεξάνδρου 4
διέπεσεν οὗτος ὁ κλῆρος ἀπὸ χρόνων Σαλίνας, τῆς καὶ | Ἀλεξάνδρας
καλουμένης, ἐπὶ τοῖς χρόνοις Ἡρώδου τοῦ βασιλέως καὶ Αὐγούστου
τοῦ Ῥωμαίων αὐτοκράτορος· ὃς καὶ διάδημα ἐπέθετο ἑαυτῷ ὁ Ἀλέ-
ξανδρος οὗτος, εἷς τῶν χριστῶν καὶ ἡγουμένων ὑπάρχων. συναφθει- 5
σῶν γὰρ τῶν δύο φυλῶν τοῦ τε βασιλικοῦ καὶ τοῦ ἱερατικοῦ, Ἰούδα
δέ φημι καὶ Ἀαρὼν καὶ πάσης τῆς τοῦ Λευί, βασιλεῖς καὶ ἱερεῖς κα-
θίστων· οὐ γὰρ διήμαρτέν τι ἀπὸ τῆς τῆς ἁγίας γραφῆς αἰνίξεως.
τότε δὲ λοιπὸν ἀλλόφυλος βασιλεὺς Ἡρώδης καὶ οὐκέτι οἱ ἀπὸ τοῦ 6
Δαυὶδ διάδημα ἐπέθεντο. μεταπεσούσης δὲ τῆς βασιλικῆς καθέδρας, 7
ἐν Χριστῷ ἐπὶ τὴν ἐκκλησίαν ἀπὸ μὲν οἴκου τοῦ σαρχικοῦ Ἰούδα καὶ
Ἰσραὴλ τὸ βασιλικὸν μετέστη ἀξίωμα, ἵδρυται δὲ ὁ θρόνος ἐν τῇ ἁγίᾳ
τοῦ θεοῦ ἐκκλησίᾳ εἰς τὸν αἰῶνα, ἐκ δύο προφάσεων ἔχων τὸ ἀξίωμα
τό τε βασιλικὸν καὶ τὸ ἀρχιερατικόν — καὶ τὸ μὲν βασιλικὸν ἀπὸ 8
τοῦ κυρίου ἡμῶν Ἰησοῦ Χριστοῦ κατὰ δύο τρόπους διά τε τὸ εἶναι
αὐτὸν ἐκ σπέρματος Δαυὶδ τοῦ βασιλέως κατὰ σάρκα καὶ τὸ εἶναι
αὐτόν, ὅπερ καὶ ἔστι, | βασιλέα μείζονα ἀπ᾽ αἰῶνος κατὰ τὴν θεότητα·
τὸ δὲ ἱερατικόν, ὅτι αὐτὸς ἀρχιερεὺς καὶ ἀρχιερέων πρύτανις —, κατα-
σταθέντος εὐθὺς Ἰακώβου, τοῦ ἀδελφοῦ τοῦ κυρίου καλουμένου καὶ 9
ἀποστόλου, ἐπισκόπου πρώτου, υἱοῦ τοῦ Ἰωσὴφ φύσει ὄντος ἐν τάξει
δὲ ἀδελφοῦ τοῦ κυρίου κληθέντος διὰ τὴν συνανατροφήν. |

4. Ἦν γὰρ ὁ Ἰάκωβος οὗτος υἱὸς τοῦ Ἰωσὴφ ἐκ ⟨πρώτης⟩ γυναι- 4,1
κὸς τοῦ Ἰωσήφ, οὐκ ἀπὸ Μαρίας, ὡς καὶ εἰς πολλοὺς τόπους τοῦτο
ἡμῖν εἴρηται καὶ σαφέστερον ἡμῖν πεπραγμάτευται. ἀλλὰ καὶ εὑρί- 2

σχομεν αὐτὸν ἐκ τοῦ Δαυὶδ ὄντα διὰ τὸ υἱὸν εἶναι τοῦ Ἰωσήφ, Να-
ζιραῖόν ⟨τε⟩ γενόμενον (ἦν γὰρ πρωτότοκος τῷ Ἰωσὴφ καὶ ἡγιασμένος)·
ἔτι δὲ καὶ ἱερατεύσαντα αὐτὸν κατὰ τὴν παλαιὰν ἱερωσύνην ηὕρομεν.
διὸ καὶ ἐφίετο αὐτῷ ἅπαξ τοῦ ἐνιαυτοῦ εἰς τὰ ἅγια τῶν ἁγίων 3
εἰσιέναι, ὡς τοῖς | ἀρχιερεῦσιν ἐκέλευσεν ὁ νόμος κατὰ τὸ γεγραμμέ-
νον· οὕτως γὰρ ἱστόρησαν πολλοὶ πρὸ ἡμῶν περὶ αὐτοῦ, Εὐσέβιός
τε καὶ Κλήμης καὶ ἄλλοι. ἀλλὰ καὶ τὸ πέταλον ἐπὶ τῆς κεφαλῆς 4
ἐξῆν αὐτῷ φορεῖν, καθὼς οἱ προειρημένοι ἀξιόπιστοι ἄνδρες ἐν τοῖς
†αὐτοῖς ὑπομνηματισμοῖς ἐμαρτύρησαν.   ›ἱερεύς‹ τοίνυν, ὡς ἔφην, 5
ὁ κύριος ἡμῶν Ἰησοῦς Χριστός ›εἰς τὸν αἰῶνα κατὰ τὴν τάξιν Μελ-
χισεδέκ‹, βασιλεύς τε ὁμοῦ κατὰ τὴν τάξιν τὴν ἄνωθεν, ἵνα μεταγάγῃ
τὴν ἱερωσύνην ἅμα τῇ νομοθεσίᾳ.   τοῦ δὲ σπέρματος Δαυὶδ κατὰ τὴν 6
Μαρίαν καθεζομένου ἐν θρόνῳ, * εἰς τὸν αἰῶνα καὶ τῆς βασιλείας
αὐτοῦ οὐκ ἔσται τέλος. ἔδει γὰρ αὐτὸν νῦν μεταγαγεῖν τὴν τάξιν
τοῦ τότε βασιλείου. καὶ γὰρ ἡ βασιλεία αὐτοῦ οὐκ ἔστιν ἀπὸ τῆς
γῆς, ὡς ἔλεγεν ἐν τῷ εὐαγγελίῳ Ποντίῳ Πιλάτῳ ›ἡ βασιλεία μου
οὐκ ἔστιν ἐκ τοῦ κόσμου τούτου‹. τοῦ γὰρ Χριστοῦ τὰ πάντα πλη- 7
ροῦντος δι' αἰνιγμάτων, ἕως τινὸς μέτρου αἱ ὑποθέσεις ἔφθανον. οὐ
γὰρ ἦλθεν, ἵνα προκοπὴν λάβῃ βασιλείας, ὁ βασιλεύων ἀεί· ἐχαρίσατο
δὲ τοῖς ὑπ' αὐτοῦ καθισταμένοις τὸ βασίλειον, ἵνα μὴ νομισθῇ ἀπὸ
τῶν μικρῶν ἐπὶ τὰ μείζονα προκόπτειν. μένει γὰρ αὐτοῦ ὁ θρόνος 8
καὶ τῆς βασιλείας αὐτοῦ οὐκ ἔσται τέλος καὶ κάθηται ἐπὶ τὸν θρόνον
Δαυίδ, τὸ βασίλειον τοῦ Δαυὶδ μεταστήσας καὶ χαρισάμενος τοῖς ἑαυ-
τοῦ δούλοις ἅμα τῇ ἀρχιερωσύνῃ, τουτέστι τοῖς ἀρχιερεῦσι τῆς κα-
θολι|κῆς ἐκκλησίας. | καὶ πολλὰ ἔστι περὶ τούτου λέγειν, ἀλλ' 9
ὅμως ἐπειδὴ εἰς τὸν τόπον ἐλήλυθα δι' ἣν αἰτίαν Ἰεσσαῖοι ἐκαλοῦντο
πρὶν τοῦ καλεῖσθαι Χριστιανοὶ οἱ εἰς Χριστὸν πεπιστευκότες, τούτου
ἕνεκα ἔφημεν ὅτι ὁ Ἰεσσαὶ πατὴρ γίνεται τοῦ Δαυίδ, καὶ ἤτοι ἐξ ὑπο-
θεσέως τούτου τοῦ Ἰεσσαὶ ἤτοι ἐκ τοῦ ὀνόματος Ἰησοῦ τοῦ κυρίου
ἡμῶν ἐπεκλήθησαν Ἰεσσαῖοι διὰ τὸ ἐξ Ἰησοῦ ὁρμᾶσθαι, μαθηταὶ αὐ-
τοῦ ὄντες, ἢ διὰ | τὸ τῆς ἐτυμολογίας τοῦ ὀνόματος τοῦ κυρίου·
Ἰησοῦς γὰρ κατὰ τὴν Ἑβραϊκὴν διάλεκτον θεραπευτὴς καλεῖται ἤτοι
ἰατρὸς καὶ σωτήρ. ὅμως τούτῳ τῷ ὀνόματι πρὶν τοῦ Χριστιανοὺς 10
αὐτοὺς καλεῖσθαι τὴν ἐπωνυμίαν ἐκέκτηντο. ἐπὶ Ἀντιοχείας δέ, κα-
θάπερ ἄνω ἐπεμνήσθημεν καὶ ὡς ἔχει ἡ τῆς ἀληθείας ὑπόθεσις,
ἤρξαντο οἱ μαθηταὶ καὶ πᾶσα ἡ ἐκκλησία τοῦ θεοῦ Χριστιανοὶ κα-
λεῖσθαι. |

5. Εὕροις δ' ἄν, ὦ φιλόλογε, καὶ τούτων τὴν ὑπόθεσιν ἐντυχὼν 5, 1
τοῖς τοῦ Φίλωνος ὑπομνήμασιν ἐν τῇ περὶ Ἰεσσαίων αὐτοῦ ἐπιγραφο-
μένῃ βίβλῳ, ὡς τούτων τὴν πολιτείαν καὶ τὰ ἐγκώμια διεξιὼν καὶ
τὰ αὐτῶν μοναστήρια ἐν τῇ κατὰ τὴν Μάρειαν λίμνην ἱστορῶν
περιοικίδι οὐ περί τινων ἑτέρων ὁ ἀνὴρ ἱστόρησεν, ἀλλὰ περὶ Χρι-
στιανῶν.   οὗτος γὰρ γενόμενος ἐν τῇ χώρᾳ (Μαρεῶτιν δὲ τὸν 2

τόπον καλοῦσι) καὶ καταχθεὶς παρ' αὐτοῖς ἐν τοῖς κατὰ τὸν χῶρον
τοῦτον μοναστηρίοις ὠφέληται. ἐν ἡμέραις γὰρ τῶν Πάσχων ἐκεῖ 3
γενόμενος, τάς τε αὐτῶν πολιτείας ἐθεάσατο καὶ ὡς τινες ἑβδομάδα
τὴν ἁγίαν τῶν Πάσχων ὑπερτιθέμενοι διετέλουν, ἄλλοι δὲ διὰ δύο
ἐσθίοντες, ἄλλοι δὲ καὶ καθ' ἑσπέραν. ἦν δὲ πάντα ταῦτα τῷ ἀνδρὶ
πεπραγματευμένα εἰς τὴν περὶ πίστεώς τε καὶ πολιτείας τῶν Χρι-
στιανῶν ὑπόθεσιν.

ὡς οὖν τότε ἐκαλοῦντο Ἰεσσαῖοι ἐπ' ὀλίγῳ χρόνῳ μετὰ τὴν ἀνά- 4
15 ληψιν τοῦ σωτῆρος καὶ Μάρκου τῇ τῶν Αἰγυπτίων χώρᾳ κηρύξαντος
κατὰ τοὺς χρόνους τούτους τινὲς ἐξεληλύθασι πάλιν, τῶν ἀποστόλων
δῆθεν ἀκόλουθοι, λέγω δὲ οἱ ἐνταῦθά μοι δηλούμενοι Ναζωραῖοι,
ὄντες μὲν κατὰ τὸ γένος Ἰουδαῖοι καὶ τῷ νόμῳ προσανέχοντες καὶ
περιτομὴν κεκτημένοι, ἀλλ' ὥσπερ ἀπὸ σκοποῦ τινες θεασάμενοι πῦρ 5
20 καὶ μὴ νοήσαντες δι' ἣν αἰτίαν οἱ τὴν πυρὰν ταύτην ἐξάψαντες ἢ
εἰς ⟨ἣν⟩ χρησιμότητα τοῦτο | ποιοῦσιν, ἢ τὰ | τῆς ζωῆς ἑαυτῶν ὀψώνια
πρὸς ἐδωδὴν διὰ τῆς πυρᾶς κατασκευάζοντες ἢ ἐπὶ ἀφανισμῷ τινων
καυστικῶν ξύλων ἢ φρυγάνων τῶν ὑπὸ πυρὸς εἰωθότων ἀναλίσκε-
σθαι, οὕτω καὶ αὐτοὶ μιμησάμενοι πῦρ ἀνάψαντες ἑαυτοὺς ἐνέπρη-
σαν. ἀκούσαντες γὰρ μόνον ὄνομα Ἰησοῦ καὶ θεασάμενοι τὰ θεο- 6
σήμεια τὰ διὰ τῶν χειρῶν τῶν ἀποστόλων γινόμενα καὶ αὐτοὶ εἰς
Ἰησοῦν πιστεύουσιν. γνόντες δὲ αὐτὸν ἐν Ναζαρὲτ ἐν γαστρὶ συλ-
ληφθέντα καὶ ἐν οἴκῳ Ἰωσὴφ ἀνατραφέντα καὶ διὰ τοῦτο ἐν τῷ
εὐαγγελίῳ Ἰησοῦν τὸν Ναζωραῖον καλεῖσθαι, ὡς καὶ οἱ ἀπόστολοί
φασιν »Ἰησοῦν τὸν Ναζωραῖον, ἄνδρα ἀποδεδειγμένον ἔν τε σημείοις
καὶ τέρασι« καὶ τὰ ἑξῆς, τοῦτο τὸ ὄνομα ἐπιτιθέασιν ἑαυτοῖς τοῦ
καλεῖσθαι Ναζωραίους — οὐχὶ Ναζιραίους, τὸ ἑρμηνευόμενον ἡγιασμέ- 7
νους. τοῦτο γὰρ τοῖς τὸ παλαιὸν πρωτοτόκοις καὶ θεῷ ἀφιερω-
θεῖσιν ὑπῆρχεν τὸ ἀξίωμα, ὧν εἷς ὑπῆρχεν ὁ Σαμψὼν καὶ ἄλλοι μετ'
αὐτὸν καὶ πρὸ αὐτοῦ πολλοί, ἀλλὰ καὶ Ἰωάννης ὁ βαπτιστὴς
τῶν αὐτῶν ἀφηγιασμένων τῷ θεῷ καὶ αὐτὸς εἷς ὑπῆρχεν· »οἶνον
γὰρ καὶ σίκερα οὐκ ἔπινεν«· ὡρίζετο γὰρ τοῖς τοιούτοις αὕτη ἁρ-

μόδιος τῷ ἀξιώματι ἡ πολιτεία. | 6. ἀλλὰ οὐδὲ Νασαραίους ἑαυ- 6, 1
τοὺς ἐκάλεσαν· ἦν γὰρ ἡ αἵρεσις τῶν Νασαραίων πρὸ Χριστοῦ καὶ
Χριστὸν οὐκ ᾔδει —· ἀλλὰ καὶ πάντες ἄνθρωποι τοὺς Χριστιανοὺς 2
ἐκάλουν Ναζωραίους ὡς προεῖπον, ὡς λέγουσι κατηγοροῦντες Παύλου
τοῦ ἀποστόλου »τοῦτον τὸν ἄνθρωπον ηὕρομεν λοιμὸν καὶ διαστρέ-
φοντα τὸν λαόν, πρωτοστάτην τε ὄντα τῆς τῶν Ναζωραίων αἱρέ-
σεως«. ὁ δὲ ἅγιος ἀπόστολος οὐκ ἀρνεῖται μὲν τὸ ὄνομα, οὐχὶ τὴν 3
τούτων αἵρεσιν ὁμολογῶν, ἀλλὰ τὸ ὄνομα τὸ ἀπὸ τῆς τῶν ἀντι-
λεγόντων κακονοίας διὰ τὸν Χριστὸν ἐπενεχθὲν αὐτῷ ἀσμένως κατα-
δεχόμενος. φησὶ γὰρ ἐπὶ τοῦ βήματος »οὔτε ἐν τῷ ἱερῷ ηὗρόν με 4
πρός τινα διαλεγόμενον ἢ ἐπίστασίν τινα ὄχλου ποιοῦντα οὐδὲ ὧν
μου κατηγοροῦσιν οὐδὲν πεποίηκα. ὁμολογῶ δέ σοι τοῦτο, ὅτι κατὰ

τὴν ὁδὸν ἥν αἵρεσιν οὗτοι φάσκουσιν οὕτω λατρεύω, πιστεύων πᾶσι τοῖς ἐν τῷ νόμῳ καὶ ἐν τοῖς προφήταις‹. καὶ οὐ θαῦμα ὅτι ὁ 5 ἀπόστολος ὡμολόγει ἑαυτὸν Ναζωραῖον, πάντων καλούντων τοὺς Χριστιανοὺς τότε τούτῳ τῷ ὀνόματι διὰ Ναζαρὲτ τὴν πόλιν, ἄλλης μὴ οὔσης χρήσεως τῷ ὀνόματι πρὸς τὸν καιρόν, | ὥστε τοὺς ἀνθρώπους ⟨Ναζωραίους⟩ καλεῖν τοὺς τῷ Χριστῷ πεπιστευκότας, περὶ οὗ καὶ γέγραπται ›ὅτι Ναζωραῖος κληθήσεται‹. καὶ γὰρ καὶ νῦν ὁμω- 6 νύμως οἱ ἄνθρωποι πάσας τὰς αἱρέσεις, Μανιχαίους τέ φημι καὶ Μαρκιωνιστὰς Γνωστικούς τε καὶ ἄλλους, Χριστιανοὺς τοὺς μὴ ὄντας Χριστιανοὺς καλοῦσι καὶ ὅμως ἑκάστη αἵρεσις, καίπερ ἄλλως λεγομένη, καταδέχεται τοῦτο χαίρουσα, ὅτι διὰ τοῦ ὀνόματος κοσμεῖται· δοκοῦσι γὰρ ἐπὶ τῷ τοῦ Χριστοῦ σεμνύνεσθαι ὀνόματι, οὐ μὴν τῇ πίστει καὶ τοῖς ἔργοις.   οὕτω καὶ οἱ ἅγιοι τοῦ Χριστοῦ μαθηταὶ τότε μαθη- 7 τὰς Ἰησοῦ ἑαυτοὺς ἐκάλουν, ὥσπερ οὖν καὶ ἦσαν· ἀκούοντες δὲ παρὰ ἄλλων Ναζωραῖοι οὐκ ἀπηναίνοντο, τὸν σκοπὸν θεωροῦντες τῶν 20 τοῦτο αὐτοὺς καλούντων, ὅτι διὰ Χριστὸν αὐτοὺς ἐκάλουν, ἐπειδὴ καὶ αὐτὸς ὁ κύριος ἡμῶν Ἰησοῦς ⟨ὁ⟩ Ναζωραῖος ἐκαλεῖτο, ὥσπερ ἔχει τὰ εὐαγγέλια καὶ αἱ Πράξεις τῶν ἀποστόλων, διὰ τὸ ἐν τῇ πόλει αὐτὸν 8 Ναζαρὲτ (κώμη δὲ τὰ νῦν οὔσῃ) ἀνατετράφθαι ἐν οἴκῳ Ἰωσήφ, γεννηθέντα κατὰ σάρκα ἐν Βηθλεὲμ ἀπὸ Μαρίας τῆς ἀειπαρθένου τῆς μεμνηστευμένης Ἰωσήφ, τῷ ἐν τῇ αὐτῇ Ναζαρὲτ μετῳκηκότι μετὰ τὸ ἀπὸ Βηθλεὲμ αὐτὸν μεταναστάντα ἐν τῇ Γαλιλαίᾳ κατοικισθῆναι.

7. Οὗτοι δὲ οἱ προειρημένοι αἱρεσιῶται, περὶ ὧν ἐνταῦθα τὴν 7,1 ὑφήγησιν ποιούμεθα, παρέντες τὸ ὄνομα τοῦ Ἰησοῦ οὔτε Ἰεσσαίους ἑαυτοὺς κεκλήκασιν οὔτε τῶν | Ἰουδαίων ἔμειναν ἔχοντες τὸ ὄνομα οὔτε Χριστιανοὺς ἑαυτοὺς ἐπωνόμασαν, ἀλλὰ Ναζωραίους, δῆθεν ἀπὸ τῆς τοῦ τόπου τῆς Ναζαρὲτ ἐπωνυμίας, τὰ πάντα δέ εἰσιν Ἰουδαῖοι καὶ | οὐδὲν ἕτερον.   χρῶνται δὲ οὗτοι οὐ μόνον νέα διαθήκῃ, ἀλλὰ 2 καὶ παλαιᾷ διαθήκῃ, καθάπερ καὶ οἱ Ἰουδαῖοι. οὐ γὰρ ἀπηγόρευται παρ' αὐτοῖς νομοθεσία καὶ προφῆται καὶ γραφεῖα τὰ καλούμενα παρὰ Ἰουδαίοις βιβλία, ὥσπερ παρὰ τοῖς προειρημένοις· οὐδέ τι ἕτερον οὗτοι φρονοῦσιν, ἀλλὰ κατὰ τὸ κήρυγμα τοῦ νόμου καὶ ὡς οἱ Ἰουδαῖοι πάντα καλῶς ὁμολογοῦσι χωρὶς τοῦ εἰς Χριστὸν δῆθεν πεπιστευκέναι. παρ' αὐτοῖς γὰρ καὶ νεκρῶν ἀνάστασις ὁμολογεῖται καὶ ἐκ θεοῦ τὰ 3 πάντα γεγενῆσθαι, ἕνα δὲ θεὸν καταγγέλλουσι καὶ τὸν τούτου παῖδα Ἰησοῦν Χριστόν.   Ἑβραϊκῇ δὲ διαλέκτῳ ἀκριβῶς εἰσιν ἠσκημένοι. 4 παρ' αὐτοῖς γὰρ πᾶς ὁ νόμος καὶ οἱ προφῆται καὶ τὰ γραφεῖα λεγόμενα, φημὶ δὲ τὰ στιχηρὰ καὶ αἱ Βασιλεῖαι | καὶ Παραλειπόμενα καὶ Ἐσθὴρ καὶ τἄλλα πάντα Ἑβραϊκῶς ἀναγινώσκεται, ὥσπερ ἀμέλει καὶ παρὰ Ἰουδαίοις.   ἐν τούτῳ δὲ μόνον πρὸς Ἰουδαίους διαφέρονται καὶ 5 Χριστιανούς, Ἰουδαίοις μὲν μὴ συμφωνοῦντες διὰ τὸ εἰς Χριστὸν πεπιστευκέναι, Χριστιανοῖς δὲ μὴ ὁμογνωμονοῦντες διὰ τὸ ἔτι νόμῳ πεπεδῆσθαι, περιτομῇ τε καὶ σαββάτῳ καὶ τοῖς ἄλλοις.   περὶ Χρι- 6

στοῦ δὲ οὐκ οἶδ᾽ εἰπεῖν, εἰ καὶ αὐτοὶ τῇ τῶν προειρημένων περὶ Κή-
ρινθον καὶ Μήρινθον μοχθηρίᾳ ἀχθέντες ψιλὸν ἄνθρωπον νομίζουσιν
ἢ καθὼς ἡ ἀλήθεια ἔχει διὰ πνεύματος ἁγίου γεγεννῆσθαι ἐκ Μαρίας
διαβεβαιοῦνται.   ἔστιν δὲ αὕτη ἡ αἵρεσις ἡ Ναζωραίων ἐν τῇ Βε- 7
ροιαίων περὶ τὴν Κοίλην Συρίαν καὶ ἐν τῇ Δεκαπόλει περὶ τὰ τῆς
Πέλλης μέρη καὶ ἐν τῇ Βασανίτιδι ἐν τῇ λεγομένῃ Κωκάβῃ, Χωχάβῃ
δὲ Ἑβραϊστὶ λεγομένῃ. ἐκεῖθεν γὰρ ἡ ἀρχὴ γέγονε, μετὰ τὴν ἀπὸ 8
τῶν Ἱεροσολύμων μετάστασιν πάντων τῶν | μαθητῶν ἐν Πέλλῃ
ᾠκηκότων, Χριστοῦ φήσαντος καταλεῖψαι τὰ Ἱεροσόλυμα καὶ ἀνα-
χωρῆσαι δι᾽ ἣν ἤμελλε πάσχειν πολιορκίαν. καὶ ἐκ τῆς τοιαύτης
ὑποθέσεως τὴν Περαίαν οἰκήσαντες ἐκεῖσε, ὡς ἔφην, διέτριβον. ἐν-
τεῦθεν ἡ κατὰ τοὺς Ναζωραίους αἵρεσις ἔσχεν τὴν ἀρχήν.

8. Πεπλάνηνται δὲ καὶ οὗτοι περιτομὴν αὐχοῦντες, καὶ ἔτι οἱ τοι- 8, 1
οῦτοι »ὑπὸ κατάραν εἰσί«, μὴ δυνάμενοι τὸν νόμον πληρῶσαι. πῶς
γὰρ δυνήσονται πληροῦν τὰ ἐν τῷ νόμῳ εἰρημένα, ὅτι »τρὶς τοῦ
ἔτους ὀφθήσῃ ἐνώπιον κυρίου τοῦ θεοῦ σου, κατά τε τὰ Ἄζυμα καὶ
Σκηνοπηγίαν καὶ τὴν Πεντηκοστήν«, ἐν τῷ τόπῳ Ἱεροσολύμων.
ἀποκλεισθέντος γὰρ τοῦ τόπου καὶ τῶν ἐν τῷ νόμῳ μὴ δυναμένων 2
πληροῦσθαι, παντὶ τῷ νοῦν ἔχοντι σαφὲς ἂν εἴη ὅτι Χριστὸς ἦλθεν πλη-
ρωτὴς τοῦ νόμου, οὐ τὸν νόμον καταλύσων, ἀλλὰ τὸν νόμον πληρώσων,
καὶ ἀφελεῖν τὴν κατάραν τὴν κατὰ τῆς παραβάσεως τοῦ νόμου ὁρι-
σθεῖσαν. μετὰ γὰρ τὸ ἐντείλασθαι τὸν Μωϋσέα πᾶσαν ἐντολὴν ἦλθεν 3
ἐπὶ τὸ τέρμα τῆς βίβλου καὶ »συνέκλεισε τὸ πᾶν εἰς κατάραν« λέγων
»ἐπι|κατάρατος ὃς οὐκ ἐμμένει πᾶσι τοῖς γεγραμμένοις λόγοις ἐν τῷ
10 βιβλίῳ τούτῳ τοῦ ποιῆσαι αὐτούς«.   ἦλθεν οὖν λύων μὲν τὰ πε- 4
πεδημένα δεσμοῖς τῆς κατάρας, | χαριζόμενος δὲ ἡμῖν ἀντὶ τῶν μικρῶν
τῶν μὴ δυναμένων πληροῦσθαι τὰ μείζονα καὶ οὐ μαχόμενα θάτερον
θατέρῳ πρὸς τὴν τοῦ ἔργου πλήρωσιν ὡς τὰ πρότερα· οὕτως γὰρ 5
κατὰ πᾶσαν αἵρεσιν φθάνοντες ἐν τῇ περὶ σαββατισμοῦ καὶ περιτομῆς
καὶ τῶν ἄλλων σχέσει πολλάκις ἐπειργασάμεθα, πῶς ὁ κύριος ἡμῖν
τὰ ἐντελέστερα κεχάρισται. πῶς δὲ οἱ τοιοῦτοι δυνήσονται ἀπο- 6
λογίαν ἔχειν, μὴ τῷ πνεύματι τῷ ἁγίῳ ὑπακούσαντες τῷ διὰ τῶν
ἀποστόλων εἰρηκότι τοῖς ἐξ ἐθνῶν πεπιστευκόσι »μὴ βάρος ἐπιτίθε-
σθαι πλὴν τῶν ἐπάναγκες, ἀπέχεσθαι αἵματος | καὶ πνικτοῦ καὶ πορ-
νείας καὶ εἰδωλοθύτου;« πῶς δὲ οὐκ ἐκπεσοῦνται τῆς τοῦ θεοῦ χάρι- 7
τος, λέγοντος Παύλου τοῦ ἁγίου ἀποστόλου ὅτι »ἐὰν περιτέμνησθε,
Χριστὸς ὑμᾶς οὐδὲν ὠφελήσει«, »οἵτινες ἐν νόμῳ καυχᾶσθε, τῆς
χάριτος ἐξεπέσατε«;

9. Ἀρκέσει γοῦν καὶ ἐν ταύτῃ τῇ αἱρέσει ἡ διὰ τῆς συντομίας 9, 1
παρ᾽ ἡμῶν διάλεξις. εὐθυέλεγκτοι γὰρ οἱ τοιοῦτοι καὶ εὐάλωτοι, καὶ
Ἰουδαῖοι μᾶλλον καὶ οὐδὲν ἕτερον. πάνυ δὲ οὗτοι ἐχθροὶ τοῖς 2
Ἰουδαίοις ὑπάρχουσιν. οὐ μόνον γὰρ οἱ τῶν Ἰουδαίων παῖδες πρὸς

τούτους κέκτηνται μῖσος, ἀλλὰ καὶ ἀνιστάμενοι ἕωθεν καὶ μέσης
ἡμέρας καὶ περὶ τὴν ἑσπέραν, τρὶς τῆς ἡμέρας ὅτε εὐχὰς ἐπιτελοῦσιν
ἑαυτοῖς ἐν ταῖς συναγωγαῖς ἐπαρῶνται αὐτοῖς καὶ ἀναθεματίζουσι,
τρὶς τῆς ἡμέρας φάσκοντες ὅτι ›ἐπικαταράσαι ὁ θεὸς τοὺς Ναζωραίους‹. δῆθεν γὰρ τούτοις περισσότερον ἐνέχουσι, διὰ τὸ ἀπὸ Ἰου- 3
δαίων αὐτοὺς ὄντας Ἰησοῦν κηρύσσειν εἶναι ⟨τὸν⟩ Χριστόν, ὅπερ ἐστὶν
ἐναντίον πρὸς τοὺς ἔτι Ἰουδαίους, τοὺς τὸν Ἰησοῦν μὴ δεξαμένους.
ἔχουσι δὲ τὸ κατὰ Ματθαῖον εὐαγγέλιον πληρέστατον Ἑβραϊστί. παρ' 4
αὐτοῖς γὰρ σαφῶς τοῦτο, καθὼς ἐξ ἀρχῆς ἐγράφη, Ἑβραϊκοῖς γράμ-
μασιν ἔτι σῴζεται. οὐκ οἶδα δὲ εἰ καὶ τὰς γενεαλογίας τὰς ἀπὸ τοῦ
Ἀβραὰμ ἄχρι Χριστοῦ περιεῖλον. ἀλλὰ καὶ ταύτην φωράσαντες 5
ὡς βληχρὸν καὶ ὀδύνης ἐμποιητικὸν διὰ τοῦ ἰοῦ σφηκίον, καταθλά-
σαντές τε τοῖς τῆς ἀληθείας λόγοις, ἐπὶ τὰς ἑξῆς ἴωμεν, ἐπιπόθητοι,
παρὰ θεοῦ αἰτοῦντες τὴν βοήθειαν. |

Appendix II: Geography

Jerome tells Augustine (*ep.* 112, 13) that the Nazarene sect is to be found among the Jews in all the synagogues of the East. At the time of writing, this would have been highly unlikely, although it may have been not so far wrong three hundred years earlier. His use of *Oriens* must in any case be limited to the areas he himself knew; that is, from Antioch south along the coast as far as Bethlehem. But what Jerome is probably saying—taking his claim in context—is that the Nazarene sect is cursed throughout the East. By the end of the fourth century, even the curse itself was most likely anachronistic and unnecessary, but liturgical usages change slowly.

Turning to more specific references, we have the Pella tradition (see Appendix III). Some Nazarenes doubtless remained there, across the Jordan, while others, perhaps led by their aging bishop Simon, returned after 70 or 73 to Jerusalem. They will not have stayed there past 135, and with the Hadrianic persecution both Jerusalem and Pella Nazarenes may have fled north.

The talmudic sources seem to return us to the area of the Galilee, where a Nazarene presence can be supposed to have been constant since the ministry of Jesus. The location of Kfar Sechania cannot be determined with complete certainty, but it was almost surely in the greater Galilee area,[1] and perhaps not far from Sepphoris. This same region, southeast of Acre, is also a possible location of the town of Chochaba, but its location is not without difficulties. It is first mentioned by Julius Africanus,[2] who puts it together with Nazara and connects it with the *desposynoi*. He does not mention Nazarenes by name, but Epiphanius quite specifically does so: "the heresy of the Nazarenes exists . . . in Basanitis in the so-called Kokabe, Chochabe in Hebrew."[3] He goes on to say that they moved there from Pella. Here we must resolve difficulties both geographical and chronological.

---

1   See B. Bagatti, *LA* 11 (1960), 300-304; J. Gutmann, *Encyclopedia Judaica* 8 (Berlin, 1931), 837f; and Klein and Neubauer, *locc. citt..* chap. 7.
2   Eusebius *HE* I 7, 14 (*GCS* II 1, 2, p. 60): Κώχαβα.
3   *Pan.* 29 7, 7. Cf. also 30 2, 7-8; 30 18,1.

It seems likely that we are dealing with more than one village named Chochaba. Bagatti sees at least three,[4] although this may be a bit ambitious. Avi Yonah[5] locates one in the western Galilee and one in the general Basanitis area, about 28 km. east of the lake. The chronological difficulties are resolved if we surmise that the western Chochaba was inhabited by Nazarenes from the beginning and that the eastern one received those who moved northward from Pella somewhere near the turn of the century.

Further confusion inheres because of the appearance of a town called Choba (Χωβα). This place is noted by Eusebius.[6] The similarity of this name to Chochaba seems to have caused the confusion. Eusebius, however, connects this town only to the Ebionites, although in his case that is no guarantee that he does not mean Nazarenes. Avi Yonah locates a Choba on the west bank of the Jordan River about a third of the way up the valley from Jericho.[7] We cannot rule this out as a possible earlier site of Nazarene habitation, but neither can we with certainty make any firm connection to the sect.

Our final bit of geographical data revolves around Beroea of Coele Syria. Epiphanius (*pan*. 29, 7) names this town (modern-day Aleppo) as a home of the Nazarenes. He does not mention it in connection with the Ebionites. Jerome, like Epiphanius, states in the present tense that the members of the sect are living in Beroea of Syria.[8] Black notes that the two presbyters for whom Epiphanius wrote his *panarion* came from Beroea in Coele Syria (*PG 41, 156*).[9] This must greatly strengthen the credibility of what he says about the place, as he would hardly have been likely to tell them something of their own town which they would know to be patently false. Neither Epiphanius nor Jerome tells us how they got there, and we can only surmise that they may have fled there during the Hadrianic persecution which ended in 138.[10] Similarly, we have no data as to the size of the group. It is here we see the last traces of the Nazarenes.

4   *Art. cit.*
5   *Gazeteer of Roman Palestine* (*Qedem* 5) (1976), 106, 107.
6   *Onomas.* 172. Jerome, *de situ et nom. loc. hebr. liber* 112, also mentions Choba, but he is directly copying Eusebius.
7   *op. cit.*, 49, 109.
8   *De vir. ill.* 3.
9   *BJRL* 41 (1959), 299.
10 We have seen above, chap. 1, that there is no connection between our Nazarenes and Pliny's *nazerini* of Coele Syria.

Appendix III: The Historicity of the Pella Tradition

Any attempt to treat the post–New Testament history of Jewish Christianity must first decide on the historicity of the reported flight of the Jerusalem church to Pella of the Decapolis.[1] Until the middle of this century, this legend was accepted almost without question. It is, of course, the underlying assumption of the present study that Jewish Christianity was not destroyed, and this writer believes that the Pella flight provides a direct historical link of continuity between the Jerusalem Nazarenes of Acts 24:5 and the sect which is the subject of this study. This appendix attempts to deal with the major objections made to the historicity of the flight.

In 1951 S.G.F. Brandon published *The Fall of Jerusalem and the Christian Church* in which he tried to show that the Jerusalem Christians suffered the same fate in 70 A.D. as their fellow-Jews: death, slavery, and dispersion. The Pella tradition had to be discarded, and as justification for doing so, Brandon raised three serious difficulties with the Pella flight. 1) Before 70 the church of Jerusalem held supreme authority; after that date it held no sway in Church affairs. If the leaders were in Pella (and perhaps returned to Jerusalem as the legend suggests) then what happened to their authority? One must conclude that they did not survive the disaster. 2) If Pella was razed by the rebels in 66, as Josephus reports,[2] then that city cannot be considered as a refuge for Jewish Christians, because either a) they were there at the time of the raid and would have been treated as traitors by the rebels, or b) they came after the raid, in which case the

---

1   Eusebius *HE* III 5,3; Epiphanius *pan.* 29, 7; 30, 2; *de mens. et pond.* 15. The very importance of this incident is reflected in the volume of modern studies it has earned: B.C. Gray, *Jour. of Eccl. Hist.* 24 (1973), 1–7; J.J. Gunther *ThZ* 29 (1973), 81–94; M. Simon, *RSR* 60 (1972), 37–54; S. Sowers, *ThZ* 26 (1970), 305–320; B. Bagatti, *Revista de Cultura Biblica* 9 (1972), 170–179; G. Lüdemann in *Jewish and Christian Self-Definition*, ed. E.P. Sanders (Philadelphia, 1980), pp. 161–173. See also the present author's unpublished masters thesis, "The Flight of the Jerusalem Church to Pella of the Decapolis" (The Hebrew University of Jerusalem, 1977).

2   *War* II 457–460.

surviving and angered Pella Greeks would have been most hostile to the arrival of Jews in any guise. 3) Brandon pointed out the extreme difficulty of leaving Jerusalem, which was guarded by Zealots, and passing through the lines of the Roman army. It would have been impossible for a community of almost any size to accomplish such a feat. A number of scholars found his proofs convincing and abandoned the legend as ancient fiction.[3] Others simply ignored him, but some have attempted to defend the tradition.[4] In 1967 Brandon, in his somewhat radical *Jesus and the Zealots*, maintained his position, strengthened it with further argument along the same lines, and pointed out that none who had written against him to date had dealt with these three main objections to the flight.

Jerusalem's loss of authority

Even a cursory perusal of the available post–70 Christian sources makes it clear that Jerusalem carried no weight of authority in the general ecclesiastical structure after Titus' victory. According to Eusebius, however, there continued to exist a Jerusalem church with an unbroken succession of bishops.[5] Eusebius makes other references to events concerning the "Jerusalem Church" after 70, a fact which Brandon calls "contradictory."[6] Is it contradictory that the Jerusalem community removed to Pella and yet Eusebius continues to write about the "Bishops of Jerusalem"? Gibbon remarked, long before Brandon's time: "During this occasional absence, the bishop and church of Pella still retained the title of Jerusalem. In the same manner, the Roman pontiffs resided seventy years at Avignon; and the patriarchs of Alexandria have long since transferred their episcopal seat to Cairo."[7] Rather than seeing an internal contradiction in Eusebius' inclusion of the list of Jewish Christian bishops (*HE* IV 5, 1–3), we should find in this another indication that some viable Jewish Christian remnant did survive Jerusalem's disaster.

If Jerusalem Jewish Christians did survive, and if the Jerusalem bishopric was important enough, as Eusebius tells us, that "those of the apostles and of the disciples of the Lord who were still alive" saw fit to return from afar to elect James's

3   G. Strecker, *Das Judenchristentum in den Pseudoklementinen* (Berlin, 1958), pp. 229ff: L. Gaston, *No Stone on Another* (Suppl. to NovTest 23), p. 142, n. 3; J. Munck, *NTS* 6 (1960), 103f; L. Keck, *ZNTW* 56 (1965), 65, n. 36; W.R. Farmer, *Maccabees, Zealots and Josephus* (New York, 1957), p. 125, n. 2; R. Furneaux, *The Roman Siege of Jerusalem* (London, 1973), p. 12lf; Lüdemann, *art. cit.*

4   Brandon himself lists some of those who ignored him in *Zealots*, p. 209, n. 1. Among those on the defense, see L.E. Elliot-Binns, *Galilean Christianity* (London, 1956), p. 67f; W. Wink, *Union Seminary Quarterly Review* 25 (1969), 37–46; B. Reicke, in *Suppl. to NovTest* 33 (1972); and Sowers, Gray, Simon, and Gunther, *artt. citt.*

5   *HE* IV 5, 1–3.

6   *Zealots*, p. 213, n. 2. See *HE* III 11; 22; 32, 1–7; 35.

7   *Decline and Fall of the Roman Empire*, II, (London, 1909), 9, n. 1. Cf. P. Carrington, *The Early Christian Church*, I (Cambridge, 1957), 250, who calls Simon "the bishop of Jerusalem church-in-exile at Pella."

successor,[8] then why did the Jerusalem church lose its former authority? Authority rests not so much in a geographical place as in a relational position. James was not the final authority because he was the Bishop of Jerusalem; rather he was chosen Bishop of Jerusalem because he was "the brother of the Lord." So it seems to have been also with the apostles. Their authority derived from the fact that they had been immediate disciples of Jesus.[9] By the same token, Simon b. Clopas was chosen to succeed James because he was Jesus' cousin, and others in the time of Domitian were considered leaders in the Chuch because of their relationship to Jesus.[10] As the apostles died or moved away, so also the authority of Jerusalem began to diminish. John, traditionally, lived out his later years in Ephesus, and with him died direct apostolic authority. By that time (c. 100), considerable attention was already being given to apostolic *writings*. Brandon is looking for an anachronism when he expects to see a continued authority recognized for the "Church of Jerusalem."[11] That is to say, if we recognize that the concept of "apostolic succession" (and its concomitant authority) did not become a working reality until at least a century later, then it is an anachronism to speak of such cathedral authority at such an early date.

Pella as a safe refuge

Here Brandon has created a far greater problem than really exists. He has tried to show that Pella could not have been safe for a band of fleeing Jerusalem Christians, because it was raided by avenging Jews in 66 and was thereafter inhabited by Gentiles made hostile to any Jews who might try to enter the town. In presenting his alternative explanation of how the Pella "foundation legend" got started, however, he has found it necessary to say that there were Christian refugees from the Galilee and Samaria who came to Pella.[12] It is clear that, if his objections to the safety of Jerusalem Christians are valid, then it would not have been any safer in Pella for Jewish Christians from anywhere else. (In Brandon's theory these refugees later claimed to be descended from the Jerusalem church, so they must have been *Jewish* Christians for such a claim to have had any

---

8   *HE* III 11.
9   Cf. Acts 1:21–26.
10 *HE* III 11; 20, 6; 32, 6.
11 Whatever authority may have inhered in the place Jerusalem itself would have died, of course, in 70. Such locational authority would have had meaning only to those of Jewish heritage; non-Jews would have had no special reason to revere "the Holy City." But in the eyes of *Jewish* Christians, we might not necessarily expect Jerusalem (without apostles or other recognized leaders) to hold special authority. In Judaism itself at this time, the authority shifted *with the leaders* to Yavne, even though Jerusalem evidently continued to be inhabited for another 65 years (see K.W. Clark, "Worship in the Jerusalem Temple after A.D. 70," *NTS* 6 [1960/61], 269–280).
12 *Zealots*, p. 213.

credibility.)[13] Either the refugees arrived and were repulsed or killed by the local populace, or—wherever they came from—they managed to settle in Pella.

The problem here centers around a single reference in Josephus' *Jewish War* (II 457–460). The inhabitants of Caesarea had just killed more than 20,000 Jews in their city. "The news of the disaster at Caesarea infuriated the whole nation; and parties of Jews sacked (διαμερίσθεντες) the Syrian villages and the neighboring cities, Philadelphia, Heshbon and its district, Gerasa, Pella, and Scythopolis" (Loeb translation). In the section immediately following, Josephus describes how various cities around the country were destroyed (καταστρεφάμενοι) or burned (ὑποπρήσαντες). Pella is not mentioned again in the lengthy following description of what happened to these and other cities, and from Josephus' words no general rule can be fixed whereby we could determine indirectly what happened to Pella's Jewish inhabitants. In Gerasa (480), for example, the Gentile inhabitants protected and aided their Jewish fellow-citizens, while in Scythopolis (466–468) the Jewish inhabitants helped to repel the raid and then were treacherously slain by the non-Jewish citizens. If nothing else, these two examples show us that the towns still continued to exist as viable entities, that διαμερίσθεντες should not be understood to mean that these towns were completely wiped out.[14] In both cases, in fact, this curiously-placed word does not seem to indicate a very great destruction.[15] In the one case (Scythopolis) the raiding party seems to have been repulsed, and in the other (Gerasa) whatever happened was not serious enough to damage the previous good relations between the Gentile and Jewish inhabitants.

We must add to this another consideration of no small importance. It is reasonable to assume that Pella may have been chosen as a place of refuge precisely because there existed there some established community of Christians which could be expected to welcome and care for the refugees. If this be granted, then we must look at what effect this would have had on the safety of those refugees during the time of Pella's troubles and thereafter. A community of Christians in Pella at this time would not only have provided food and shelter, but also would have raised its voice on behalf of harboring and protecting the refugees. It is to be remembered that Pella was primarily a Gentile town, and we should expect to find mostly Gentile Christians there. While it may be true that a band of refuge Jews (Christian or otherwise) might not expect to find a warm reception in

---

13   Gray, *art. cit.*, p.5.

14   It was naively suggested by Elliot-Binns (*op. cit.*, p. 67) that the Gentile residents of Pella were perhaps all destroyed, leaving the city open for resettlement by the fleeing Jerusalem Christians.

15   The archeological work by Smith, McNicoll, and Hennessey has found much evidence of the burning of Pella by Alexander Yannai in 83/82 B.C. Significantly, however, they report no such evidence at all for the period around the Jewish revolt. See the *Bulletin of the American Schools of Oriental Research* 240 (1980), 63–84; 243 (1981), 1–30; 249 (1983), 45–78.

a Gentile city during the time of rebellion, the picture is altered completely when we consider that their hosts there may have been Greek Christian citizens.

Getting out of Jerusalem

Rabbinic tradition tells how Rabban Yoḥanan b. Zakkai was smuggled out of Jerusalem in a coffin so that he might have an audience with Vespasian.[16] This story is repeatedly brought by Brandon and his school to demonstrate how difficult it was to leave the city because the Zealots were guarding all exits and killing any who were suspected of trying to desert.[17] A close reading of Josephus with the view in mind that those Jews who had come for the Feast of Unleavened Bread were all inextricably trapped will indeed yield numerous places where the historian gives this picture.[18] However, if one then re-reads the *Jewish War* looking for the time when it became impossible to escape, one finds that Josephus recounts stories of escapes throughout the siege, almost into the final days.

The cumulative picture provided by these notices is impressive in its portrayal of the continuous escape from the city by thousands. One may refer to *War* II 538 and 556 (November 66); IV 353 (2000 at one time), 377ff, 397, 410 (all in the winter of 67/68, before Passover); V 420ff, 446–450, 55lf (June 70). Right up until the end, in August 70, we read (VI 113–115) that "there were others who, watching their opportunity for escaping in safety, made off to the Romans. Among these were the chief priests Joseph and Jesus, and certain sons of the chief priests. . . Many others also of the aristocracy went over with the chief priests." As result of this, Joseph records (116–117), the rebels had to spread a rumor of the death of these escapees, in order to deter further desertions. 118: The Romans countered by bringing them back so the people could see them alive, "whereupon great numbers fled to the Romans."[19] Not until after the Temple was burned did Titus declare that there could be no more desertions (VI 352), and yet even after this as many as 40,000 fled to the Romans and were allowed to go free (VI 383–386).

It may be objected here that Josephus is writing for a Roman audience, under the patronage of the Flavians, and that he simply wants to put the actions of the Romans in as good a light as possible. For that reason he frequently mentions desertions so that he can describe how well the deserters were treated by the magnanimous conqueror. There is, no doubt, some truth in this. However, this

---

16 Avot de R. Nathan, Version I, iv; *ibid.*, Version II, vi; Midrash Lamentations, 1, 31; Gittin 56a–b; Midrash Proverbs, xv.

17 Brandon does not list the references specifically, but they are *War* IV 410; 377ff; 556; 564–565; V 29f; 423; 448; 512; VI 421.

18 *War* VI 421. But cf. IV 88, where the large numbers are those who "had flocked from the seat of the War" to Jerusalem.

19 Josephus translations by Thackeray in the Loeb series.

possible exaggeration is more than balanced by Josephus' hatred of the Zealots. It is just as likely that he is overstating the completeness of the zealot seal on escapes from the city. In order to present the Zealots in as bad a light as possible, he repeatedly mentions their cruel prohibition forbidding their fellow-Jews the freedom of escape.

List of Abbreviations

Altaner	B. Altaner and A. Stuiber, *Patrologie* (1966)
ANCL	*Ante-Nicene Christian Library*
Av. Zar.	Avodah Zarah
Bardenhewer	O. Bardenhewer, *Geschichte der altkirchlichen Literatur* (1913–1932)
BJRL	*Bulletin of the John Rylands Library*
Brach.	Brachot
BZ	*Biblische Zeitschrift*
Cath. Enc.	*Catholic Encyclopedia* (1967)
CC	*Corpus Christianorum*
CSEL	*Corpus Scriptorum Ecclesiasticorum Latinorum*
DTC	*Dictionnaire de Théologie Catholique*
ep.	*epistula*
Epiph.	Epiphanius
ERE	*Encyclopedia of Religion and Ethics* (Hastings)
Eus.	Eusebius
GCS	*Die Griechischen Christlichen Schriftsteller*
GenR	Midrash Genesis
GH	Gospel according to the Hebrews
GN	Gospel according to the Nazarenes
HE	*Historia Ecclesiastica*
H-S	E. Hennecke (W. Schneemelcher) *New Testament Apocrypha* (1963)
HTR	*Harvard Theological Review*
HUCA	*Hebrew Union College Annual*
Hull.	Hullin
j	Palestinian (Jerusalem) Talmud
JBL	*Journal of Biblical Literature*
JJS	*Journal of Jewish Studies*
JQR	*Jewish Quarterly Review*
JTS	*Journal of Theological Studies*
K-R	A.F.J. Klijn & G.J. Reinink, *Patristic Evidence for Jewish Christian Sects* (1973)

LA	*Liber Annuus*
Liddell-Scott	H.G. Liddell, R. Scott, H.S. Jones, *Greek-English Lexicon* (1968)
M	Mishnah
NovTest	*Novum Testamentum*
NT	New Testament
NTS	*New Testament Studies*
ODCC	*Oxford Dictionary of the Christian Church*
OT	Old Testament
pan.	panarion
PG	J.P. Migne, ed., *Patrologia Graeca*
PL	J.P. Migne, ed., *Patrologia Latina*
RAC	*Reallexikon für Antike und Christentum*
RB	*Révue Biblique*
REJ	*Révue des Études Juives*
RGG	*Die Religion in Geschichte und Gegenwart*
RSR	*Recherches de Science Religieuse*
Sanh.	Sanhedrin
Shabb.	Shabbat
T	Tosefta
ThDNT	*Theological Dictionary of the New Testament*
ThZ	*Theologische Zeitschrift*
TLZ	*Theologische Literaturzeitung*
TU	*Texte und Untersuchungen zur Geschichte der altchristlichen Literatur*
VC	*Vigiliae Christianae*
ZATW	*Zeitschrift für die alttestamentliche Wissenschaft*
ZNTW	*Zeitschrift für die neutestamentliche Wissenschaft und die Kunde des Urchristentums*

Bibliography

Abbott, E.A. *The Fourfold Gospel* II ("The Beginning"). Cambridge: University Press, 1914.

Albright, W.F. "The Names 'Nazareth' and 'Nazarene'." *JBL* 65 (1946), 397–401.

Alon, G. *Studies in Jewish History*. Tel Aviv: Hakibutz Hameuchad, 1957. In Hebrew.

———. *The Jews in their Land in the Talmudic Age*. Jerusalem: Magnes, 1980.

Altaner, B. "Augustinus und Epiphanius von Salamis." *TU* 83 (1967), 286–296.

Aspects du Judéo-Christianisme. Travaux du centre d'études supérieurs spécialisé d'histoire des religions de Strasbourg, 1964.

Bacher, W. "Le mot 'Minim' dans le Talmud designe-t-il quelquefois des Chrétiens?" *REJ* 38 (1899) 38–46.

Bacon, B.W. *Studies in Matthew*. London: Constable, 1930.

Bagatti, B. *The Church from the Circumcision*. Jerusalem: Franciscan Printing Press, 1971.

———. "Richerche su alcuni antichi siti Giudeo-Cristiani." *LA* 11 (1960/61), 289–314.

Bardy, G. "Saint Jérôme et ses Maitres hébreux." *Révue Bénédictine* 46 (1934), 145–164.

———. "Philastre de Brescia." *DTC* 12 (1935), c. 1398–1399.

———. "St. Jérôme et l'Évangile selon les Hébreux." *Mélange de Science Religieuse* 3 (1946), 5–36.

Barr, J. "St. Jerome's Appreciation of Hebrew." *BJRL* 49 (1966/7), 281–302.

Basset, R. "Nusairis." *ERE* IX (1917).

Bauer, J.B. "Sermo peccati / Hieronymous u. das Nazaräerevangelium." *BZ* 4 (1960), 122–128.

Bickerman, E.J. "The Name of Christians." *HTR* 42 (1949), 109–124.

Black, M. "The Patristic Accounts of Jewish Sectarianism," *BJRL* 41 (1958/9), 285–303.

———. *An Aramaic Approach to the Gospels and Acts*. Oxford: Clarendon, 1967.

Bousset, W. "Noch einmal der 'vorchristliche Jesus'." *Theologischer Rundschau* 14 (1911), 373–385.

Brandon, S.G.F. *The Fall of Jerusalem and the Christian Church*. London: SPCK, 1951.

———. *Jesus and the Zealots*. New York: Scribner, 1967.

Brandt, W. *Elchasai, ein Religionstifter und sein Werk*. Leipzig: Hinrichs, 1912.

Broydé, I. "Min." *Jewish Encyclopedia* VIII (1904), 594–596.

Büchler, A. "The Minim of Sepphoris and Tiberias in the Second and Third Centuries."

Studies in Jewish History, Memorial Volume. London: Oxford, 1956, pp. 245–274. First published in *Festschrift für Hermann Cohen.* Berlin, 1912, pp. 271–295.

Bugge, C. "Zum Essäerproblem." *ZNTW* 14 (1913), 147–174.

Burkitt, F.C. *Christian Beginnings.* London: University of London, 1924.

Cameron, R., ed. *The Other Gospels: Non-Canonical Gospel Texts.* 1982.

Carroll, K.L. "The Fourth Gospel and the Exclusion of Christians from the Synagogues." *BJRL* 40 (1957/8), 19–32.

Caspari, W. "Ναζωραῖος Mt 2:23 nach alttest'n Voraussetzungen." *ZNTW* 21 (1922), 122–127.

Cullmann, O. *The Christology of the New Testament.* London: SCM, 1959.

Daniélou, J. *The Theology of Jewish-Christianity.* London: Darton, Longman and Todd, 1964.

Davies, W.D. *The Setting of the Sermon on the Mount.* Cambridge: University Press, 1964.

Dodd, J.T. *The Gospel According to the Hebrews.* London: Search, 1933.

Dussaud, R. *Histoire et religion des Nosairis.* Paris: Bouillon, 1900.

Ehrhardt, A.A.T. "Judaeo-Christians in Egypt, the Epistula Apostolorum and the Gospel to the Hebrews." *Studia Evangelica (=TU* 85) (1964), 360–382.

Elliot-Binns, L.E. *Galilean Christianity.* London: SCM, 1956.

Enslin, M.S. "Nazarenes, Gospel of the." *Interpreter's Dictionary of the Bible.* Ed. G.A. Buttrick. 1962.

Finkel, A. "Yavneh's Liturgy and Early Christianity." *Jour. of Ecumenical Studies* 18 (1981), 231–250.

Finkelstein, L. "The Development of the Amidah." *JQR* 16 (1925/6), 127–170.

Fortesque, A. "Apollinarism." *ERE* I (1908).

Friedländer, M. "Encore un mot sur Minim, Minout et Guilionim dans le Talmud." *REJ* 38 (1899), 194–203.

Gärtner, B. "Die rätselhaften Termini Nazoräer u. Iskariot." *Horae Soederblomianae* 4 (1957), 5–36.

Gevaryahu, C.M.Y. *"Birkat ha-mînîm." Sinai* 44 (1958/9), 367–376. In Hebrew.

Ginzberg, L. "Die Haggada bei den Kirchenvätern VI. Der Kommentar des Hieronymus zu Jesaja." *Jewish Studies in Memory of George A. Kohut.* New York: A. Kohut Memorial Foundation, 1935, pp. 279–314.

Goldstein, M. *Jesus in the Jewish Tradition.* New York: Macmillan, 1950.

Grabius, J.E. *Spicilegium SS. Patrum, ut et Haereticorum.* Oxford: 1698.

Graetz, H. *The History of the Jews.* Philadelphia: Jewish Publication Society, 1956 [1893].

Grant, F.C. *The Earliest Gospel.* New York: Abingdon-Cokesbury, 1943.

Grant, R.M. "The Problem of Theophilus." *HTR* 43 (1950), 179–196.

Grego, I. *La reazione ai Giudeo-Cristiani nel IV secolo negli scritti patristici e nei canoni conciliari.* Jerusalem: Franciscan Printing Press, 1973.

Gressmann, H. "Die Aufgaben der Wissenschaft des nachbiblischen Judentums." *ZATW* 43 (1925), 1–32.

Grotius, H. *Annotationes in quatuor Evangelia et Acta Apostolorum. Opera Theologica*, Tomi II, vol. I. London: Pitt, 1679.

Grützmacher, G. "Jerome" *ERE* VII (1914), 497–500.

Guignebert, C. *Jesus.* London: Paul, Trench, Trubner, 1935.

Gundry, R.H. *The Use of the Old Testament in St. Matthew's Gospel.* Suppl. to *NovTest* 18. Leiden: Brill, 1967.

Handmann, R. "Das Hebräer-Evangelium." *TU* 5, Heft 3 (1888).

Harnack, A. *Geschichte der altchristlichen Literatur.* Leipzig: Hinrichs, 1904.

———. "Review of W. Brandt's *Elchasait.*" *TLZ* 37 (1912), c. 683–685.

———. *History of Dogma.* New York: Dover, 1961 (1900).

Hedegård, D. *Seder R. Amram Gaon.* Lund: Lindstedt, 1951.

Hennecke, E. and Schneemelcher, W. *New Testament Apocrypha.* Eng. trans. ed. by R.M. Wilson. Philadelphia: Westminster, 1963.

Herford, R.T. "The Problem of the 'Minim' Further Considered." *Jewish Studies in Memory of George A. Kohut.* New York: A. Kohut Memorial Foundation, 1935, pp. 359–369.

———. *Christianity in Talmud and Midrash.* New York: Ktav, 1975 [1903].

Hilgenfeld, A. *Die Ketzergeschichte des Urchristentums.* Leipzig: Fues, 1884.

———. *Judentum u. Judenchristentum. Eine Nachlese zu der* Ketzergeschichte des Urchristentums. Leipzig: Fues, 1886.

Hirschberg, H. "Allusions to the Apostle Paul in the Talmud." *JBL* 62 (1943), 73–87.

———. "Once Again—the Minim." *JBL* 67 (1948), 305–318.

Hoennicke, G. *Das Judenchristentum im ersten und 2. Jahrhundert.* Berlin: Trowitzsch, 1908.

Holl, K. *Die handschriftliche Überlieferung des Epiphanius (Ancoratus und Panarion).* *TU* 36, 2, 1910.

Horbury, W. "The Benediction of the Minim and the Early Jewish–Christian Controversy." *JTS* 33 (1982), 19–61.

Hort, F.J.A. *Judaistic Christianity.* London: Macmillan, 1904.

Jocz, J. *The Jewish People and Jesus Christ.* Grand Rapids: Baker, 1979 [1949].

Jones, A.H.M. *The Cities of the Eastern Roman Provinces.* Oxford: University Press, 1971.

Judéo-Christianisme: Recherches historiques et théologiques offertes en homage au Cardinal Jean Daniélou. RSR 60 (1972).

Juster, J. *Les Juifs dans l'Empire Romain.* Paris: Geuther, 1914.

Katz, S.T. "Issues in the Separation of Judaism and Christianity after 70 C.E.: A Reconsideration." *JBL* 103 (1984), 43–76.

Kelly, J.N.D. *Jerome.* London: Duckworth, 1975.

Kennard, J.S. "Nazoraean and Nazareth." *JBL* 66 (1947), 79–81.

Klijn, A.F.J. "Jerome's Quotations from a Nazoraean Interpretation of Isaiah." *RSR* 60 (1972), 241–255.

———, and Reinink, G.J. *Patristic Evidence for Jewish–Christian Sects.* Suppl. to *NovTest* 36. Leiden: Brill, 1973.

Koch, G.A. "A Critical Investigation of Epiphanius' Knowledge of the Ebionites: A Translation and Critical Discussion of Panarion 30." Dissertation, 1976.

Kohler, K. "The Origin and Compilation of the 18 Benedictions with a Translation of the corresponding Essene Prayers in the Apostolic Constitutions." *HUCA* 1 (1924), 387–425.

Kraus, J. "Filastrius." *Lexikon für Theologie u. Kirche* 4 (1960), c. 124f.

Krauss, S. "The Jews in the Works of the Church Fathers." *JQR* 5 (1892/3), 122–157; 6 (1894), 82–99, 225–261.

———. "Zur Literatur der Siddurim." *Aron Freimann Festschrift.* Berlin: 1935, pp. 125–140.

Kuhn, K.G. "Giljonim und Sifre Minim." *Judentum, Urchristentum, Kirche. Festschrift für Joachim Jeremias.* Berlin: Töpelmann, 1964, pp. 24–61.

Lagrange, M.-J. "Évangile selon les Hébreux." *RB* 31 (1922), 321–349.

———. *Le Messianisme chez les Juifs, 150 B.C.–200 A.D.* Paris: Lecoffre, 1909.

Laible, H. *Jesus Christus im Talmud.* Berlin, 1891.

Lammen, H. "Les Noṣairis." *Études religieuses*, 1899.

Lawlor, H.J., and Oulton, J.E.L. *Eusebius.* London: SPCK, 1928.

Lessing, G.E. "Neue Hypothese über die Evangelisten, als bloss menschliche Geschichtschreiber betrachtet." *Theologischer Nachlass* (1778) in *Lessings sämtliche Werke.* Ed. H. Göring. Bd. XVIII, pp. 203–220. Stuttgart.

Levi, J. "Le mot 'Minim' désigne-t-il jamais une secte juive de Gnostiques antinomistes ayant exercé son action en Judée avant la destruction du Temple?" *REJ* 38 (1899), 204–210.

Lidzbarski, J. "Nazoraios." *Zeitschrift für Semitistik u. verwandte Gebiete* 1 (1922), 230–233.

Lightfoot, J.B. *The Apostolic Fathers.* New York: Olms, 1973 [1890].

Longenecker, R.N. *The Christology of Early Jewish Christianity. Studies in Biblical Theology*, 2nd Series, no. 17. Naperville: Allenson, 1970.

Mann, J. "Geniza Fragments of the Palestinian Order of Service." *HUCA* 2 (1925), 269–338.

Manns, F. *Essais sur le Judéo-Christianisme.* Jerusalem: Franciscan Printing Press, 1977.

———. *Bibliographie du Judéo-Christianisme.* Jerusalem: Franciscan Printing Press, 1978.

Marmorstein, A. "Judaism and Christianity in the Middle of the Third Century." *HUCA* 10 (1935), 223–263.

Marx, A. "Untersuchungen zum Siddur des Gaon R. Amram." *Jahrbuch der jüdischliterarischen Gesellschaft* 5 (1907). Hebrew section, pp. 1–38.

Massignon, L. "Nuṣairi." *The Encyclopedia of Islam*, III (1913), 2.

Mattingly, H.B. "The Origin of the Name *Christiani.*" *JTS* 9 (1958), 26–37.

Médebielle, P.A. "'Quoniam Nazaraeus Vocabitur' (Mt II 23)." *Miscellanea Biblica et Orientalia.* Rome: Herder, 1951, pp. 301–326.

Meyer, E. *Ursprung und Anfänge des Christentums.* Stuttgart: Cotta, 1921–4.

Moore, G.F. "Nazareth and Nazarene." *The Beginnings of Christianity* I. Eds. H.M. Jackson and K. Lake. London: Macmillan, 1920, pp. 426–432.

———. *Judaism.* Cambridge: Harvard, 1946–48.

Munck, J. "Jewish Christianity in Post-Apostolic Times." *NTS* 6 (1960), 103–116.

————. "Primitive Jewish Christianity and Later Jewish Christianity: Continuation or Rupture?" *Aspects du Judéo-Christianisme.* Strasbourg, 1965, pp. 77–91.

Murphy, F.X. "St. Jerome." *Catholic Encyclopedia* VII (1967), 872–874.

Neusner, J. *A History of the Jews in Babylonia.* Leiden: Brill, 1968.

Nicholson, E.B. *The Gospel According to the Hebrews.* London: Kegan Paul, 1879.

Parkes, J. *The Conflict of the Church and the Synagogue.* New York: Athanaeum, 1977 [1934].

Pieper, K. *Die Kirche Palästinas bis zum Jahre 135.* Köln: J.P. Bachem, 1938.

Pines, S. *The Jewish Christians of the Early Centuries of Christianity according to a New Source.* Jerusalem: Israel Academy of Sciences and Humanities, 1965.

Pritz, R.A. "On Brandon's Rejection of the Pella Tradition." *Immanuel* 13 (1981), 39–43.

————. "The Jewish Christian Sect of the Nazarenes and the Mishnah." *Proceedings of the Eighth World Congress of Jewish Studies.* Division A (1982), pp. 125–130.

Quispel, G. "Das Hebräerevangelium im gnostischen Evangelium nach Maria." *VC* 11 (1957), 139–144.

————. "The 'Gospel of Thomas' and the 'Gospel of the Hebrews'." *NTS* 12 (1966), 371–382.

Rembry, J.G. "'Quoniam Nazaraeus vocabitur' (Mt 2/23)." *LA* 12 (1961/2), 46–65.

Repo, E. *Der "Weg" als Selbstverzeichung des Urchristentums. Eine traditionsgeschichtliche und semasiologische Untersuchung.* Helsinki: Suomalainen tiedeakatemia, 1964.

Rubinstein, A. "The Appellation 'Galileans' in Ben Kosebha's Letter to Ben Galgolah." *JJS* 6 (1955), 26–34.

Rueger, H.P. "NAZARETH/NAZARA NAZARENOS/NAZORAIOS." *ZNTW* 72 (1981), 257–263.

Safrai, S. "Pluralism in Judaism of the Yavne Period." *Deot* 48 (1980), 166–170. In Hebrew.

Schaeder, H. "Ναζαρηνός, Ναζωραῖος." *ThDNT* 4, (1942), 874–889.

Schäfer, P. "Die sogenannte Synode von Jabne." *Judaica* 31 (1975), 54–64.

Schechter, S. "Geniza Specimens." *JQR* 10 (1897/8), 654–659.

Schlatter, A. *Synagoge und Kirche bis zum Barkochba Aufstand.* Stuttgart: Calver, 1966.

Schmidtke, A. *Neue Fragmente und Untersuchungen zu den judenchristlichen Evangelien. TU* 37/1, Leipzig, 1911.

————. "Zum Hebräerevangelium." *ZNTW* 35 (1936), 24–44.

Schoeps, H.J. *Theologie und Geschichte des Judenchristentums.* Tübingen: Mohr, 1949.

————. *Urgemeinde Judenchristentum Gnosis.* Tübingen: Mohr, 1956.

————. *Jewish Christianity.* Philadelphia: Fortress, 1969 [1964].

Schonfield, H.J. *The History of Jewish Christianity.* London: Duckworth, 1939.

Schweizer, E. "Er wird Nazoräer heissen." *Judentum, Urchristentum, Kirche: Festschrift für Joachim Jeremias.* Berlin: Töpelmann, 1964.

Schwen, P. "Nazareth u. die Nazoräer." *Zeitschrift für wissenschaftliche Theologie* 54 (1912), 31–35.

Simon, M. *St. Stephen and the Hellenists in the Primitive Church.* London: Longmans, Green, 1958.

———. *Verus Israel.* Paris: Boccard, 1964 [1948].

Simon, R. *Histoire Critique des principaux commentateurs du Nouveau Testament, depuis le commencement du Christianisme jusque à nôtre temps: avec une dissertation critique sur les principaux Actes Manuscrits qui ont été cités dans les trois Parties de cet Ouvrage.* Rotterdam, 1963.

Sperber, D. "Min." *Encyclopedia Judaica* XII (1971), 1–3.

Stemberger, G. "Die sogenannte 'Synode von Jabne' und das frühe Christentum." *Kairos* 19 (1977), 14–21.

Stern, S.M. "Quotations from Apocryphal Gospels in Abd al-Jabbar." *JTS* 18 (1967), 34–57.

———. "Abd al-Jabbar's Account of How Christ's Religion was Falsified by the Adoption of Roman Customs." *JTS* 19 (1968), 128–185.

Strack, H.L. *Jesus, die Häretiker u. die Christen nach den ältesten jüdischen Angaben.* Leipzig: Schriften des Institutum iudaicum in Berlin (fasc. 37), 1910.

———, and Billerbeck, P. *Kommentar zum Neuen Testament aus Talmud und Midrasch.* Munich: Beck, 1926–28.

Strecker, G. *Das Judenchristentum in den Pseudoklementinen.* Berlin: Akademie, 1958.

———. "On the Problem of Jewish Christianity." Appendix I to W. Bauer, *Orthodoxy and Heresy in Earliest Christianity.* London: SCM, 1971, pp. 241–285.

Sutcliffe, E.F. "St. Jerome's Hebrew Manuscripts." *Biblica* 29 (1948), 195–204.

Tatum, W.B., "Matthew 2:23—Wordplay and Misleading Translations." *Biblical Translator* 27 (1976), 135–138.

Taylor, R.E. "Attitudes of the Fathers toward Practices of Jewish Christians." *Studia Patristica* IV (=*TU* 78), 1961, 504–511.

Testa, E. *Il Simbolismo dei Giudeo-Cristiani.* Jerusalem: Franciscan Printing Press, 1962.

Waitz, H. "Das Evangelium der zwölf Apostel (Ebionitenevangelium)." *ZNTW* 13 (1912), 338ff; 14 (1913), 38–64, 117–132.

———. "Das Buch des Elchasai, das heilige Buch der judenchristlichen Sekte der Sobiai." *Harnack-Ehrung.* Leipzig, 1921, pp. 87–104.

Waitz, W. "Neue Untersuchungen über die sogenannten judenchristlichen Evangelien." *ZNTW* 36 (1937), 60–81.

Weiss, B. *Die Apostelgeschichte. TU* 9, vol. 3/4, 1893.

Wilkinson, J. "L'apport de saint Jérôme a la topographie." *RB* 81 (1974), 245–257.

Winter, E.K. "Das Evangelium der Jerusalemitischen Mutterkirche. Aufgaben der Matthäus Forschung." *Judaica* 9 (1953), 1–33.

Winter, P. "'Nazareth' and 'Jerusalem' in Luke chs. i and ii." *NTS* 3 (1956/7), 136–142.

Wirthmüller, J.B. *Die Nazoräer*, Regensburg: Pustet, 1864.

Young, F.M. "Did Epiphanius know what he meant by 'Heresy'?" *Studia Patristica* I, 199–208.

Zimmern, H. "Nazoräer (Nazarener)." *Zeitsch. der deutschen morgenländischen Gesellschaft* 74 (1920), 429–438.

Zöckler, O. *Hieronymus.* Gotha: Perthes, 1865.

Zuckschwerdt, E. "Nazoraios in Matth. 2, 23." *ThZ* 31 (1975), 65–77.

INDICES

SCRIPTURE REFERENCES

HEBREW BIBLE

Gen. 49:10 *31*
Exod. 23:17 *34*
Lev. 10:10 *61*
Deut. 17:18 *66*
    27:26 *34*
Josh. 8:32 *66*
Jud. 13:5,7 *12*
   16:17 *12*
2Kgs. 22:14 *66*
2Chron. 34:22 *66*
Ps. 31:7 *67*
   60:12 *100*
   131:11 (132:11) *30*
Prov. 5:14 *69*
   8:21 *27*
   8:23 *27*
Isa. 6:2,3 *22*
   8:10 61
   8:12,13 *61,66*
   8:14 *58-62*
   8:20-21 *62-64*
   9:1-4 *64-65*
   11:1 *12-15, 41, 54,*
      108
   11:1-10 *13*
   29:17-21 *54*
   29:19 *68*
   29:20-21 *65-68*
   31:6-9 *54, 68-70*
   33:8 *61*

42:14 *61*
49:8 *61*
61:4 *61*
Ezek. 22:26 *61*
   32:24 105
   48:15 61

NEW TESTAMENT

Matt. 1:22-23 *12*
   2:5-6 *12*
   2:15 *12*
   2:17-18 *12*
   2:23 *11-14, 33*
   3:13-15 *93*
   4:1 *90*
   4:15-16 *65*
   5:17 *88*
   7:14 *14*
   10:5,6 *88*
   13:53-58 *54*
   13:54 *80*
   13:57 *54*
   15:24 *88*
   16:18 *70*
   18:22 *93*
   26:71 *11*
   27:9 *57*
   27:9-10 *57*
Mk. 3:18 *101*
   7:5-9 *63*

JEWISH SOURCES

CHRISTIAN SOURCES

MODERN AUTHORS

SUBJECTS